Advertising Writing

Advertising Writing
Putting Creative Strategy to Work
THIRD EDITION

W. Keith Hafer
Adjunct Professor
Florida Institute of Technology

Gordon E. White
Professor
University of Illinois
at Urbana—Champaign

West Publishing Company
ST. PAUL   NEW YORK   LOS ANGELES   SAN FRANCISCO

Copyeditor: Rosalie Maggio
Cover Image: Courtesy of D'Arcy Masius Benton &
    Bowles, Inc. Design by Intergroup Marketing and
    Promotions
Cover Design: Deborah Gallagher
Composition: Carlisle Communications, Ltd.

Library of Congress Cataloging-in-Publication Data

Hafer, W. Keith
    Advertising writing : putting creative strategy to work / W. Keith
Hafer, Gordon E. White.—3rd ed.
        p.   cm.
    Bibliography: p.
    Includes index.
    ISBN 0-314-46532-4
    1. Advertising copy.   I. White, Gordon E.   II. Title.
HF5825.H28 1989
659. 13'22—dc19   88-27648
                    CIP

CONTENTS

Foreword   xi
Preface   xiii
Acknowledgments   xiv
About the Authors   xv

1 What Makes Good Advertising and Good Advertising Writers   1

Criteria for good advertising writing ■ What is the good advertising writer like? ■ Acquiring the qualities of a good copywriter

■ Case History: Alexander Proudfoot

2 What You Should Know About Customers "Up Front": Preparation for Creative Strategy   19

Market research ■ People research ■ Consumer behavior ■ Selectivity ■ Attitudes ■ Repetition

■ Case History: Safety Belt Campaign
■ Case History: Kemper Insurance
■ Case History: VISA
■ Case History: Kleenex Softique

3 Where Advertising Writing Begins: Creative Strategy   39

Key to successful advertising ■ Creative strategy/creative tactics ■ Purpose of creative strategy ■ Simplified creative strategy ■ Example of creative strategy ■ Personal Profile ■ Emphasis on goals ■ Necessity for planning

■ Case History: U.S. Marine Corps
■ Case History: Emery Worldwide
■ Case History: Pearle Vision Center
■ Case History: State Farm Insurance

4 **Some Obvious Questions to Ask: How to Discover Ideas for Copy** 57

Information search ■ Sensible questions ■ Engineers versus salespeople ■ Seasonal buying ■ Benefits versus features ■ Cardinal sin in copywriting ■ Background brief ■ Guarantees and warranties ■ Previous advertising ■ Competitor's advertising ■ Know your customer ■ Where the advertising appears ■ Creative strategy ■ Isolating the main selling idea

■ Case History: Mazda
■ Case History: Coors Premium Beer
■ Case History: Jamaica Tourist Board
■ Case History: Pledge

5 **Setting the Stage for Creativity** 77

Writer involvement in research ■ Best source of inspiration ■ Organized research ■ Research example ■ Development of a single ad ■ Inspiration follows footwork ■ Origin of creative ideas

■ Case History: O'Keefe & Merritt

6 **Headline and Visual: Indivisible** 83

Copy-art team ■ Visual/verbal together ■ Total communication ■ Illustration and headline in combination ■ Importance of thinking visually ■ What a layout is ■ Seven basic layout categories ■ The function of an illustration ■ Twelve ways of using illustrations ■ Art or Photography? ■ Responsibilities of the art director ■ Three chief headline categories

■ Case History: The Travelers
■ Case History: Gold'n Plump Poultry
■ Case History: Maker's Mark Bourbon

7 **Completing the Writing Assignment** 111

Function of body copy ■ Forms of body copy ■ Length of body copy ■ Specifics versus generalities ■ Claims versus facts ■ Ways of building belief ■ Suggested

format for typing copy ▪ Creed for copyriters
▪ Emphasis on basic selling idea ▪ Strive for the
unexpected ▪ Magazine ads versus newspaper
ads ▪ Creating folders and brochures

▪ Case History: *The Wall Street Journal*
▪ Case History: Carnival Cruises
▪ Case History: Michelin Tires

8 Modern Miracle: Desk-Top Ad Making   131

Do-it-yourself ads ▪ Creative software ▪ High-
resolution reproduction

▪ Case History: David Shih—Hunger, Literacy Campaigns

9 Writing Advertising for Radio   137

How radio has changed ▪ Stations rather than programs
▪ The tools of radio writing ▪ Creating pictures in the
mind's eye ▪ The fleeting message ▪ Concentration on
one theme ▪ Example of repeated key elements ▪ The
medium of the imagination ▪ Eighteen rules for writing
radio copy ▪ Suggested script form ▪ Identifying scene
and characters ▪ Basic broadcast terms ▪ Use of music
and sound effects ▪ Timing the commercial
▪ Importance of writing it "short" ▪ Reading copy
aloud ▪ Types of radio commercials ▪ Writing for local
AM and FM stations

▪ Case History: Kelly Services
▪ Case History: Radio Advertising Bureau

10 Writing Advertising for Television   155

Achieving one total impression ▪ What TV does best
▪ Expressing your TV idea ▪ Suggested TV script
form ▪ Camera terms for script writer ▪ Indicating
distances ▪ Transition methods ▪ Various effects ▪ Use
of voice-over ▪ Importance of writing it "short" ▪ The
storyboard and its uses ▪ Importance of pre-production
meeting ▪ Basic forms of television production

▪ Case History: French's Mustard
▪ Case History: Mercury

- Case History: Dannon Yogurt
- Case History: Bud Light
- Case History: Raid

11 The Direct Approach 183

Direct marketing ▪ Famous examples ▪ Reasons for recent boom ▪ Thoroughly tested copy ▪ Direct marketing via direct mail ▪ Advantages of direct mail ▪ Typical direct mail package ▪ Copywriter as salesperson ▪ Direct marketing catalogs ▪ Other direct marketing media ▪ Constant testing ▪ Long copy versus short copy ▪ Ways to increase selling power ▪ Other uses of direct mail

- Case History: Black, Gillock & Langberg
- Case History: *Urge* Magazine

12 Writing Business-to-Business Advertising 201

Business talking to business ▪ Business advertising and personal selling ▪ Types of business publications ▪ Different reader attitude ▪ News and information ▪ Capabilities not products ▪ Soliciting inquiries ▪ How copywriter prepares ▪ Guidelines for effective copy ▪ Understanding the reader's job function ▪ Twenty ways to improve business advertising ▪ Comparison to consumer advertising

- Case History: United States Gypsum Company
- Case History: United Technologies

13 Writing Retail Advertising 213

Retail share of ad budget ▪ Retailing is local ▪ Four essentials of retail copy ▪ Store image ▪ Price ▪ Immediacy ▪ Specifics and details ▪ The crucial executive ▪ Tight deadlines ▪ Special advertising activities ▪ Media of retailing ▪ Creative staffs in retail ▪ Help from manufacturers ▪ Differences between retail and national advertising ▪ "Retail" covers many businesses

- Case History: Spiegel
- Case History: The Plastic and Aesthetic Surgery Center at Jewish Hospital, Louisville

14 Writing Copy for Sales Promotion 225

Reasons for sales promotion boom ∎ What sales promotion achieves ∎ Copywriter's contribution ∎ Forms of sales promotion ∎ Example of sweepstakes ∎ What sales promotion can and cannot do

∎ Case History: L'Oréal Studio Products
∎ Case History: NFL Properties: "Fun, Food, and Football"

15 Other Copywriting 235

Variety of copywriting chores ∎ Point-of-purchase advertising ∎ Forms of point-of-purchase ∎ After-sale advertising ∎ Reinforcing the purchase decision ∎ Yellow Pages advertising ∎ Transit advertising ∎ Fashion advertising

∎ Case History: Spuds MacKenzie

16 The Nutshell Principle: Key to Success 243

The nutshell principle ∎ Billboard viewing ∎ Demands on creative person ∎ Marriage of picture and words ∎ Strip away unessentials ∎ Product as signature ∎ Helpful hints ∎ Expanding on poster idea ∎ Good poster ideas adapt

∎ Case History: Fischer Packing Company

17 Advertising Copy Research 249

Copy testing ∎ Various research techniques ∎ Checklists ∎ Suggestions for testing ∎ Forms of pretesting ∎ Consumer panels ∎ Coupon or inquiry tests ∎ Split-run tests ∎ Market tests ∎ Theater testing ∎ Forms of posttesting ∎ Starch Readership Surveys ∎ Gallup-Robinson ∎ Burke Day-After recall ∎ Motivation research

∎ Case History: Home Box Office

18 Advertising to Foreign Markets 265

Expanding markets ∎ Past mistakes ∎ Bilingual personnel ∎ Purchase of foreign agencies ∎ America's own "foreign" market ∎ Size of Hispanic market

19 Advertising Writers: Where They Work and What They Do   269

Five obvious businesses for copywriters ■ Writing for an agency ■ Writing for a retailer ■ Writing for the media ■ Writing as a free-lancer ■ Writing for direct marketing ■ Writing for a manufacturer ■ Other option: public relations ■ Public relations assignments ■ Public relations as a career

20 Hints on Seeking an Ad-Writing Job and Other Jobs   281

Preparing the sample book ■ Special target audience ■ The portfolio ■ Writing the résumé ■ Writing the cover letter ■ The interview ■ Hints on seeking any job ■ Doing research ■ Zeroing in on the target ■ Persistence is the key ■ Use of contacts ■ Vocational questionnaire

Appendix I Writing for New Business   297

Meaning of term "new business" ■ The lifeblood of agencies ■ Acquiring new business ■ Organizing new business ■ Questions regarding new business prospect ■ Research for new business ■ The new business presentation ■ Agency house campaigns ■ Books as new business tools ■ How to keep new business ■ Where do new business writers come from?

■ Case History: J. H. Benedict & Associates

Appendix II Tips for the New Ad Writer Who Works Alone   309

Art direction and production for the amateur ■ Working with local suppliers ■ Typefaces and measurements

Epilogue *Ethics and Social Responsibility*   *315*

Glossary *319*
Bibliography   *327*
Index *331*

FOREWORD

Never before have I read a book on advertising writing that was put together by such highly qualified professionals.

The combined experience of Keith Hafer and Gordon White includes years of advertising writing for some of America's largest corporations plus years of experience in teaching advertising writing at universities. These men know how to write advertising and how to teach others to write it.

In this book they begin by stressing creative strategy—that all-important process of digging, analyzing, and planning that precedes good advertising.

They explain what qualities a writer needs in order to be successful as well as how to think up ideas, how to get attention, how to involve a reader or viewer, and how to change people's attitude toward a product.

The authors tell how to get the information you need to write effective copy, how to stimulate the creative process and think up ideas. The book contains a detailed step-by-step case history of how a successful advertising campaign was developed through research and interviews.

The actual creation of an advertisement or a broadcast commercial is explained—how to start, how to chose effective illustrations, and how anyone can make a rough layout—how to combine headline and illustrations to build a powerful message.

One chapter covers the growing field of direct response advertising, mail order advertising, rules for preparing effective direct mail copy, and the various forms of direct mail letters.

The chapters on radio and television writing contain the best instructions I have ever read on producing effective broadcast advertising. The methods described are simple, clear, logical, and extremely effective.

Other areas covered in the book are retail advertising, business publication advertising, posters, brochures, booklets, and ads in the yellow pages.

In addition, the authors cover advertising copy research. The writer is given methods for testing copy, including opinion tests, coupon tests, sales market tests, and simulated market tests. Post-testing, readership reports, recall tests, and motivation research are also explained.

Finally they tell the rich rewards awaiting the ad writer, where the advertising jobs are, and how to go about applying for them. To the aspiring copywriter this information alone is worth many times the price of the book.

Most important, the material in the entire volume is *current, up to date*—not the methods of the 1960s or the 1970s, but the newest methods of the 1980s and beyond.

The book contains numerous illustrations as well as thirty-nine modern and timely case histories that bring to life the comments in the text.

This volume can be a boon to students who are just beginning the study of advertising writing. Teachers of advertising and people who are already in advertising will also benefit.

In summary, this book is the most practical, complete, yet concise text on the writing of advertising that I ever read. It is a book I wish I had had when I first went into advertising. It would have put me years ahead.

By JOHN CAPLES, former Vice-President
Batten, Barton, Durstine & Osborn, Inc.;
Member of the Advertising Hall of Fame

PREFACE

Advertising Writing: Putting Creative Strategy to Work is practical and concise, and is meant to be of value to writers of advertising with little or no formal training in the art. This simple text examines the need for a disciplined approach to advertising writing via primary application of sound creative strategy. We have tried to combine the most valuable elements of advertising writing theory with the most important aspects of its practice.

Toward this end, the book was conceived as a bridge between rules and suggestions for writing advertising and actual advertisements that have been run or aired. We include thirty-nine creative case histories— actual print and broadcast advertisements that have succeeded in their purpose. To make these ads more meaningful to students, they are integrated into the text with a detailed summary of their (a) marketing problems and goals, (b) creative solutions, and (c) results in the marketplace. Each is introduced by a brief analysis of the advertising principles that the particular case best expresses.

In selecting chapter topics and ads highlighting those topics, we wanted to present only the essentials of advertising writing, its forms and purposes. Since no book on advertising can hope to cover all its aspects, it should be stressed that this is not a detailed study on art direction, broadcast production, or the mechanics of producing print advertisements. It is not a text on marketing, research, or consumer behavior. Nor is it an outline of the legal, social, or moral aspects of advertising.

Instead, it is our hope that the text will serve as a guide to students and practitioners to help them attain proficiency in writing advertising copy for all media. We hope, too, that by clarifying the function and techniques of advertising writing, their jobs can be made a little easier.

Without underestimating intuitive writing insights, it is hoped students will understand and respond to the imperative directive woven into the fabric of this book: that no advertising writers can hope to succeed unless their efforts are first firmly grounded in sound creative strategy—with its knowledge of customer needs, product benefits, and advertising objectives.

W. Keith Hafer
Gordon E. White

ACKNOWLEDGMENTS

The advice offered in this book would not be nearly so meaningful without the demonstrations provided by advertising professionals. Acknowledgement is made with gratitude for the understanding and cooperation of the many practitioners who submitted superb material for this volume. We sincerely thank the following advertisers, advertising agencies, and advertising service organizations: The Advertising Council, Inc.; Batten, Barton, Durstine & Osborn, Inc.; J. H. Benedict & Associates; Black, Gillock & Langberg; Leo Burnett Company; Carnival Cruise Lines; Clarity Coverdale Rueff; Communications Diversified of New York; Adolph Coors Company; The Dannon Company, Inc.; D'Arcy Masius Benton & Bowles, Inc.; DDB Needham Worldwide; Department of Transportation; Doe-Anderson Advertising Agency; Emery Worldwide; William Esty Company; Fallon McElligott; Fischer Packing Company; Foote, Cone & Belding; R. T. French Company; Gold'n Plump Poultry; HDM Advertising Agency; HDM Dawson Johns & Black; Home Box Office; Jamaica Tourist Board; Jewish Hospital, Louisville; S. C. Johnson & Son, Inc.; Kelly Services, Inc.; Kemper Group; Kimberly-Clark; Kobs & Draft Advertising, Inc.; Lincoln-Mercury Division of Ford Motor Company; L'Oréal; Maker's Mark Distillery; Marstrat, Inc.; Mazda; Michelin Tire Corporation; NFL Properties; Pearle Health Services, Inc.; Alexander Proudfoot Organization; Radio Advertising Bureau; Specialty Advertising Association International; Spiegel; State Farm Insurance Companies; J. Walter Thompson; The Travelers; United States Gypsum Company; United States Marine Corps; United Technologies; *Urge* Magazine; Visa U.S.A., Inc.; Young & Rubicam.

We are grateful to Mary Lowrey and James Ferguson, University of Illinois, for help in the final preparation of the book. And very special thanks to John Caples, that magnificent fifty-year veteran copywriter and member of the Advertising Hall of Fame, for his kind foreword to this book.

ABOUT THE AUTHORS

W. KEITH HAFER studied painting at the Hawthorne School of Art in Provincetown, Massachusetts, and at the Washington, D.C., Art League before earning a J.D. at George Washington University and an M.A. in psychology at New York University. After further graduate work at Harvard and the Universities of Virginia, Georgia, and Texas, he received a Ph.D. from Walden University. From 1970 through 1978, he was a full-time teacher of advertising at the Universities of Puerto Rico, Virginia, Georgia, and Texas, and currently enjoys semi-retirement in Satellite Beach, Florida, where he serves as a part-time consultant to a psychiatric hospital, writes a weekly newspaper column titled "Coping With Life," and is at work on a novel about the advertising business. He has also written seven books, many magazine articles, national and regional magazine and newspaper columns, and a weekly critique of advertising for *New England Advertising Week* and two metropolitan daily newspapers.

Keith Hafer's career in advertising has included free-lance writing and design, radio writing, advertising management, and advertising research with Gallup & Robinson. His agency experience spanned ten years in the Philadelphia, New York, Hollywood, and the San Francisco offices of N.W. Ayer and the Silton Co. of Boston; his agency roles included writing, account supervision, business development, and creative direction.

Before entering the agency business, Hafer spent fifteen years in industry, serving as vice-president, member of the board of directors, and director of human relations and communications for Fischer & Porter Co., and as president of Chalfant Crafts, Inc.

GORDON E. WHITE received his A.B. from the University of Alabama and his M.S. and Ph.D. from the University of Illinois. He has taught at the University of Alabama, at Northwestern University, and at the University of Illinois. He has been teaching advertising creative courses at the latter institution since his retirement from the advertising agency business at the end of 1967.

His advertising agency career spanned thrity-one years—nearly six years as a copywriter with Campbell-Ewald Company of New York, Inc., and more than twenty-five years with Batten, Barton, Durstine & Osborn, Inc., in New York and Chicago. He was vice-president in charge of creative work in BBDO-Chicago for many years.

He is co-author of *Basic Advertising* and author of *John Caples: Adman*. He has been a contributor to *Coronet, Printer's Inc, Advertising Agency Magazine, Journal of Marketing, Journal of Advertising*. He has twice been a speaker at the annual Creative Workshop sponsored by *Advertising Age*. He is a former chair of the board of directors of the *Journal of Advertising*. He is a Fellow of the American Academy of Advertising.

1

What Makes Good Advertising and Good Advertising Writers

Chapter Topics

Criteria for good
advertising writing
What is the good
advertising writer like?
Acquiring the qualities of a
good copywriter

Key Terms

Pivotal person
Integrity
Objectivity
Empathy

Case History

Alexander Proudfoot

WHAT IS GOOD ADVERTISING WRITING?

Advertising is selling, pure and simple. As an advertising writer, you are a salesperson, primarily of goods and services, only occasionally of social or political ideas. The general public seems to realize that advertising is selling, and accepts it for what it is. Be prepared to do likewise.

It is a rare enterprise in today's society—whether industrial companies or government bureaus or health facilities or political parties—that does not employ writers of advertising in an effort to communicate, to persuade, to sell. If your goal is to be a writer of good advertising, you'll find yourself a member of an ever-expanding field of communication.

In determining what form good advertising should take, no single standard has been acceptable to all writers and never will be. Although every creative person has strong opinions about what constitutes good advertising writing, each realizes that what is the right solution for one marketing situation is not necessarily correct for another because no two marketing situations are ever precisely the same. A beginning copywriter can draw some solace from the knowledge that even in the copywriting halls of fame there has always been a difference of opinion as to what sort of copy is best.

Who is right? To whom should you, as a beginning advertising writer, listen? The answer may surprise you. Once you have done adequate fact-finding research, you should listen only to your own instincts, your own inspiration, because you are now in a creative world . . . a world that rewards individuality.

In spite of this creative license, there are criteria to guide you in developing good advertising writing. Among them are the following:

1. It must offer a benefit or reward for reading.
2. It must be easily understood.
3. It must be honest and believable.
4. It must inform and motivate.
5. It must be memorable.
6. It must be appropriate to the product or service.
7. It must reflect favorably on the overall image of the advertiser.
8. It must succeed in its planned objective.

Any advertising that meets all these requirements has done its job well, and the writer can take justifiable pride in the work.

Some advertisers and their agencies boast about their award-winning advertising. And although it is ego-building to capture medals, trophies, and professional acclaim, awards are meaningless unless the advertising meets its sales goals.

There are great rewards in learning to be a skillful advertising writer—whether you work for an agency, a direct marketing firm, a retail store, a manufacturer, or one of the media. And although money is surely one of the rewards, there is also a rich return that comes from knowing you have solved a sticky communications problem, that you have created messages that reach out, touch, and motivate others.

No matter where you end up writing copy, you will seldom spend all day chained to your typewriter, grinding out golden words and phrases. As an advertising writer you are a professional, part of a working organization, with obligations that are a part of that role. You must attend training sessions, briefing sessions, planning sessions. You must keep in tune with administrators, sales managers, and buyers. You must get out into the field to call on the trade from time to time. Often you may have to hire and supervise specialized creative talent (artists, musicians, actors) and deal with suppliers who mechanically reproduce the creative material of advertising (printers, broadcast producers). You will have to get up on your own two feet and present, explain, or otherwise sell advertising ideas to administrative boards, to clients, and to sales and management groups. As an advertising writer you are going to have to be very much an all-around person.

The copywriter is truly a pivotal person, once described as "the one in the middle"—in the middle of a vast commercial or social enterprise, in the middle of a basic communications process. The writer is the point of contact between buyer and seller. And while the writer's advertising message may be spoken with the tongue of angels, the writer speaks not for self but for others.

Advertising writing is done in and for nearly every private and public segment of our world. Because of this great variety of tasks and the great need for competent writing, an ambitious advertising writer willing to learn the craft well can find a niche where individual talent can develop and flower, and where the rewards of good work can make life truly worthwhile. Attractive as that prospect may be, it is only fair to point out that not everybody is suited to a copywriting career. The successful copywriter will be a sort of Renaissance person. You may not have to be a paragon of virtue, but the craft does demand certain special qualities in its practitioners.

WHAT IS THE GOOD ADVERTISING WRITER LIKE?

No two experts agree on exactly what makes a good advertising writer, but there is a consensus on one point: without an innate *interest in words* you're not likely to become a good writer. This interest is almost always natural and basic. Just as people who dislike figures seldom become accountants, those who don't enjoy the magic of words seldom become writers.

Along with this natural appreciation of language, you will want to have an *aptitude* for expression and a reasonable reservoir of experience or education, or both. Like interest, aptitude usually results from heredity or environment. Unlike interest, it can be influenced greatly by a rich cultural background upon which you can draw for information, vocabulary, reference, and analogy.

There is some agreement that a study of the humanities, including languages, will enhance your writing skills and provide a reference bank for a nontechnical writer. Scientific courses—especially in fields of engineering—provide solid background if you work for industrial rather than consumer products.

Most advertising authorities also agree that study in the social sciences can contribute to a writer's skill. Specifically, courses in psychology, sociology, and anthropology are useful in providing you with insights that bear directly on the motivating power of advertising writing.

In addition to natural aptitude and educational preparation, individual personality and innate qualities and abilities will affect your writing skill. Personal characteristics found to favorably influence writing ability include:

- intelligence
- imagination
- highly developed powers of observation
- objectivity
- determination
- persistence
- self-discipline
- patience
- curiosity
- interest in human nature
- self-confidence
- integrity
- verbal skills
- humility
- empathy
- capacity for criticism
- mental and physical stamina.

ACQUIRING THE QUALITIES OF A GOOD COPYWRITER

Of these qualities, some are inborn and cannot be changed. Others can be acquired or modified to a degree.

Intelligence

Although commonly held to be hereditary, intelligence, or potential brain power, is not always constant; it can fluctuate in response to environmental factors such as sleep, general health, health habits, diet, vocational and domestic happiness, social compatibility, and self-satisfaction. Fortunately, intelligence, which is essential to a writer, is possessed in generous quantity by virtually all creative people. As Gary Steiner writes in *The Creative Organization:*

> General intelligence seems to bear about the same relation to on-the-job creativity at the professional level as weight does to ability in football. You have to have a lot of it to be in the game at all; but among those on the team—all of whom have a great deal of weight to begin with—differences in performance are only slightly, if at all, related to weight.[1]

Imagination

Imagination is the most difficult characteristic to modify, but you can acquire a creative outlook by the process of consciously using your mind in an imaginative way. As Hanley Norins writes in *The Compleat Copywriter,* a creative advertising writer is the kind of person who sees camels in clouds.[2]

One way of stimulating your imagination is through peaceful meditation. Today, a number of successful firms set aside private rooms where employees who work with their minds can be alone in a quiet atmosphere. Those who use these facilities daily for fifteen or twenty minutes of quiet meditation report encouraging results and often find solutions to creative problems requiring the use of imagination.

Although there may be no limit to imagination and ways to expand it, advertising writing tends to use the imagination only in narrow, practical terms to help solve highly specific marketing problems.

Observation

Observation is one characteristic you can greatly develop through discipline and application. For most of us, the mind records little of what the eye beholds and often makes its own interpretation of the little it does happen to retain.

This was dramatically illustrated for one of the authors when he was a student. During a lecture on circumstantial evidence, one door of the classroom burst open and a young woman, screaming loudly, raced down one aisle and up the other, pursued by two men (or was it

---

1. Gary A. Steiner, ed., *The Creative Organization* (Chicago: University of Chicago Press, 1956), p. 6.
2. Hanley Norins, *The Compleat Copywriter* (New York: McGraw-Hill, 1966), p. 10.

one?). Immediately after the interruption, the professor asked the students to summarize what they had observed. Four hundred different versions were submitted.

You can, however, train yourself with relative ease to take deliberate note of all that you see.

Objectivity

Objectivity involves looking at more than one side of a situation that affects you personally. Like observation, objectivity can be increased through a conscious effort to put ourselves in the other person's place. Consistent practice in examining questions from two or more sides is bound to result in a broadened perspective. This is crucial when dealing with human factors.

Determination and Persistence

Although closely related, determination and persistence are different. Determination is the resolve to tackle a problem by making a start. Persistence is the steady application of effort toward a goal. Because these characteristics are centered in the human will, they respond to motivation, either self-induced or supplied by others. Sufficient emphasis on the goal produces determination as well as persistence.

Self-Discipline

Can you regulate yourself to schedules? Do you have the self-discipline to meet those never-ending deadlines?

Patience

No copywriter can long endure without the human quality of patience. Perhaps patience can best be described as a serene conviction that no matter how long it takes to find the idea or the words you need, they will, in the end, appear in your mind. Patience is generally a by-product of experience as a copywriter. It comes—even to the most impetuous—from the day-to-day exposure to the revisions and corrections that are an integral part of the copywriting craft.

Curiosity

Like observation, curiosity can be developed through desire and consistent application. By training yourself to seek facts and insights about people, ideas, and things, curiosity can become the backbone of research as well as an intriguing source of ideas.

Interest in Human Nature

An interest in human nature is of paramount importance. Without it, much of human motivation will remain obscure; with it, critical insights will give greater power to your efforts to inform and persuade.

Self-Confidence

Self-confidence tends to be acquired very early in life, and results from a feeling of being appreciated as well as from successful experience at every developmental level. The surest way to acquire confidence is to work persistently toward worthwhile goals until they are achieved. Each new success bolsters your self-esteem, making the next upward step easier to attain. Self-confidence helps sustain you through those cycles when your ad ideas are greeted with disdain.

Integrity

Integrity in a writer of advertising usually stems from the central core of one's being. Uncertain moral guidelines can be compensated for only by self-imposed laws requiring rigid observance of honesty in thought and expression. At times you will be sorely tested. Much of the criticism leveled at advertising for dealing in half truths can be avoided by a resolve to write only what you know to be demonstrably true. In the end, truth well told is the only thing that really sells a product or an idea and *keeps* it sold.

Verbal Skills

Verbal skills stem from a large and growing vocabulary as well as from self-confidence, and are essential even for a beginning copywriter. You can constantly sharpen, improve, and expand these skills by reading widely and by making it a practice to learn the meaning of new words added to your arsenal.

Humility

Humility acts as a balance for your self-confidence. Each is necessary to a well-integrated human personality. The successful advertising writer requires and generally has a high ego drive, which provides the inner motivation to succeed in an often lonely and anonymous occupation. Humility, on the other hand, provides the perspective that makes it possible for writers to distinguish reality from fantasy, and to function as responsive and responsible members of the business and social structure. Unfortunately, humility is not easy to acquire and is particularly difficult to retain in the face of success, which can come very early to copywriters. However, since the process of living generally includes failures as well as successes, it is from these failures and their attendant self-appraisals that humility springs. So when you fail at something—as all of us inevitably must—take solace in the knowledge that your capacity to write persuasively has been enhanced by your personal understanding of what it means to try and not succeed.

Empathy

Every lesson in humility is, in effect, a lesson in empathy—the one quality that is absolutely essential to successful communication. It is empathy that enables you to see your selling proposition from the customer's point of view.

Hanley Norins contends that the advertising writer must play the role of both parties in the transaction. It is Norin's belief that an advertisement is actually a dialogue in which the copywriter does all the verbalizing.[3] Leo Burnett, who strongly held empathy to be the crux of effective advertising, once told the Chicago Copywriters Club: "If you can't turn yourself into your customer, you probably shouldn't be in the advertising business at all."[4]

One way of developing an appropriate level of empathy is to acquire extensive *personal knowledge* of the products or services about which you write, knowledge of the prime prospects to whom you write, and as much *personal experience* as possible in observing and participating in the actual selling and using experiences. In this way, the needs and feelings of the customer (and the salesperson) will take on new meaning, giving you new insights in preparing effective copy.

Capacity for Criticism

How tough skinned are you? Do you have a capacity for accepting criticism? Professor S. Watson Dunn and others stress the ability to take criticism[5] and come up smiling. Advertising writing is no field for sensitive souls.

Advertising writing is a combination of fiction (which draws only on the personal imagination of the writer) and non-fiction (which is based largely on research), and has room for countless ways of expression. It is inevitable that copy supervisors, creative directors, and client personnel all have their own ideas on how the advertising should be presented. It is not unusual for a piece of copy to be changed a half

---

3. Ibid., p. 15.
4. Leo Burnett, *Communications of an Advertising Man* (Chicago: Leo Burnett Co., 1961), p. 19.
5. S. Watson Dunn, *Advertising Copy and Communication* (New York: McGraw-Hill, 1956), p. 17.

dozen or more times between its first writing and its ultimate trip to production.

If or when your ideas are dumped on, you will want to grit your teeth and vow to come back strong another day.

Mental and Physical Stamina

Two final requirements for significant success as a copywriter are mental stamina and physical stamina. Without the capacity to keep the mind clicking at a steady pace over time, the often frenetic demands of the advertising business cannot be met. To parrot a famous advertising slogan, you have to *be sharp and feel sharp.* To cope with the pressure, you don't have to live like an Olympian, but it pays to take good care of all your faculties all the time. Almost without exception, the successful person in this business has boundless physical drive.

The purpose of this book is to help you find your way among the choices and techniques of the copywriting art. Its chapters attempt to set down suggestions, insights, and guidelines enabling you to attain your chosen goal as quickly and as surely as possible. You will find the career of advertising writing stimulating, demanding, and rewarding. It is almost never dull. And of this you can be certain: everything that you have ever done, or read, or seen, or thought, or been, will be of value to you. As you develop your capacities in this intriguing craft, you will see that no single human experience is ever wasted.

CASE HISTORY
ALEXANDER PROUDFOOT

Courtesy of Alexander Proud-foot and Alexander Proudfoot Communications.

Anyone who aspires to be a first-rate persuasive copywriter can learn much from this plain but potent print campaign for Alexander Proudfoot, an extremely high-level international management consultant organization.

These ads ran only in the *Wall Street Journal* and *Forbes*. They were directed to a very small target market—top management officers of substantial corporations.

Assume you're a top corporate officer and see if these headlines shake you up. The first ad, the 100 percent efficiency ad, drew this phone call from a CEO. "I read your ad yesterday in the *Wall Street Journal,* which said that if I didn't sleep last night I should call you this morning. Well, I didn't sleep last night." Another CEO phoned and said, "I saw your 'discontent' ad at least two months ago and haven't been able to get it out of my mind."

The ads averaged about fifty responses a month, which is most unusual in a business where the minimum fee is about $500,000. Obviously, the Proudfoot organization selects from the fifty respondents those businesses it would prefer to add to its roster.

Here are the headlines of the ads in the order in which they appeared: 1) "There is no business operating at 100% efficiency—including yours," 2) "The more money your company makes, the more likely it is to *lose* money," 3) "Discontent. The most valuable management asset, the most difficult to keep," 4) "The CEO who's always ready for bad news always has good news for stockholders," 5) "Don't-do-anything-about-it-and-maybe-it'll-go-away is no way to run a business," and 6) "The trouble with a money leak in your business is you can't hear it."

Every headline was precisely directed to the head person on the corporate ladder. Each headline touched the prospect's self-interest. Each headline was provocative. Each headline hinted of the promise of a solution. Each headline impelled a prospect to read on.

The body copy was just as provocative as the headline. It was crisp. It was challenging. It drew responses from people difficult to reach.

These ads were consistently among the ten best noted and best read and among the four best remembered campaigns published in the *Wall Street Journal,* according to the *Journal's* own research.

These ads worked because the writer did an impressive amount of preliminary investigation before attempting to write them. He spent two months talking with Proudfoot clients learning how Proudfoot had benefited them. He called on a number of CEOs of major

ALEXANDER PROUDFOOT

Continued

corporations to learn their attitudes toward management consulting and what might be most likely to interest them in management consulting. He spoke with editors of the business press and with other management consultants. It was only after all this up front digging that he felt he could determine the nature of the advertising that would most benefit his client.

It's only fair to tell you that these ads were written by a master copywriter, Walter Weir. He has been a successful advertising craftsman for over fifty years. He'd be the first to tell you that there's magic in mere words, that you don't have to be fancy to be effective. But you do have to do your spadework first.

The more money your company makes,
the more likely it is
to <u>lose</u> money

Nothing succeeds like success, "they" say.

Nothing *fails* like success, we say.

Think about it. We spend a lot of time finding ways to be successful. And once we make it, all we think about is how to *stay* successful.

So we stop doing what *got* us there— not being satisfied with the way things were; looking for what we could do to make more money come in; finding every way *possible* to increase sales, production, profits.

The incentive—lack of success, of enough money—is gone. You can now take it a little easier, not be as concerned about efficiency. In all areas.

And—oddly enough—you have nobody to do *for* you the things *you* once did. Even though you can now afford it.

You may have nobody. But *we* have.

Alexander Proudfoot

Specializing in the Installation of Productivity Improvement and Profit Enhancement

The Alexander Proudfoot Worldwide Family of Companies. Founded 1946. Executive Offices: 249 Royal Palm Way, Palm Beach, FL 33480 (800-843-4877). Operating in the United States, Canada (Toronto 416-862-7543), Mexico (Mexico City 905-254-6711), Brazil (Sao Paolo 011.283.2533), Great Britain, France, Belgium (Brussels 02.511.0640), Federal Republic of Germany, Italy, Spain, Portugal, Denmark, Ireland, Luxembourg, The Netherlands, Hong Kong, Singapore (65.225.4646), Malaysia, Australia. This message prepared by Proudfoot Communications.

Discontent

The most valuable management asset,

the most difficult to keep

When is management most likely to lose the discontent that alone keeps a company climbing?

Usually after it's become—or even gotten close to becoming—the industry leader.

There's a great difference between *getting* there and *being* there.

Something happens to the discontent.

It's never too late to revive it. Or to have somebody—like us, for example—show you *why* and *how* to revive it.

Chances are, of course, your first discontent will be with *us*.

Over why we didn't let you hear about us sooner.

Alexander Proudfoot

Specializing in the Installation of Productivity Improvement and Profit Enhancement

The Alexander Proudfoot Worldwide Family of Companies. Founded 1946. Executive Offices: 249 Royal Palm Way, Palm Beach, FL 33480 (800-843-4877). Operating in the United States, Canada (Toronto 416-862-7543), Mexico (Mexico City 905-254-6711), Brazil (São Paulo 011.283.2533), Great Britain, France, Federal Republic of Germany, Italy, Spain, Portugal, Denmark, Ireland, Luxembourg, The Netherlands, Belgium (Brussels 2.511.0640), Hong Kong, Malaysia, Singapore (65.225.4646). This message prepared by Alexander Proudfoot Communications. L.P.

(In Florida Call 305-655-9300.)

"Don't-do-anything-about-it-and-maybe-it'll-go-away" is no way to run a business

In the management hot seat, nothing is more vital—no matter what happens—than keeping your cool.

And the best way to keep your cool is to know *what* to do. And *why*.

That's where we come in.

And uncertainty goes out.

Our experience in *making possible* the certainty a CEO needs for making critical decisions adds up to a number of lifetimes.

Someday you may be interested in adding a number of lifetimes of invaluable experience to your own.

When you are, we'd like to hear from you.

Alexander Proudfoot

Specializing in the Installation of Productivity Improvement

and Profit Enhancement

2

What You Should Know About Customers "Up Front": Preparation for Creative Strategy

Chapter Topics

Market research
People research
Consumer behavior
Selectivity
Attitudes
Repetition

Key Terms

"Up front" research
Focus groups
VALS
Perception
Novelty and contrast
Closure
Learning theory
Attitude measurement
Attitude change
Repetition with variations

Case Histories

Safety Belt Campaign
Kemper Insurance
VISA
Kleenex Softique

The subtitle of this book is "How to Put Creative Strategy to Work." But in order to have creative strategy at all, there has to be *knowledge*—not just knowledge of the product and its benefits, but, above all, knowledge of your potential customers. Knowledge comes from research (which is essentially just an organized way of gathering information).

STRATEGY: "UP FRONT" RESEARCH

In advertising there are two kinds of research. One of them, research on the effectiveness of the advertising itself, is covered in a later chapter. The other kind of research, which is far more important, is referred to as "up front research." This is the research on which strategy decisions are based.

Market Research

Simmons.   One phase of "up front research" studies the size and scope of the marketplace for a particular product. Who buys it? Who might buy it? How often? The most widely adopted source of market information today is the Simmons Market Research Bureau. National advertisers and agencies who subscribe to the Simmons service receive a "library" of booklets reporting on usage of many categories and brands of products every six months. The information on brands is comprehensive, covering age and family size groups, geographic distribution, degree of usage (light, heavy), frequency of purchase. Along with the product usage reports, Simmons issues booklets that detail the media usage of these same consumers. A brief study of Simmons research on almost any product will tell you which age group buys the most, what area they live in, what magazines they read, what television programs they watch.

Survey of Buying Power.   Another highly respected source of similar information for national advertisers is the annual *Survey of Buying Power* issued by *Sales and Marketing Management Magazine*.

Two of the other suppliers of market information are *Selling Areas-Marketing, Inc.* and *Mediamark Research, Inc.* These sources can arm you with an incredible amount of information before you start devising strategy.

People Research

Market researchers' reports about your customers are largely demographic—age, sex, education, income, and similar statistics. They tell little about your customers as people. More "up front research" is thus sought by today's advertisers.

Focus Groups. One of the simplest ways to learn more about customers as persons is through the use of *focus group interviews.* A focus group is a small assemblage of logical prospects for your product. These eight or ten people gathered together are given a topic of discussion by a researcher. They might discuss a certain aspect of your product or they might discuss what they don't like about a particular product category. In the group talk session, one comment prompts another. And another. A participant might hitchhike on somebody else's idea. The conversation is uninhibited. The researcher lets the respondents talk, largely without prompting, and taperecords the whole session. Occasionally such sessions also are filmed through a two-way mirror. Focus group interviews give you a remarkable insight into how your customers think and feel. If nothing else, the very language your customers use in ordinary conversation can lead to more real, more believable advertising copy.

VALS. On the assumption that you can never know enough about your customers, a number of the most sophisticated agencies and advertisers rely on yet another research system known as VALS (values and life styles), developed by Stanford Research Institute. Based on intensive "depth" interviews, VALS divides up potential customers into segments of the marketplace or general national audience. The VALS series of socio-economic-psychographic groups begins at the base of the market chart with Survivors (people barely able to keep body and soul together) and Sustainers (people who are just managing, with little hope of improvement). Next up the VALS scale come the Belongers (the great majority of the population, composed of hard-working, home-owning, church-going, patriotic people), and the Achievers (the second largest segment of the population, formed by people aggressively trying to better themselves). Among the groups in the VALS population is a small collection of individualists known as the "I-Am-Me" group. And there is a select group known as the "Societally-Conscious." Strange as some of those group designations may sound, you can see the practicality of VALS in preparing communications. For example, previous Merrill Lynch advertising said, "Merrill Lynch is bullish on America," and showed a herd of cattle. That's a Belonger's sentiment. It was not strong enough, or selfish enough, for the Achievers. Yet it is Achievers, persons actively concerned with their own welfare, who buy stocks. So the theme line was changed to "Merrill Lynch: A Breed Apart," and the commercials showed a single bull. The single bull remains; the theme now says, "Merrill Lynch believes your world should know no boundaries." Experience has proven that the VALS kind of research brings the writer close to the prospect as a live human being.

Housecalls, Inc. A quite recent, highly innovative form of "up front" research is named Housecalls, Inc. From a list of logical prospects, a dozen to two dozen people are selected for depth interviews in their homes. The difference in the Housecalls system is that the respondents are *videotaped* as they *use the product* and comment on it. After a minute or two, respondents forget about the presence of the camera. They act and talk very freely; their actions and reactions are natural and revealing. Once the interviews are completed, the managing director of Housecalls, a former agency creative head, analyzes them for both product and communications ideas. He then suggests concepts for future advertising by his clients.

You can learn a great deal about your particular customer from good "up front research," from various bits of marketing statistics. But it is also well for you to know something about people in the aggregate— particularly that phase of human behavior that social scientists call *consumer behavior,* especially as it relates to advertising.

UNDERSTANDING CONSUMER BEHAVIOR

What makes consumer behavior a legitimate study for scientists and scholars as well as for advertising practitioners? For many people in our society, the role of consumer is a key role. Consider, for example, the men and women who spend much of their time, effort, and judgment acting as purchasing agents for their families. Or those in the business world who must make many consumer decisions. For each and every one of us, whether we care to admit it or not, the way we behave as consumers gives us one means of expressing ourselves to the world.

Motivation

An analysis of sales figures will reveal *who* is buying the product or service, and that information is valuable. Of even more value, however, is *why* the product's customers chose to part with their money. This knowledge is essential if you want to turn prospects into customers.

It would appear that we consistently act to achieve certain goals, that we have been motivated in a particular direction since childhood. For many Americans the basic physiological needs of hunger and thirst have been reasonably satisfied and thus we tend to be motivated (usually by our parents) to satisfy higher-level needs: getting good grades in school, entering a profession, being an executive, making a lot of money. But these are not the only motives. Many of today's young people are motivated on a higher plane—dedicated to benefiting all of society rather than just themselves. Once the seed is planted it is difficult to uproot; some motives remain with us all our lives, becoming a key part of our psychological make-up.

The late Pierre Martineau, research director of the *Chicago Tribune,* contended that in many fields the dominant, powerful motives are so deeprooted that they are not apparent in any superficial manner. Martineau once studied what motivates intelligent people to smoke cigarettes, even when fear of death would seem an overriding motive *not* to smoke. His survey found that people smoke for a wide variety of reasons:

1. To demonstrate effectiveness (to indicate virility and vigor, productive maturity, sexual potency);
2. For mouth pleasure or oral indulgence (as in chewing gum and sucking mints);
3. To express possessiveness (a particular brand is highly personal property, an extension of self);
4. To be self-expressive (with distinctive smoking mannerisms);
5. For social poise (to have something to do with your hands);
6. As a reward for effort (when you've finished the job, you've earned a cigarette);
7. As proof of daring (particularly in a youngster);
8. For social meanings (the offer of a cigarette is a gesture of friendliness);
9. As a symbol of sophistication (it demonstrates worldliness);
10. For relaxation (for taking a break or enjoying the after-dinner period.)[1]

Perception

Like motivation, perception and response are elements of behavior. However, motivation when known, can be used to produce behavior, but it seldom can be altered by advertising; perception, on the other hand, although difficult to predict, can be influenced by the right advertising messages, presented in the right place at the right time.

Perception is the impression made on the human brain by all stimuli with which it comes in contact. In the process of this contact, the brain catalogues or classifies the stimuli in relation to its past experience.

The first time we become aware of a stimulus, it may impress us strongly. With repetition, we become accustomed to it and grow less responsive. So it is with sensational advertising. The first time we see it, our interest is excited by the impact. After repeated exposure the novelty is gone, and the message becomes blurred through our loss of interest.

We react to change in stimuli when change is pronounced. For example, a large change on a small item is far more apparent than the

1. Pierre Martineau, *Motivation in Advertising* (New York: McGraw-Hill, 1957), pp. 58–61.

same change on a larger item. And we abide by certain rules of constancy. These rules never change: a lemon is yellow, a book is rectangular in shape, and the walls of a room are perpendicular. We *know* this, in spite of what appearances might indicate at any given time. We wear constancies like a cocoon, which probably is a blessing of some consequence, considering all the different stimuli directed at us each day.

In order to break through this kind of mental protective barrier, it is necessary for the communicator to do something at least a little bit out of the ordinary. Thus, the writer employs novelty as a device to stop us by showing us what we don't expect, such as placing a black and white advertisement among full-color ads (or vice versa). It stands out by contrast.

Novelty and Contrast.   Attention to advertising can be captured in an infinite number of ways: an unusual picture, an odd-shaped illustration, a distinctive voice or accent. Noblia Citizen wristwatch showed a human hand painted to look like a zebra. Chivas Regal showed a sand castle in the shape of a Chivas Regal bottle. Dodge Colt inserted Japanese words into English headlines. Xerox used one page of a two-page spread to show an empty room with a blank wall and an electric wall plug, where the Portable Copier had been plugged in before somebody rolled it away to use elsewhere.

These are dramatic examples of pictures used in a novel way to create impact. However, attention can be attracted equally well by using a compelling and memorable slogan. The oldest and one of the best-known examples is that of Ivory Soap's restrained (and therefore credible) message "99 and 44/100 percent pure." More modern examples are General Electric's "We Bring Good Things to Life" and the Ford Motor Company institutional line "Quality is Job 1."

Size.   Although design of an advertisement can influence its impact regardless of size, size alone can generate a higher level of attention by readers. Using this insight, many advertisers employ one full page, two facing pages (a spread), or multiple successive pages to herald their advertising messages. Some advertisers have even used elaborate pop-up messages that are impossible for a reader to miss. In an ad itself, one enormous close-up photograph is more likely to catch the eye than several smaller illustrations.

Placement.   Of equal importance with size is placement of an advertisement, and print media charge a price that varies according to where the ad is scheduled to appear. Thus the back cover of a magazine, the inside front cover, and the inside back cover, positions consistently reported by Starch Readership surveys as attaining the most impact among readers, carry the highest premiums. These positions are frequently selected to introduce a new product, a new product use, or a special offer. Placement of the ad within the body of a publication is also important. A fashion advertisement should get more attention from potential buyers in the women's section of the newspaper than in the sports section. A television commercial will probably be more effective when positioned within the body of a program than during the clutter of a station break.

Color.   Color is used in many ways to gain more attention for an advertisement. Traveler's Insurance used a red umbrella in black and white ads for added impact. Most food advertisers use full color to provide realism and appetite appeal. And manufacturers who have made dramatic changes in packaging colors (such as Rheingold beer with its white can years back, or Pringles Potato Chips with its bright red canister) have reaped a rich harvest in increased interest.

The Familiar Stands Out.   All human beings have the inclination to see things whole rather than in part, especially familiar things. For example, a familiar object will stand out no matter how diffuse the background. You can immediately pick out your sweetheart in a crowd; you can instantly spot the Coca-Cola bottle on the soft drink shelves.

Closure.   The universal human tendency to report a complete figure for an incomplete one is called closure. In fact, the very act of completing the figure may register it more sharply in the mind. In advertising, this comes under the heading of audience involvement or audience participation. Some television commercials once featured a lovely woman floating through a flowery meadow singing "You can take Salem out of the country, but." There her sound stopped deliberately because the advertiser was certain that most people in the audience would automatically complete the lyric "You can't take the country out of Salem." *That* is closure. Some experts contend that advertising is more effective when the main point is implied rather than stated because it involves the reader or viewer. This presumes that the consumer will fill the gap and thus get the point more clearly—a dangerous presumption perhaps, as most consumers haven't the time or interest to complete the thought.

We Perceive Selectively.   While perception is an ever-present factor in determining how each of us adjusts to the world around us, we each perceive according to our own background. And we cannot possibly absorb all the stimuli that surround us—there simply is not room in the brain—so we must ignore much of what we perceive. But we do not do this at random; we do it selectively. In the final analysis, we see and hear what we *want* to see and hear.

Advertisers Can Be Selective, Too.   Lest all this sounds discouraging to the prospective advertising writer, consider the other side of the coin. Advertising can be selective too—at least, to a degree. Advertising can select a certain audience segment at which to beam a message. It may reach that particular audience through the use of selective media. And it certainly can feature selective headlines aimed only at the prospects it wants to reach.

Quaker State Motor Oil has practiced selectivity with great skill. One of its headlines was directed "To the Owners of Cars Which Don't Get Much Exercise." The accompanying photograph showed a sweet but proper suburban matron standing alongside her shiny and immaculate antique Packard sedan. Another Quaker State advertisement had the headline "To the Owners of Cars That Stay Out All Night." The picture underneath was a night shot of a crowded city street in an apartment-house neighborhood.

Learning

Buying behavior is a form of learning. Awareness and knowledge of certain advertising is a form of learning. The wise copywriter can sometimes apply the rules of learning to great advantage.

Repetition.   Most prominent among the principles of learning is repetition. From childhood on, we learn through repetition—how to tie our shoelaces, how to say our ABCs, how to hit a ball with a bat. We practice. We do it over and over again. Repetition is the chief reason for the campaign approach in advertising. When people see a long-running series of ads make a claim time after time, they "learn" it.

Generalization.   Generalization is a response elicited by a stimulus that is *different* from but *similar* to a familiar one. When we judge on the basis of a stereotype, we are generalizing (all Scots are thrifty). Through generalization we form images—of a retail store, for example. Several satisfactory buying experiences enable us to declare that Marshall Field's is the best store in the country. If we like our Chevrolet, we are inclined to accept General Motors as a great company. Generalization may make us quick to accept Pepsi when the soda fountain is out of Coke (or vice versa, of course).

Discrimination.   On the other hand, the learning principle of discrimination enables us to *avoid* making the same response to a similar but somewhat different stimulus. Shrewd marketers do not want consumers to accept a substitute so they emphasize the uniqueness of their product and how it differs from their competitor's. The shrewd marketer wants customers to be discriminating. Certainly the ingenious "Bud Light" campaign on TV is the epitome of urging discrimination.

Reinforcement or Reward.   Reinforcement or reward is usually necessary for learning, but not always. Many people who do not own a Volkswagen or a Polaroid camera are well aware of the benefits of each, thanks to superb advertising over a long period of time.

Once we learn something, it is almost impossible to persuade us to *unlearn* it. This indicates that it should be somewhat easier for an advertiser to sell a prospect a *new* product than to unsell the prospect's current product.

Several years ago, Professor Steuart Henderson Britt of Northwestern University wrote an article entitled, "How Advertising Can Use Psychology's Rules of Learning."[2] In examining just a few of his rules, we see how they apply to specific advertising cases.

Rule: "Unpleasant things may sometimes be learned as readily as pleasant things, but the most ineffective stimuli are those which arouse little or no emotional response." Consider some of those irritating television commercials for headache remedies. We may hate those pounding hammers, but we remember the product when we have a headache.

Rule: "The order of presentation of materials to be learned is very important." Studies indicate that points at the *beginning* and *end* of a message are remembered better than those in the middle. Might such considerations even affect the placement of television spots in a show?

Rule: "If material to be learned is different or unique, it will be better remembered." Recall how perception is increased through the use of novelty and constrast. Consider unusual sounds in radio or TV, like the sing-songy treatment of the derisive term "Wimpy! Wimpy! Wimpy!" for Hefty trash bags. Consider the black eye-patch on the "Man in the Hathaway Shirt."

Rule: "Learning is aided by active practice rather than passive reception." If you can get your audience members to participate in your sales message, they are much more likely to remember your brand. Consider how the use of a well-known tune pulls the audience along. Certainly the "I heard it through the grapevine" song was a smashing success for California raisins because the audience joined in. Consider how certain key advertising phrases get picked up and used in general conversation (e.g., "Where's the Beef?").

Personality

If the rules of learning can be employed advantageously by a copywriter, can the writer trace and appeal to personality characteristics of consumers? The study of human personality—that mystifying combination of motives and response traits—is fascinating, but until now the practical applications for marketing and advertising have been somewhat elusive. There is little solid evidence that personality measures can predict buying behavior.

One personality measure explored by sociologist David Riesman in the pursuit of consumer insight is susceptibility to social influence. In

2. Steuart Henderson Britt, *Printer's Ink* 252 (September 1955): 74, 77, 80.

his book *The Lonely Crowd,* Riesman suggests that the social character of people can be divided into three kinds: (a) tradition-directed (behavior that is oriented toward the past or resistant to change); (b) inner-directed (behavior that is guided by internalized personal values); and (c) other-directed (behavior that strongly depends on others for leadership and guidance). The evidence suggests that other-directed people are susceptible to social influence, that they are strongly influenced by their peers, and that they are constantly striving for approval. Any advertising based on the underlying idea of Keeping up with the Joneses is likely to have some impact on them.

A number of tests have been made that correlate brand choice with personality characteristics. Results have been largely inconclusive. Even if there were direct correlation, it would be difficult to pinpoint and reach an audience of consumers with a common personality make-up. But it is not impossible. Until recent years, available media were measured almost exclusively on the basis of demographics—age, income, education, and the like; now, however, media measurement services are exploring sociographic dimensions such as lifestyle and self-concept.

Attitude Formation

Short of measuring the influence of advertising on *sales,* the next most accepted measurement would be advertising's influence on *attitudes.* A number of behavioral scientists might disagree, but the majority would probably conclude that our attitudes are reasonable predictors of our behavior.

Because our attitudes are formed early in life, they are often an integral part of our personalities, difficult and painful to change, highly resistant to pressure intended to modify them.

Attitude Measurement

Although attitudes also resist measurement, psychologists are forever trying to measure them, and have developed several attitude scales that do a reasonable job of quantitative measurement in survey research. One of these is the Semantic Differential Scale, originated by Professor Charles Osgood of the University of Illinois. It is based on pairs of adjective opposites that assess meaning in terms of *evaluation* (good-bad); *potency* (strong-weak); *activity* (fast-slow). The Semantic Differential Scale offers seven categories of agreement for each concept: 1 and 7 signify "extremely"; 2 and 6 signify "quite"; 3 and 5 signify "slightly"; 4 signifies "neutral." For example:

Big Ten Football

dull *1 2 3 4 5 6 7* exciting

The Semantic Differential Scale has achieved widespread use in recent years for very good reasons. It is quick and easy to administer; it gives quantitative answers; it measures the intensity as well as the direction of attitudes.

Attitude Change

Measuring attitudes is difficult; *changing* attitudes is a monumental task. One reason involves *selective perception,* which can sidetrack incoming information three ways; (a) we ignore or avoid messages counter to our own point of view; (b) we twist messages to fit our point of view; (c) we quickly and conveniently forget messages that conflict with our point of view.

Granted all the difficulties, how can the advertiser hope to produce attitude change? Unhappily, advertising itself is universally recognized as a biased source of information. We are far more likely to pay attention to recommendations of relatives and friends. Some scholars have postulated a two-step flow of communication, whereby the message flows from the mass media to local opinion leaders (physicians, bankers, lawyers, teachers) and then to the friends, family, colleagues, and followers of the opinion leaders. It is an old saying—but true nonetheless—that the best advertising is word-of-mouth advertising.

A number of psychological studies in persuasion have been done on such topics as one-sided versus two-sided arguments, fear appeals, non-overt appeals, and the like. You find them detailed in almost any good current book on consumer behavior. The conclusions arrived at by these studies are interesting, but do not necessarily constitute gospel for the writer of advertising.

Repetition.   Since people learn through repetition, advertising repetition appears to be almost an essential for attitude change. Also, any sizable market keeps changing constantly. As David Ogilvy points out, the market you are advertising to is not a crowd but a passing parade.[3]

But while repetition may make people better acquainted with you, it does not ensure that their liking for you will increase steadily. Many times the opposite may occur. For example, a humorous television commercial may give you a chuckle the first time you see it. After a dozen or more times, it becomes deadly boring.

Repetition with Variations.   What is the best plan to follow in attempting to produce attitude change through advertising? If you study the advertising you admire personally, you will notice that it shrewdly repeats one basic appeal or theme, *with variations.* Most successful advertisers adopt this policy. Recall, for instance, the many inventive variations on the Coca-Cola and Pepsi-Cola themes.

Forced Use.   It is also possible to change attitudes through a forced use of the product via sampling. Procter & Gamble invest heavily in

---

3. David Ogilvy, *Confessions of an Advertising Man* (New York: Dell, 1963), p. 123.

sampling of new products in the hope that temporary use may lead to permanent change. Forced use may also be achieved with coupons, price offers, premiums, or contests. In this way, *behavioral* change would precede *attitude* change.

Reinforcement. It is sobering to realize that after you may have influenced an attitude change you have to work to *keep* that attitude changed. Festinger's theory of *cognitive dissonance* indicates that people go through a mental and emotional struggle to keep all their attitudes in balance. They stew for weeks, perhaps, before making a major purchase—weighing every argument, every consideration. Then, having made a decision, they do not breathe a sigh of relief. Instead, they immediately start worrying about whether it was really the *right* decision. So the advertising writer not only has to lead the prospect to the right decision, but must keep on beaming the advertiser's messages at the customer in order to reinforce that decision.

Combining a knowledge of human behavior with "up front research" on people and "up front research" on the marketplace gives you a pretty good idea of what your advertising must do. Thoroughly immersed in background knowledge you are ready to tackle strategy decisions, decisions made long before you touch pencil to paper. Now you begin to know what to be creative about.

CASE HISTORY
SAFETY BELT CAMPAIGN

Courtesy of Department of Transportation, the Advertising Council, and Leo Burnett Company.

This public service campaign from the Advertising Council and the Department of Transportation has as its theme line, "You Could Learn a Lot from a Dummy." Copywriting students could learn a lot from studying the subtleties of this advertising.

The objective of the campaign was to increase the frequency of seat belt use by people who occasionally buckle up—about 70 percent of all drivers. Consumer surveys of previous safety belt messages indicated that people were repelled by blood-and-gore advertising, that they didn't want to be preached to, and that they didn't want to be equated with a statistic.

The creative people at the Leo Burnett agency decided to try a totally different tack—humor. This was humor with a point, featuring two crash dummies talking to one another rather than somebody in authority talking directly to the viewer.

Because there was some natural concern over the use of humor to address the serious subject of highway safety, the campaign idea was tested first among members of the safety community. Obviously, the cooperation of safety professionals is essential to the Department of Transportation's efforts to promote the use of seat belts.

Overall, their reaction was positive. A common top-of-mind reaction was that the campaign was unique and different from previous seat belt advertising efforts. Most of the advertising that safety professionals had seen took a more serious approach. The use of humor was a clear and welcome departure from the serious tradition. It was also seen as a way of getting and keeping attention, making the message more acceptable, and causing people to think about the issue more than they had in the past. Comments on the use of humor included: "It humanizes the issue and makes it more acceptable." "It's a new twist on an old theme. Humor adds appeal and we know scare tactics don't work." "I like the use of humor. It masks the medicine taste."

The two dummies, Vince and Larry, offered several benefits. Since they are dummies they can use puns and double entendre ("You'd die if you had our job") that drive the message home but that real people could never say. They also permit the use of crash sequences without any of the horror that results when real people are in real crashes.

The fact that Vince and Larry deliver the message via dialogue was also seen as a benefit. Since the dummies are talking to each other, viewers

31

SAFETY BELT CAMPAIGN

Continued

don't feel they are being lectured on yet another thing they should do for their own good. As one respondent put it, "People don't want to be told what to do. But here the dummies are talking to each other, not preaching. You hear the message but it doesn't preach. That makes it more effective."

Finally, there was a sense that the use of dummies was particularly appropriate because dummies are a tool of the trade of safety professionals.

All these subtle touches combine to provide humor with an impact—an impact that may save a life.

"YOU'D DIE IF YOU HAD MY JOB."

BUCKLE YOUR SAFETY BELT.

CASE
HISTORY
KEMPER INSURANCE

Courtesy of Kemper Group.

One of the fundamentals of advertising success is that when you have a good thing going for you, *stay with it*. Since 1974 Kemper Insurance has been sticking with a good thing.

Probably the most basic of all communications goals is to create awareness. Kemper advertising was challenged to meet that goal and succeeded in creating a lasting image.

Up until 1974 the insurance-buying public was not very aware of the Kemper name. Not only that, Kemper was being outspent by as much as three to one by its better-known, more heavily advertised competitors. Kemper management set a tough task for its ad people: increase awareness among potential policyholders without increasing media expenditure relative to competitors' and develop a theme that is uniquely Kemper's, that relates to the overall concept of insurance, that is flexible enough to cover any kind of insurance.

The creative solution? A cavalry troop representing the employees of the Kemper Group led by a buckskin-clad cavalry scout who represents Kemper's independent agents. Who better than the cavalry symbolizes protection and help when you need it? These are the very qualities an insurance company needs to be known for. Not only that, but the symbolism of the cavalry and cavalry theme adapts to any insurance product situation from auto to home to business.

Since this colorful television campaign was launched, Kemper's corporate awareness level has more than doubled among the company's primary target audience. Today Kemper is definitely one of the better-known insurance companies. Along with its increase in awareness has been a rapid increase in sales of its property and casualty insurance products.

Success has come because the advertising has concentrated on projecting this single unique image for the company. Little wonder that the Kemper Cavalry continues to ride through the years.

CASE HISTORY
VISA

Courtesy of Visa U.S.A., Inc., and its agency, Batten, Barton, Durstine & Osborn, Inc.

For a beautiful example of positioning in advertising, Visa is everything you'd want it to be.

Going into 1985, Visa's business was very healthy and it was the leader in retail credit cards. But despite volume and cardholder growth, Visa was experiencing an image decline in consumer perception, low advertising awareness levels, and the competitive introduction of a new, strong retail credit card.

A new advertising campaign was called for, a campaign with multiple objectives. It had to regain the perceptual advantage that Visa had traditionally enjoyed versus Master Card as the best overall card for key payment situations. It had to maintain Visa's advertising awareness levels despite its severe competitive spending disadvantage. It had to maintain Visa's retail appropriateness in the face of the new Discover card competitive threat. And it had to improve consumer perception of Visa as appropriate for upscale travel and entertainment use. This last point provided the key to the new campaign.

The creative strategty recognized that Visa and Master Card were viewed as retail-oriented cards without the superior prestige of American Express and its upscale travel and entertainment usage. Visa decided to align itself with the category image leader, American Express, on a key performance advantage—acceptance. (Visa is accepted at four times as many establishments as American Express.) Focusing on this functional benefit allowed Visa to claim superiority over American Express, thereby gaining much needed prestige and positive user imagery from the comparison. By comparing Visa to American Express, the other credit cards are dismissed out of hand and relegated to a position of lesser stature.

Executions of the creative strategy take advantage of Visa's acceptance superiority over American Express by featuring the upscale, interesting, and unique establishments that accept Visa, "but don't take American Express." Each establishment is gloriously highlighted, even romanced, throughout the commercial so that viewers aspire to it as some place they want to be. This quality build-up adds importance to the competitive reference at the end of the commercial, expressed in the recurring theme line: "Visa. It's Everywhere You Want to Be."

The production qualities of the commercials are superb. The settings are lovingly photographed; the copy is brilliantly written.

Since the introduction of Visa's "It's Everywhere You Want to Be" campaign in October 1985, the brand has successfully achieved every one of its four campaign objectives.

A triumph of positioning. A treat to watch.

VISA®

It's everywhere you want to be.™

Client: VISA
Product: CLASSIC VISA CARD

Title: "BERMUDA"

Time: 30 SECONDS
Comml. No.: NZVCO285

If you take the Somerset Road

all the way out to Mangrove Bay

you'll find a very special place.

Captain John's Boat Yard,
one of the only places in Bermuda

you can rent a boat and a
motor, and spend the day

out over the coral,
looking for fish,

or out on the flats, just looking.
But remember two things . . .

Bring some sandwiches

and your Visa card.

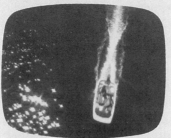

Because Captain John doesn't sell food,
and he doesn't take American Express.

It's everywhere you want to be.

Visa. It's everywhere you want to be.

CASE HISTORY
KLEENEX SOFTIQUE

Courtesy of Kimberly-Clark and its agency, Foote, Cone & Belding.

Throughout this book you are urged to "Strive for the Unexpected." What could be more unexpected than a nose with feet? A running nose, indeed. Could there be a better way to communicate the importance of softness in a tissue?

It took imagination to think of the nose with feet in the first place. It takes imagination on the part of the viewer to become involved with the message. This unusual concept could be done only with animation. Animation allows the advertiser to heighten the demonstration of product performance. Animation enables the commercial to dramatize the major benefit of Softique—that it is soothing.

The lovable animated Running Nose character made its first appearance in a 1984 Clio-winning commercial and since then has starred in a series of other commercials. One of the more recent, "Noses Run Wild," appealed to viewers with allergies. After suffering through a variety of painful experiences (including a buzz saw), our hero finds comfort by sinking into a luxurious stack of Softique tissues. The tag line for all these bizarre adventures is a natural: "Softness that's right on the nose."

At the time this engaging little creature was created, Softique faced a severe marketing challenge. Its softness superiority claim was no longer valid. A rival, Puffs, was firmly established as the leader of the premium segment. Softique advertising on the air was seen as average, at best. Levels of brand awareness and benefit association were low, calling for an *exceptionally intrusive,* distinctive effort. Advertising needed to raise the level of involvement between consumer and product. It needed to force, via the executional technique, a greater recognition of product and its benefit.

The running nose with feet came running to the rescue. And in 1985 the judges for the Clio awards selected "Nose to Nose" as the best animated commercial in the world.

FCB

Kleenex Softique.

"Runny Nose Rev."/Ordinary Tissues-New
KKKS 4113

1. (MUSICAL FANFARE)
ANNCR (VO): Introducing Kleenex®
Softique® tissues and "The Runny
Nose".

2. (SFX: CRASH) NOSE: Achoo!

3. ANNCR (VO): No wonder runny
noses get sore.

4. NOSE: Ooh! Aah!

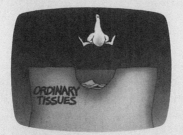

5. ANNCR (VO): Many tissues are
really irritating.

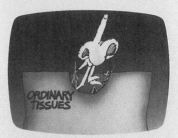

6. NOSE: Ow! Ow! Ow!

7. ANNCR (VO): But now, sensitive
noses can run into...
(SFX: BONK)

8. ...new Kleenex® Softique® tissues.

9. NOSE: Achoo! Achoo!

10. ANNCR (VO): Unlike ordinary
tissues, Softique® has special softness
fibers fluffed up for the softest touch
ever from a Kleenex® tissue.

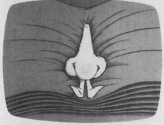

11. NOSE: Ahhhhhh...

12. ANNCR (VO): New Softique®.
For softness that's right on the nose.

3

Where Advertising Writing Begins: Creative Strategy

Chapter Topics

Key to successful
  advertising
Creative strategy/creative
  tactics
Purpose of creative
  strategy
Simplified creative strategy
Example of creative
  strategy
Personal profile
Emphasis on goals
Necessity for planning

Key Terms

Creative strategy
Creative tactics
Principal benefit
Principal target
Principal objective
Strategy statement
Personal profile
DAGMAR
Communications objective
Marketing objective

Case Histories

U.S. Marine Corps
Emery Worldwide
Pearle Vision Center
State Farm Insurance

If you are already interested in writing advertising, you are probably creative, imaginative, something of a poet or dramatist, a dreamer, a constant thinker-upper of ideas. All well and good. Advertising writing is indeed a creative process. But you'll discover in this chapter that the key to successful advertising writing is *knowing what to be creative about*. This is where creative strategy comes in—right at the start of the ad-making process, *after* the "up front" research.

There is a difference between advertising creative strategy and advertising creative tactics. Creative strategy comes first. Suppose, for example, you were one of the country's largest banks about to issue a credit card that could be used everywhere in America. Stressing that universal usage point is *strategy*. How you stress that point in advertising is a matter of *tactics*. Bank Americard chose to do it on radio with lively music, reciting all the names of all the states. It was memorable.

Creative strategy is a matter of determining *what* the advertising is to say. Creative tactics is a matter of *how* the advertising says it. If your creative strategy is correct, you are very likely to have effective (if not sensational) advertising. But if your creative strategy is wrong, you are likely to end up with ineffective advertising.

Creative strategy is not just some vague and lofty term; it embodies a set of rules and procedures long followed by most of our major advertising organizations. In fact, major or minor, there's hardly an intelligent advertiser who does not follow these principles—by whatever name.

Although no two advertising organizations outline creative strategy in precisely the same way, all base their analytical procedures on two essential factors: (1) knowledge of the customers that make up their market, as expressed in the needs and wants of the most logical prospects, and (2) knowledge of how their product benefits those customers in some special way. Almost all creative strategies are accompanied by a personal profile (a biographical sketch) of the most likely customer, a device we will examine shortly.

The purpose of the creative strategy is to give advertising copywriters and art directors one concise but complete document telling exactly what these creative people need to know in order to turn out great advertising. The creative strategy also bears the input and the approval of all the management people involved, so there is general agreement right from the start. As long as the creative person complies with the creative strategy, all is well.

A review of many recommended creative strategy outlines reveals that all of them identify the most likely customer and the wants, needs, and problems of that customer; all identify the special benefit of the product in helping solve the customer's problems; and all identify the effect the advertising should produce. Some creative strategies define the competitive situation; some call for proof of the benefit; some call for a "positioning" statement on how the product is already seen in the consumer's mind (luxury car or economy car); some call for a short analysis of media channels that might be used; some suggest a method for testing results; some may even indicate the general tone and manner of the creative approach. Most are accompanied by a personal profile. Some prominent advertising practitioners screen several strategy options before finally settling on a single creative work plan.

The creative strategy, which is agreed to by all interested parties before the creative work is begun, is generally a crisp and clear series of statements not exceeding one page in length. It is single-minded, concentrating on what is *most* important. And the creative strategy is always put in writing for ready reference as time goes on. Nowadays it is commonplace to hear an account executive ask, when shown new copy and layout, "Is this idea on strategy?"

An advertising creative strategy is simply an organized way of looking at all the facts and factors surrounding a marketing problem that must be solved. And while the principle of applying creative strategy is standard practice in the most sophisticated advertising circles in America, the analysis it involves is basic to every advertising problem anywhere. Advertising creative strategy can and should be applied on Main Street just as it is on Madison Avenue. It is the professional, commonsensical way to proceed. We suggest that you attack your various advertising problems by using the following simplified creative strategy outline.

SIMPLIFIED CREATIVE STRATEGY

Strategy Statement

Terse and to the point, the strategy statement embraces the following three points: (1) It spotlights your unique selling proposition as a consumer benefit, and factually supports that claim of benefit. (2) It describes the most likely prospect and how that prospect should react to the advertising. (3) It will probably refer to the way the product is currently positioned in the public mind if it is an established product, or how the company wants it positioned if it is a new product. The strategy statement lays out *what* is to be said in the advertising, but not *how* it is to be said. However, it is likely to indicate the general tone or manner of the proposed advertising.

1. **Principal Benefit.** How does the distinctive feature of your product or service meet consumer wants and needs in a way that differentiates it from competitors? What is your unique selling proposition? What can you say about your product benefit that a competitor cannot say or does not say? (Always look at a product's features in terms of consumer benefits. On a clock, the luminous dial is a *feature*. The *benefit* is that it can be read in the dark.)

2. **Principal Target.** Who is the most likely prospect for your product or service? Create out of statistics a single individual to whom you can talk directly in your advertising. In other words, draw up a personal profile.

3. **Principal Objective.** How do you want the customer to think, feel, and act after receiving your message? These goals are chiefly communications goals as opposed to marketing goals (a point we will examine directly), and they can be measured.

Let us review the key points of our creative strategy outline as they might apply to the creative case history of the United States Marine Corps. Read the case history at the end of this chapter with its distinctive commercial, and see if you can reconstruct what might have been the creative strategy. Do this with every case history in the book. Each is an authentic, detailed report of creative strategy applied in the marketplace. You can learn as much, or more, from a study of these experiences as you can from the main text.

Simulated Creative Strategy Analysis: Marine Corps

1. **Principal Benefit.** The Marine Corps offers a respected career for a young person about to finish high school.

2. **Principal Target.** High school seniors of good character who are uncertain about their futures.

3. **Principal Objective.** To perpetuate the generally held image of Marine Corps superiority over the other branches of the service.

Strategy Statement.   The United States Marine Corps offers an exciting yet respected career for a 17- or 18-year-old high school senior with no definite future plans. It offers adventure and glamour of particular appeal to a small-town kid at loose ends or a city kid trapped in drab surroundings. It offers the instant respectability of belonging to a select group. The advertising should strongly register the exclusivity of the organization.

In many instances this one-page creative strategy is accompanied by a personal profile. Just as the creative strategy is designed to help a writer know *what* to write about, the personal profile is designed to help a writer know *whom* to address. It is difficult to argue with the theory that a writer can communicate more naturally and more convincingly when talking to just one individual rather than to a mass audience. The fact that this individual is manufactured does not matter. The individual *could* be real, because the person is created from statistics bearing on the target market. The individual is given a name and a detailed family history that could indeed be true. This personal profile, which is created from a mass of marketing data and statistical information, comes partly out of demographics—age, sex, education, income, occupation, residence—and partly out of psychographics—lifestyles, innovativeness, social consciousness. The single customer in question is also developed from: focus group interviews, a study of buying patterns, a review of letters to management, good human insights, and a tiny bit of imagination.

So much emphasis is placed on the personal profile today that—in one notable instance—a store-window mannikin was used to deliver, via audiotape, her own "buyer's biography" at an agency-client presentation in the board room.

Imagine how this same technique might have been used for Marine Corps recruiting. A well-built, freckle-faced young male mannikin might have said:

> Hi. My name is Jerry Jones and I'm from Jackson, Tennessee. Well, not Jackson exactly, but from a farm a couple of miles outside. We have a small farm and a big family. Mother, Dad, five brothers, and three sisters. I'm the fourth oldest boy and I'll be finishing at Jackson High this spring. Don't know what to do after that. I'm a pretty good baseball player, but not good enough to earn a living at it. There really isn't much for me to do on the farm, and there sure isn't anything for me to do in Jackson. Pump gas, maybe. Or clerk in the supermarket. My grades are good enough to get me into college, but we haven't got that kind of money. And, besides, I'm not sure I'm ready to hit the books again just yet. I'd really like to get away for a while and see what life is like in the outside world.

Now here is a person you can like, understand, sympathize with, and want to help. Here is also a person you can easily communicate with.

If that little recital had been a typed, third-person descriptive personal profile, it might have been dotted with footnotes referring back to the statistical material that formed the basis for a particular comment.

The personal profile is a tremendous aid to the advertising writer because it encourages genuine person-to-person communication.

Like every other form of writing, advertising writing is creative and offers abundant opportunity for imagination. However, unlike non-commercial writing, advertising strategy establishes a fixed set of objectives or goals that must be met by the copy. Obtaining these strategic objectives is the only legitimate purpose of advertising.

STRATEGY: UNDERSTANDING OBJECTIVES

Advertising writers control only the content of the message; they have no control over the medium through which the message is transmitted, or the conditions under which it is received by the audience. Therefore, advertising writers must do everything possible to make sure of their ground before beginning the writing task. This in turn makes it essential that advertising writing focus on a specific objective.

Until a generation ago, most advertising practitioners would have said flatly that the objective of any advertisement was to sell goods. Then in 1961, the Association of National Advertisers published a potent little booklet by Russell Colley. *Defining Advertising Goals for Measured Advertising Results* (commonly called DAGMAR) advocated a more precise measurement of advertising effectiveness than sales results alone. Because so many variables that have nothing to do with advertising can affect final sales (product, price, packaging, retailer cooperation, competitive efforts, general economic conditions, weather, and the like), DAGMAR recommended sharply-defined *communications goals* (creating awareness, for example) as a reasonable expectation of advertising. DAGMAR sharply distinguishes between communications objectives and marketing objectives. "To increase share of market from seven to ten percent in one year" is a marketing objective. "To teach consumers new uses for a product" is a communications objective. If an advertising campaign were designed to establish a new company slogan, for instance, then measured public awareness of that slogan would be a valid test of the advertising's success.

DAGMAR contends that a new product or a new advertising approach begins at a point of total unawareness by the general public and moves to a state of awareness, then to comprehension, then to conviction, and finally to action. First the public must see your message. Then it must understand your message. Next it must be convinced by your message. And finally the public must act upon your message. DAGMAR states that advertising can have a goal in any of those four stages—awareness, comprehension, conviction, action.[1]

Here, according to DAGMAR, are ten of the legitimate and measurable communications goals that are not directly measurable in terms of sales.[2]

1. Create awareness of the product's existence.
2. Create a favorable emotional disposition toward the brand.
3. Implant information about benefits and features.
4. Combat or offset competitive claims.
5. Correct a false impression or misinformation.
6. Build familiarity with and easy recognition of the package and trademark.
7. Build the corporate image and favorable attitudes toward the company.

---

1. Russell H. Colley, *Defining Advertising Goals for Measured Advertising Results* (New York: Association of National Advertisers, 1961), p. 55.
2. *Ibid.*, pp. 62–68.

8. Establish a reputation platform for launching new brands or product lines.

9. Register a unique selling proposition in the minds of consumers.

10. Develop leads for salespeople.

Advertising objectives are almost limitless, and there may even be more than one objective for a single advertisement. If you examine good advertising, the objective quickly becomes apparent. Perhaps you once saw an unusual Campbell Soup advertisement headlined "Soup On the Rocks." Its goal was to get the public to think in a new way about an old favorite, beef bouillon. Another ad, headlined "Soup For Breakfast," had the objective of getting people to eat soup at different times. You can test your own perception of advertising objectives against the creative case histories in this book. You'd probably agree, for instance, that the Marine Corps advertising is designed to project an image of the Corps that instills pride in its new recruits. Coors Beer advertising is designed to build an aura of quality about the product in a way that differentiates it from the frenetic appeals of other beers. Every State Farm ad reiterates and reinforces its long-term slogan: "Like a good neighbor, State Farm is there." Dannon Yogurt advertising promotes the image of the brand as a pioneer. French's Mustard advertising good-naturedly plants the idea of superiority for its yellow mustards. Kleenex advertising is designed to foster a favorable emotional disposition toward the brand. Raid advertising strongly registers a unique selling proposition on the minds of consumers. Emery advertising implants information about benefits and features. The Jamaica Tourism advertising is designed to correct a false impression. After examining the other case histories, you can probably rattle off the appropriate objective or objectives in each case. Your objectives will always be determined, however, by the particular marketing/advertising problem you are trying to solve at the time.

STRATEGY: WORKING TO A PLAN

It is vital that the creative person knows what to be creative *about*. Every product or service exists to help human beings solve a particular problem. The parent organization, which knows why it is in business and where it hopes to go, has an overall marketing strategy that considers product, price, packaging, and distribution, among other factors. The company's advertising creative strategy must be tailored to fit that overall marketing strategy. The advertising itself must be created according to strategy or plan, and that plan must be written. In turn, each individual copywriter tackling each individual assignment must work to a plan or strategy, and that plan—whether elaborate or informal—should be written.

Primarily the writer plans in order to achieve a certain objective—generally a communications objective that ties in with the parent company's overall marketing and advertising objectives.[3] Particular objectives aside for the moment, the necessity for the writer to apply creative strategy first is obvious for a number of reasons:

1. There is no single, sure-fire copy formula to meet each selling situation. What works in one set of conditions does not necessarily work in others.

2. Advertising is only one element in the selling process, sometimes a minor element. The writer must relate the copy to all other elements of marketing strategy. And the writer must be aware of and take into consideration the importance of salespeople, wholesalers, and retailers in the success of the advertising efforts.

3. Strategy and planning force a writer to use background information.

4. Strategy and planning focus attention on copy objectives, without which the advertising has no sense or direction.

5. Strategy and planning force the writer to work within a sensible pattern. One of the most talented and successful copywriters in New York agency circles began every project by propping up in front of her a time-worn hand-lettered card. On the card were these five lines:

    > What *is* it?
    > What does it *do?*
    > *How* does it do it?
    > *Where* can I get it?
    > *How much* does it cost?

    By answering these basic consumer questions to herself, she wrote copy in a sensible pattern.

6. Strategy and planning provide the writer with a basis for defending copy. At some point in a business situation, a top administrator is likely to ask, "Why did you do it this way?" Woe to the advertising writer who stammers, "Well, the idea sorta grabbed me."

You have now been introduced to creative strategy and the personal profile, and can understand and appreciate the purposes of both. You are familiar enough with the form or outline of a strategy to compose a creative strategy and a personal profile of your own. But you can take this step only after you have the proper background information. This leads us to the next point of discussion: Where do ideas for ads come from? You'll see that ad ideas often follow the asking of some very obvious questions.

---

3. S. Watson Dunn, *Advertising Copy and Communication* (New York: McGraw-Hill, 1956) pp. 58–61.

CASE HISTORY
U.S. MARINE CORPS

Courtesy of United States Marine Corps and its agency, J. Walter Thompson.

One of the old bromides in American folklore is the expression, "Tell It to the Marines." The 1980s have certainly shown that the Marines know how to tell it to America in dramatic, distinctive advertising.

The U.S. Marine Corps competes with other military services primarily for seventeen- to twenty-one-year-old males, putting overall emphasis on quality recruits. With the economic outlook including employment, fairly stable in recent years, a greater challenge was presented to the enlistment of quality recruits since more nonmilitary jobs were available. Furthermore, there has been a decline in the target market population and a decline in the target market's propensity to join a military service.

Marine Corps advertising was expected to (a) attract quality recruits; (b) maintain an unaided advertising awareness measurement range from 55-60 percent among the target group; (c) create a positive disposition among seventeen- to twenty-one-year-old males toward the Marine Corps; (d) integrate advertising support into the systematic recruitment system; and (e) establish a perceived superiority for the U.S. Marine Corps, and thus differentiate it from the other military services.

Marine Corps recruitment advertising had three target audiences. First, for enlisted recruits, the primary target audience was male high school seniors or graduates, ages seventeen to twenty-one. Second, for officer recruits, the target group was male college undergraduates, ages eighteen to twenty-one, and minority college students, eighteen to twenty-one. The third target audience was a group called the "influencers," consisting of parents, coaches, school counselors, Marines, and former Marines.

In the overall United States recruitment advertising budget, the Marine Corps has approximately 11 percent. (U.S. Army spending is approximately five times U.S. Marine Corps spending.)

Facing this set of conditions and challenges, the Marine Corps introduced a dramatic and memorable advertising effort known as the "Sword" campaign in 1984. The results have been spectacular.

In 1985 the enlistment of quality recruits (defined as high school graduates) rose to a historical high of approximately 97 percent. Advertising awareness goals were met among the target market even though there had been no increase in spending. Marine Corps slogan recognition with the target audience was at an all-time high. The "Sword" campaign

U.S. MARINE CORPS

Continued

has received tremendous reviews by the U.S. Marine Corps recruiting force and has, in fact, served to energize and motivate them. Research has shown that the primary criterion for a recruit's decision to join the Marine Corps versus another branch of the service is the prestige of the Marine Corps and its perceived elite image as exemplified in the "Sword" campaign.

In addition to its effectiveness in the U.S. Marine Corps recruiting efforts, the "Sword" campaign has won the highest accolades and awards from the advertising industry itself.

CASE HISTORY
EMERY WORLDWIDE

Courtesy of Emery Worldwide and its agency, J. Walter Thompson.

One of the most difficult tasks facing an advertising program is that of trying to *regain* position lost to a clever and aggressive competitor. This was the task facing Emery in 1985.

Once upon a time there was a pioneer in air cargo called Emery Air Freight. Emery was *it* in air cargo for many years. Then, not so terribly many years ago, along came Federal Express. The business changed from cargo to overnight delivery of letters and packages. Emery quickly lost its leadership position. By the end of 1984 Federal Express dominated the market in both awareness and sales revenues. In unaided advertising awareness the lead for Federal over Emery was 83 percent to 47 percent. In unaided brand awareness the gap was 76 percent to 42 percent. In sales revenue, Federal's margin over Emery was nearly three to one.

Nowadays Federal is perceived as the standard of performance in an industry where reliability is paramount. Federal can deliver superior performance because its resources outstrip Emery on the ground and in the air. Federal leads Emery in number of employees, planes, trucks, and drop boxes. Federal's dominance is so great that it is virtually generic for overnight delivery. Emery faced other barriers in addition to the dramatic gaps in awareness and resources. Federal's share in lightweight office-type mailings exceeds Emery's ten to one. Overall market growth is slowing, thereby putting a greater emphasis on share of market as a source of revenue. Finally, the public perception of Emery was that of a high-priced air freight company that could not match Federal's performance capability.

Emery's new advertising had to strengthen Emery's value perception and make the brand a relevant choice to the mass of lightweight shippers, the so-called "Office America." No small task.

To counter Federal's heavy spending, market dominance, and highly successful use of humor and negative office calamities, Emery chose the positive, upbeat campaign known as "9 to 5."

The objectives of the "9 to 5" campaign were to (a) increase unaided advertising awareness by 25 percent; (b) increase unaided brand awareness by 15 percent; (c) increase unduplicated customer trial by 15 percent; (d) significantly improve Emery's value perception as an overnight provider of quality service for "Office America"; and (e) increase total shipments 23 percent and lightweight shipments 40 per-

EMERY
WORLDWIDE

Continued

cent by expanding the customer base and generating more business from current customers.

Even though outspent by Federal at least two to one the new Emery "9 to 5" campaign was successful on every count. In fact, the percentage goals originally set by Emery were dramatically exceeded. For the first nine months of the "9 to 5" campaign, total shipments far exceeded objectives and lightweight business went through the roof. In fact, Emery's envelope-sorting facility, which had operated at 60 percent of capacity the previous year, jumped to full capacity. A second line had to be added to handle the increased shipments.

EMERY
WORLDWIDE

Title: One Of Those Days   **Length: 30 Seconds**   **Code: YEFC 5013**

(MUSIC)

SINGERS: Spilled a cup of coffee.

Ruined a sweater.

Boss is screaming where's that letter.

Call Emery and it's as good as there!

Emery's on the case so you don't have to worry.

We go anyplace and get it to you in a hurry.

From the biggest

to the smallest

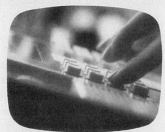

it's as good as there, just call us.

EXECUTIVE: Hi Emery . . .

SINGERS: It's as good as there.

CASE HISTORY
PEARLE VISION CENTER

Courtesy of Pearle Health Services, Inc., and its agency, Foote, Cone & Belding.

All good advertising touches the emotions in some manner and to some degree. But few television commercials have the emotional appeal and impact of those for Pearle Vision Centers.

"The idea behind the Pearle Vision campaign is not just to sell eyeglasses. The idea is *trust*," explains the creative director. Each commercial presents a different scenario in which a loved one is in need of glasses or contact lenses. The creative team came up with situations and characters that capture the attention of viewers and gain their sympathy. A Little Leaguer unable to hit the ball, a grandfather who struggles to read a fairytale to his granddaughter, and a little girl who breaks her glasses before a piano recital all have their sight problems resolved by going to Pearle Vision. As the themeline reiterates musically, "Nobody cares for eyes more than Pearle."

Great creative ideas often evolve from the personal experiences of the creator. So it was with the commerical entitled "Fear Strikes Out." The agency's executive creative director tells the story of his son's first starting assignment as goalie in a junior hockey league game. The boy was covered from head to toe with the tools of the trade. He couldn't skate a lick, but he was determined to show his father what he could do.

The youngster had a rough afternoon. He watched twenty-two goals zip past him, and his team finished on the short end of a 22-0 pasting. In the car on the ride home, the boy turned to his ad-executive father with tears in his eyes and said, "Dad, I stink."

In all the Pearle Vision Center commercials the dialogue between the characters is very natural. The creative director emphasized that the writing is critical: "If there are dialogue lines that are sappy and unbelievable, no matter how good the film, the situation is going to seem false." Commenting on the magical dimension of television, he said, "A lot of times, a look in someone's face will tell you more than what you could ever do with dialogue. It's more emotional because you can read into it how you would feel in that situation."

These commercials have rung true not only to the home viewer but to advertising critics as well. The Pearle Vision Center spots earned a Bronze Medal award at the New York International Film Festival.

PEARLE™ vision center

"FEAR STRIKES OUT"

"Nobody cares for eyes more than Pearle"

SONG: YOU CAN SEE IT IN HIS EYES.

HE SET HIS SIGHTS SO HIGH. (Music under) UMPIRE: Strike 3!

SONG: WE'LL SEE YOU THROUGH THOSE TRYING TIMES

THAT COULD MAKE A GROWN MAN CRY.

KID: I stink.

ANNCR (VO): When the right glasses could make all the difference,

more people trust Pearle than anywhere else.

SONG: YOU'LL SEE IT IN HIS EYES (SFX: CRACK)

WHEN HIS HOPES

ARE REALIZED.

NOBODY CARES FOR EYES

MORE THAN PEARLE.

CASE HISTORY
STATE FARM INSURANCE

Courtesy of State Farm Insurance Companies and its agency, DDB Needham Worldwide.

It takes foresight, patience, and resolve to present a consistent image to the public in advertising. But those advertisers who do so over time win loyalty that is priceless. Consider the case of State Farm Insurance.

For many years, State Farm built its auto insurance business by offering low rates to careful drivers who lived in small towns and rural areas. By the late 1960s State Farm's rate advantage had narrowed or disappeared. Neither a rate story nor a general advertising focus on "State Farm is all you need to know about insurance" was enough to distinguish State Farm from its strengthening competition.

The advertising challenge at that time was to position State Farm in a unique way versus growing competition in order to maintain current policy holders, attract quality prospects, and serve as a role model for State Farm's agent force.

Research indicated that, particularly for home and auto insurance, consumers placed a great deal of importance on the competency, availability, and attitude of the agent who sold and serviced the insurance. To position State Farm with these attitudes in mind, a new campaign was launched in 1971 with the theme "Like a Good Neighbor, State Farm Is There."

In the beginning, actors were used to portray agents. Later, experimental spots using real agents were produced to see if the naturalness of their approach added to the quality of communication. Research confirmed that this latter approach did increase advertising effectiveness, so since 1973 real agents in real-life situations have been used exclusively. This unique selling idea has clearly separated State Farm from all its competition.

Since the inception of this campaign, slogan awareness has increased more than 75 percent, in spite of advertising expenditures that are traditionally less than those of State Farm's nearest competitors. Further, consumers continue to play back positive opinions about both the agent-presenter and the image of the company.

Advertising plays an important, but not dominant, role in the marketing of State Farm Insurance; however, the "Good Neighbor" message has been very effective in positioning State Farm to policy holders, prospects, and agents alike. This marketing and advertising approach has strongly contributed to growing advertising and company awareness, a positive company image, and maintenance of the company's number one position in the auto and home insurance business.

In this case, consistency has proved a gem.

NEEDHAM HARPER WORLDWIDE, INC.   303 E. Wacker Drive Chicago, IL 60601 (Phone: 312—861-0200)

Client: State Farm Insurance
Product: Multi Insurance   Length: :30
Film Title: "'85 Multi/Pomey (Check-Up)"
Film #:   OQMA-1730   Date: February, 1986

1. (Music under) ANNCR (VO):
Life is full of changes and State Farm
is there.

2. POMEY: I'm State Farm Agent
George Pomey.

3. If your family is like mine,
you'll find reminders of how
fast things change.

4. Wasn't so long ago...

5. ...my daughter Jill was riding
in this.

6. Now she drives this.

7. Look around you. If you see
your insurance needs have changed,
Auto - ...

8. ...Home - Life - or Health,...

9. ...see your State Farm Agent
for a family insurance check-up.
The advice is free...

10. SINGER: AND LIKE A GOOD
NEIGHBOR...

11. POMEY: ...and the decisions
are yours.

12. SINGER: ...STATE FARM
IS THERE.

4

Some Obvious Questions to Ask: How to Discover Ideas for Copy

Chapter Topics

Information search
Sensible questions
Engineers versus
    salespeople
Seasonal buying
Benefits versus features
Cardinal sin in copywriting
Building belief
Guarantees and warranties
Previous advertising
Competitor's advertising
Know your customer
Where the advertising
    appears
Creative strategy
Isolating the main selling
    idea

Key Terms

Company archives
Sales outlets
Regional differences
Seasonal patterns
Performance records
Customer correspondence
Customer benefits
Credible source
Field tests/use tests
Special fame
Competitive claims
Customer patterns
Media differences
"Gathering raw materials"
Prime prospects

Case Histories

Mazda
Coors Premium Beer
Jamaica Tourist Board
Pledge

The beginning student of advertising writing may be overwhelmed by the enormity of the task ahead. The writer understands the general principles expounded by the text, but may not know what specific steps to take. What are my goals, the writer may ask. Where do I find a background study? The writer may feel alone, isolated, as though the entire load of spotting and solving the problem is on the writer's back.

But this is not so, as you will discover when you face a real-life advertising problem for the first time. In practice, you will be part of an ongoing activity, and the enterprise to which you are attached will provide the necessary goals, guidance, information, and support. As you become more immersed in the enterprise, you will be better able to understand it and interpret it to the public.

You can turn for information to your company's library or archives, to its sales records, the data it has on its competitors, its research on consumers and markets, and its standards for manufacturing and testing what it makes. You begin the quest for information by asking many simple questions and researching many simple facts about the product. Here are some of them.

WHO MAKES THE PRODUCT?

The most obvious question is: Who makes the product? What is the background of the company that produced it?

Every product and every company has a history. A long history is a good sign that the company has pleased the buying public. When a company with a long history introduces a new model, it is fair to announce it a being "Backed by 100 years of experience." For a company with a track record for innovation the writer might say, "Now, from the same company that created the three-speed ratchet and the isotonic wedge, comes the newest idea in widgets." Was the founder of the company a pioneer in the field? Does the company make a broad line of products? Is it famous for a particular model? For example, "Moonbeam—an entirely new way to wake up—brought to you by the makers of Big Ben." Notice how often Ford refers to "Thunderbird styling" or reminds us in its advertising of the Model T and the Model A. Cluett Peabody is still getting mileage out of the chisel-chinned "Man in the Arrow Collar" who dates back to World War I days. The beginning copywriter can begin by studying history. It pays.

HOW IS THE PRODUCT MADE?

Products don't spring forth full-blown. They have to be designed, engineered, and produced, and you can learn much by talking to those responsible for these three basic steps. Why is the product a particular height, weight, or shape? Is there a consumer advantage there? For example, "The lunchbox that fits in the glove compartment of your car." Of what materials is the product made? Do they give you a benefit to talk about? If so, you might say something like, "Half as light, twice as strong as other pocket radios."

You will soon learn that engineers and production managers are not as competitive as salespeople and advertising copywriters. Engineers are very pragmatic scientists. They understate and are more likely to stress similarities than differences between products. But you must keep the engineers talking; pump them thoroughly. Eventually you will learn tidbits—facts, figures, even philosophies—that can be turned into persuasive sales copy.

HOW IS THE PRODUCT SOLD?

The copywriter who talks to a company salesperson is talking to a kindred soul. Unlike the engineer, the salesperson is definitely competitive, interested chiefly in moving merchandise. From the salesperson, you want to know how the product gets into the hands of the consumer. Through what kinds of outlets is the product sold—department stores, supermarkets, drug stores? What kind of distribution does the product have? Is it sold nationwide? Is it sold in many stores in a single town, or is there one franchise to a community? Is it a product that requires service—like an automobile? Is service close at hand? Are replacement parts readily available? This kind of examination leads to such copy claims as the Midas Muffler boast: "We have to do a better job. We're specialists." And since they **are** "specialists," Midas must also reassure prospects by boasting of how many shops it has across the country. It is a discouraging fact of business life that the finest advertising copy in the world cannot do much to help a product that does not have adequate distribution.

WHEN AND WHERE IS THE PRODUCT SOLD?

All companies keep sales figures, which can reveal many idiosyncrasies of the marketplace. You may find regional differences that are obvious (due to climate, perhaps) and regional differences that are subtle and fascinating (due to some sociological influence). You must understand and reflect these differences. (If metropolitan New York accounts for the bulk of instant coffee sales, that's where the bulk of the advertising effort should be applied.) But you must try to seek out and understand the *why* behind these differences. (Such effort may lead to a new selling theme that will also increase the consumption of instant coffee in Phoenix.) You can learn a great deal from the "pockets of resistance" revealed by sales figures and may even devise a new way to penetrate them. You may also learn that it is more practical to switch the efforts elsewhere.

Some years ago, one of the authors worked on the advertising for Chicago's leading brewer. Sales figures were analyzed regularly, and each single driver's route was studied. Here and there would be a "dry" pocket surrounded by high sales areas. Why? The quality of the beer was uniform. The driver-salespersons were, for the most part, equally skilled and efficient. Examination confirmed that the population of the neighborhood was changing. Ethnic groups were shifting. Certain of them either didn't drink beer at all or strongly preferred some other brand.

The purchase of many products follows a seasonal pattern. Some of these are obvious—outercoats in winter, suntan lotions in summer—but other products fall under the heading of "gift items" and live or die for the year on the basis of their sales in November and December. A clock or watch is a practical item, an essential item, relied upon all day, every day. Yet the overwhelming majority of clocks and watches in America are sold at three distinct periods of the year—the wedding-graduation season, the back-to-school season, and the Christmas season. The same pattern holds true for fountain pens. The shrewd copywriter adapts, and does not try to fight an established pattern.

HOW HAS THE PRODUCT PERFORMED?

Every product seems perfect when it leaves the drawing board and the factory, but how does it work in use? Perhaps an early model of the product is still performing valiantly. If so, you might say something to the effect that it "Started working when Harding was President; still on the job today." In the early 1980s the Volvo motor car boasted loudly about the number of its original shipment to the United States that were still on the road. Actual use may indicate advantages that even product engineers didn't anticipate. Perhaps a washing machine completes the rinse cycle two minutes faster than similar machines. Perhaps a car driven at a steady sixty-five miles per hour gives 2 percent greater mileage than average. You may learn of these developments from company salespeople and dealers, an excellent source of information on what happens to products after they get out in the field. And copy based on actual performance in use is far more convincing than the most glowing promises from a manufacturer.

WHAT DO CUSTOMERS SAY ABOUT THE PRODUCT?

Every well-run enterprise keeps a file of correspondence from customers. This is precious feedback. You can learn from both the letters of complaint and the hymns of praise. Knowing what bothers people most about a product category can help provide a more persuasive approach. In the early days of fast-food franchises, people complained about limited choices. That situation has changed dramatically. In fact, many letters from customers can be used intact in ads or as the basis for ads. Ford once made capital from the letter of a woman who had received a parking ticket on which the police officer identified her car as a Cadillac rather than a Ford. Check the letters to find out *what* people say about the product and *how* people say it.

A popular mechanism with research departments today is the focus group interview in which several randomly selected prospects talk informally and candidly about the product while their comments are recorded on audiotape. A playback of these tapes not only reveals attitudes and suggests ad themes, but gives the alert writer a true-to-life vocabulary that may help make the copy more believable.

WHAT'S THE BIG ADVANTAGE TO THE CUSTOMER?

Every product has a reason for being; it was created to answer some human need or want. Even the much-joked-about buggy whip was a hot item in its day. With a plethora of products for every human need, today's copywriter must endow the *basic* advantage of the product category with the *special* advantage of the product. All cars provide transportation, but all cars are not alike. There are differences in purchase price, driving mileage, capacity, comfort, styling, and image. People do not buy Cadillacs for the same reasons others buy Yugos, and this is quite apparent in the advertising for the two cars. All television sets show pictures, but all TV sets may not offer remote tuning.

In pursuing the copy homework, think first and foremost in terms of customer *benefits*—not features, per se, but benefits. A clock's musical alarm is a *feature*. The fact that the clock wakes you gently is a *benefit*. When Zenith introduced remote tuning for television, the headline did more than simply feature the miraculous new device. It stressed the *benefit:* "Now turn off those long, annoying commercials from across the room." Not all features can be directly translated into selling benefits. The fact that a clock has hands is a feature, but it is not an impressive benefit and it is certainly not a *competitive* benefit.

The key word in persuasive advertising is *differentiate*. The copywriter must analyze the background information and the evidence in the light of discovering what makes the particular product *different* from that of competitors. Many a creative director insists that *the cardinal sin in copywriting is to create a message that could be signed by a competitor*. This kind of competitive attitude makes the organized search much simpler: you quickly discard the ordinary and concentrate efforts on the extraordinary.

Suppose, for example, that two lightweight travel bags are identical in capacity and shape. Each tucks neatly under a plane seat, but one has a carrying handle and the other has a carrying strap that can be adjusted for over-the-shoulder use. Benefit? With the over-the-shoulder strap, the owner's *hands are free* for showing tickets, digging out a passport, making change. This is a different and demonstrable benefit, a definite advantage.

HOW DO WE PROVE THE BIG ADVANTAGE?

In advertising, it is not enough to discover and announce a significant advantage. That advantage must be believed, and the advertising must prove the advantage—a difficult task, since all advertising is an obvious form of self-pleading, that is, a biased source of information.

The wise copywriter seeks some kind of credible source to substantiate every claim; people pay more attention to what somebody else says about you than what you say about yourself. You might, for instance, search background information for evidence of product use or approval by a leading authority. What kind of golf club does the U.S. Open champion use? What kind of stereo system does the top recording star listen to? What kind of family car does the Indianapolis 500 winner drive?

Check quality control for the methods and results of manufacturing tests. Volkswagen's classic "Lemon" ad was based on the manufacturer's stringent quality control testing system—the story of a beautiful new car that "flunked."

Even more convincing are tests done by independent testing firms like United States Testing Company and Good Housekeeping Institute. The results of field tests or use tests can be very dramatic. One automotive parts manufacturer, Motorcraft, reported periodically on use of their products by an independent taxicab company in several large cities—use running into the millions of miles.

Satisfied customers offer evidence of proof, which is why so many industrial advertisers adopt the case history technique for advertising their appliances or machines. A case history is basically a news-type report of an actual installation—replete with facts and figures of specifications, performance, and economics. Not only is a case history impressive because it is factual, it is, in truth, a third-party endorsement. Company salespeople automatically report major installations, and generally send in snapshots. When an ad-worthy installation is found, you may be sent to make an on-the-spot investigation. The more facts and details unearthed and reported, the more easily prospects will believe the big advantage of the product being sold. Big advantages are proved by small details that you have searched out in an effort to differentiate the product.

HOW IS OUR BIG ADVANTAGE SUPPORTED?

Sometimes the most convincing sales argument of all is a guarantee or warranty. Learn how the company handles returns, repairs, and replacements. How are such requests expedited? What kind of charges are made? The Sheaffer Pen Company, for example, had a special department dedicated to "keeping alive" older, top-of-the-line pens about which the owners had become very sentimental. This sort of integrity on the part of a corporation can make a convincing, highly persuasive argument. (In Sheaffer's case, it also unearthed some fantastic human interest stories.)

HAS THE PRODUCT BEEN SINGLED OUT FOR SPECIAL PRAISE?

In some product categories, there are outside institutions that award universally accepted recognition. If a product has received genuine acclaim, it is not immodest to remind the public of the fact. Pabst still wears its Blue Ribbon, while Schlitz reminded us that it was the beer that made Milwaukee famous. The practice of displaying awards is not uncommon among food products. Today, automobiles vie for and promote the "Car of the Year" designation received from an independent automotive magazine. What Oscar-winning movie doesn't proclaim that fact in its ads? It is sound selling to employ third-person endorsement, and the more exalted that endorsement, the more convincing the sales story.

WHAT HAS PREVIOUS ADVERTISING SAID?

How can a beginning copywriter compose an intelligent advertisement today without knowing what the company's advertising has said to the public in the past? Advertising is certainly a large contributing factor to brand image. A favorable brand image is precious, and the wise copywriter will not wander too far afield from what has contributed to public acceptance over the years.

A review of past advertising may save you the embarrassment of proposing a "new" idea that was used before you were born. Or the proofbook of past advertising may reveal a golden old idea that can be given a fresh and contemporary twist. Arrow Shirts frequently resurrects old Leyendecker paintings of the legendary "Arrow Collar Man." A short time back, Camel cigarettes built an entire campaign around "I'd walk a mile for a Camel"—a theme introduced generations ago. For years Westclox built its advertising on "personalizing" clocks, following a pattern set by the first "Big Ben" copy in the early part of this century.

WHAT IS THE COMPETITOR'S ADVERTISING LIKE?

The copywriter must constantly study the advertising and promotional efforts of competitors in order to combat competitive claims and in order not to approximate a competitor's stance or "look." If, for example, a competitor is using artwork in advertising, you may insist on photography in an attempt to differentiate. It would ill behoove any cigarette but Marlboro to feature cowboys.

A salesperson or copywriter cannot know everything about a competitor, but it is inexcusable not to be familiar with what the competitor is saying in public.

WHAT ARE THE CUSTOMERS LIKE?

To add to the information bank gleaned by a study of product and company background, every copywriter wants to know as much as possible about the customers and their buying habits. One giant advertising agency approaches the preparation of advertising with the basic creed: "Know Your Customer." The same agency urges its copywriters to think of customers as "person" rather than "people."

Sales analysis can tell the writer a lot about customers in the aggregate. Talking to company salespeople—particularly those in direct contact with the buying public—can be revealing. Many companies have permanent consumer juries or panels, some of which involve purchase diaries. When a company conducts survey research on any given topic, it almost always includes a breakdown of the respondents geographically and by demographics—such factors as age, education, income, occupation. As you read in Chapter 2 about VALS, in recent years researchers have been attempting to determine what they consider to be more meaningful classifications—social class, lifestyle, psychological drives. You "meet" your customers fairly intimately by listening to tapes of focus groups interviews. And, of course, the wise copywriter makes every effort to talk to some customers face to face. The more informal the meeting, the more revealing the conversation.

What do you learn from this constant scrutiny of consumers? Mostly you learn obvious facts—that *families* buy four-door sedans, that young *swingers* buy sports cars. You also learn that there are exceptions to all insights into human behavior: that age can be a state of mind as well as a condition of years; that income can be a matter of how one spends rather than how much one earns. You learn that the real reasons for purchase are not always apparent, particularly where luxury items are concerned. A young bank executive on the rise may buy a four-door Cadillac; and elderly bank president might buy a Mustang. The least privileged of our citizens will sometimes buy the most expensive and prestigious automobile—and economics has nothing to do with it. The family that drinks Local Beer X day in and day out may buy Premium Beer Y on the weekend because they expect company. One hard-bitten advertising executive described this as a case where a person could buy social prestige for a nickel per glass. A copywriter who was aware of this situation could slant the advertising approach accordingly.

Consumers will sometimes buy and use a product for purposes other than those the manufacturer originally intended. A case in point is Arm & Hammer Baking Soda. The public was using the product as a refrigerator deodorant long before the company exploited the fact. A few years back, Waring mixers had a sudden and mysterious spurt in sales. Why? Because the young women of America had suddenly become entranced with organic cosmetics, and an electric blender was crucial in the home manufacturing process.

Every item of information about the product and about the prospect helps you focus in more accurately on the objectives and enables you to be on target and to strip away nonessentials from both thinking and writing. In the end, this kind of methodical searching or digging explains why Chivas Regal advertising shows yachts and caviar, while Budweiser advertising shows sweaty railroad yardmen after a hard day's work—each with superb creative flair.

WHERE WILL THE ADVERTISING BE SEEN AND HEARD?

In addition to learning as much as possible about the product and its customers, you want to know as much as possible about the media in which the advertising will appear. You are aware of the obvious or mechanical differences between the media—that radio is a sound medium and television is a picture medium; that broadcast copy is fleeting while print copy can be permanent.

Far more important are differences *among* the various media. What kind of editorial content does that magazine have? What kind of audience does this program reach? To what lifestyle does a given publication appeal? It is not illogical to talk one way to a woman who reads *Good Housekeeping* and talk quite another way to a woman who reads *Cosmopolitan.* A television spot for use on NFL Monday Night Football might be quite different from a spot used on a public affairs show, or even on a soap opera.

Any copywriter concerned about the nitty-gritty of media can refer to the Standard Rate and Data directories, which are basic equipment in most advertising operations—a complete source of mechanical requirements. There certainly are times, in the beginning stages of an idea, when it pays to know what a publication will accept and what it will not accept. For instance, it's helpful to know such things as how much a publication charges for bleed, whether it offers gatefolds, if it can handle a split run.

FROM QUESTIONS COME ANSWERS

The beginning copywriter is not likely to learn the answers to all these questions overnight, but is constantly learning with each new assignment. The copywriter who asks and answers the sorts of questions outlined above cannot avoid learning a great deal and quickly seeing logical directions and distinctions take shape.

Although the objectives and purposes of the advertising have been pretty well set in the higher echelons of the marketing-advertising chain of command, you should still always clarify the purpose of a particular ad. The purpose may be to increase awareness of a new product feature or to encourage participation in a contest. Whatever it may be, never lose sight of the purpose, because each single advertising message is tied to an overall company selling strategy.

A famous copywriter, James Webb Young, referred to digging for facts as "gathering raw materials." These key facts are assembled into a rather concise document, known in some agency quarters as a campaign brief or background memo or situation report. Whatever it is called, it furnishes the basis for the next step. The next step involves a term with which you are quite familiar by now—the creative strategy.

CREATIVE STRATEGY

The creative strategy generally sets the tone covering an advertiser's entire program. For those who are still seeking a foothold in the creative world, we suggest the use of a bare bones creative strategy for *each* advertisement you prepare. It helps you organize your information and your thoughts so that you can decide ahead of time exactly what you are going to say, to whom, and with what desired effect.

When the finished ad is compared with the creative strategy, there should be no discrepancies. Carry out in practice what is outlined in your strategy. The duller and stuffier the business atmosphere in which you function, the more benefit the creative strategy will be in selling ad ideas. Even people who have difficulty writing a personal letter can see the efficacy of copy written to a plan. At many universities teaching advertising copy, a written strategy statement is required with each advertisement. Preparing a strategy, whether formal or informal, is a businesslike practice.

ISOLATING THE MAIN SELLING IDEA

By the time the creative strategy is firmed up, the writer has definite understanding of the advertising's main selling idea; for example, Kleenex Softique is gentle on your nose. It is arrived at largely through the steps outlined in this chapter, through knowledge of customer and product.

While most advertising strategies are based on answering customer *wants* and *needs*, the Batten, Barton, Durstine & Osborn agency advocates strategy based on *solving a problem*. In other words, instead of asking people what they think they want or need, BBDO asks people what problems they have with a particular product category. BBDO concentrates on prime prospects—that small group of people who account for the major share of goods consumed in any given product category. For example, roughly 20 percent of beer drinkers consume 80 percent of the beer.

The problems expressed by these prime prospects must score high on three points: (1) the frequency with which the problem occurs; (2) the intensity of the customer's concern with it; (3) the preemptibility of the solution. Can you be first with a solution and so exploit it in advertising that the public infers exclusivity? This formula of problem analysis has led BBDO to several highly successful campaigns.[1]

Once the main selling idea is determined, the next step is purely creative and each writer will handle the execution of the strategy in his or her own way. A thousand copywriters, given the very same problem, would probably produce a thousand different ads.

---

1. Richard Mercer, A.A.A.A. Conference, Biltmore Hotel, New York, November 19, 1974.

CASE
HISTORY
MAZDA

Courtesy of Mazda and its agency, Foote, Cone & Belding.

What does a company do when its innovative marketing and advertising direction has been followed so much by competitors that the original advertising loses its distinction? That's the dilemma that Mazda faced in 1986. In an effort to differentiate its advertising from that of competition, Mazda turned to a well-loved representative. They chose their representative not just because he was famous but because he was an automotive enthusiast and a serious racing car fan. They turned to James Garner, a solid, friendly, straight talker whose personal attributes exactly meshed with Mazda's corporate philosophy. Garner not only admired the Mazda products, he had, in fact, already bought an RX7 for his daughter, Gigi. Garner could talk about Mazda with honesty and conviction. The match was a natural, but the agency assigned its top two creative people to work closely with Garner in fine-tuning the dialogue to fit his personality. He is very much like the character "Maverick" that he played on television for years, and that is the tone of voice used in the commercials.

The copy theme, "So Special It's Not for Everyone," was an extension of the "cut-above" positioning that Mazda had had for several years. This theme was presented by Garner with a number of variations such as "Are you ready for something this special? You should be . . .'' and "It's pretty special. Like you and me." The introductory spots all opened featuring Garner behind-the-scenes at Mazda, followed by a beauty shot of the product on a specially constructed light box the size of an entire studio. The price of each product was included.

The second series of television spots took Garner away from behind-the-scenes at Mazda and out into the world where the viewer lives, works, and plays. It is here that Garner's natural warmth and playfulness shines through. In fact, members of his own family appeared in two of the spots—his daughter, Gigi, and his brother, Jack.

The Garner/Mazda spots are directed toward a target market of men aged 25 to 54 who have graduated from or attended college, and who are in a household with an income in excess of $40,000 per year. To reach this target audience, Mazda focuses on weekend television programs—sporting events, weekend movies, and highly rated, male-oriented, upscale prime-time shows such as "60 Minutes," "Sunday Night Movies," "20/20," "Miami Vice," "Hunter." On cable television, Mazda particularly seeks out selected L.P.G.A. and Senior PGA golf events.

The television effort is supplemented with a print schedule of large, handsome, and informative full-color ads. Most fre-

MAZDA

Continued

quently these are five-color, two-page spreads, but Mazda also uses four-page and twelve-page six-color preprinted inserts. (The extra color provides Mazda's distinctive silver background.) Every print ad features a coupon to be mailed in and a toll-free phone number offering a twenty-six-page catalog. The objective is to get as much information as possible into the hands of the reader as quickly as possible. In addition to a strong magazine schedule, Mazda also uses four-color spreads in *U.S.A. Today*. The impact of four-color spreads in a large newspaper-sized format is outstanding.

However, it is James Garner who has become the face of Mazda to the general public. The first year of the Garner commercials was the most successful in Mazda history, both in terms of sales and share of mind. Garner's believability and credibility tested extremely high; he continues for Mazda.

Garner has been an outstanding celebrity representative for Mazda because he is a perfect fit with the product.

MAZDA

626 GT TURBO COUPE INTRO
"Test Track" :30

GARNER: Don't tell me you know about turbos

until you go have some fun with *this* little puppy. The turbo on Mazda's new 626 GT

is a special new design that lights up at low RPM's and *stays* lit.

NATURAL SFX

GARNER: But maybe you're not ready for this much fun.

MUSIC UP
ANNCR VO: Introducing Mazda's new 626 GT Turbo with

high-performance wheels and tires. Auto-adjusting suspension. 9-way adjustable sport seat.

$12,245

M.S.R.P. excludes taxes, license, freight, dealer charges and options.

And a price thousands less than Volvo's or Audi's turbos.

GARNER: Be careful.

This one's mine!

CASE HISTORY
COORS
PREMIUM BEER

Courtesy of Adolph Coors Company and its agency, Foote, Cone & Belding.

In advertising, one way to get attention is to do the opposite of what all your competitors are doing. Coors Beer followed that principle with Mark Harmon and the "Coors Is the One" campaign.

Almost without exception, major brewers were running frenzied lifestyle campaigns that were almost exhausting to watch and listen to—and very difficult to differentiate one from another. The pace was hectic, the music was deafening. Qualities of the product were barely hinted at.

All of a sudden there appeared on the advertising scene a lone man in the serene outdoors. He spoke quietly and earnestly. He told us about a unique beer and what went into it—the purity of the water, the aging process, the particular barley used.

The lone man was Mark Harmon: rugged, handsome, totally masculine, believable. The settings were the Colorado mountains, valleys, and streams. His story was a straight sales story—low-key, perhaps, but a straight sales story, direct and honest.

Therein was the magic that made Coors stand apart from other brands as the distinctive product it is. Each commercial in the series focuses on one point of difference about the product. This difference was explained by Harmon in a quiet, unhurried manner.

The simple, straightforward approach proved a welcome change of pace from the frenetic beer ads crowding the airways. In a fight for survival against well-established, national big-spending breweries, Coors certainly succeeded in capturing the attention of the beer-drinking audience. They did so by deliberately being different, by reverting back to one-on-one selling of the utmost simplicity.

FCB

DATE: July, 1985

CLIENT: Adolph Coors Company
PRODUCT: Coors Premium
FILM NO.: YCPP5243
FILM TITLE: "Bandwagon"

FILM LENGTH: :30

1. (NATURAL OUTDOOR SFX UP AND UNDER)

2. MARK HARMON: Y'know, I've been a beer drinker for a bunch of years.

3. And, like you, I've seen a lot of beer commercials.

4. But there's one beer people loved before it was even advertised.

5. Y'see, Coors was kind of <u>the</u> beer at my folks' place.

6. People thought it was different... special.

7. And that was true long before there were any jingles or promotions.

8. (SFX: POP)

9. It's the product people love, not the hoopla.

10. You think about that.

11. How many products can you say that about?

12. Coors is the one.

CASE HISTORY
JAMAICA TOURIST BOARD

Courtesy of Jamaica Tourist Board and its agency, Young & Rubicam.

Even an island paradise can have its problems. Such was the case with Jamaica in the late 1970s and early 1980s when the one-time elite tourist attraction and premier vacation destination fell into a difficult economic and political period of decline. For years the number of tourist/visitors remained static while the remainder of the Caribbean enjoyed healthy growth.

By December 1980, the already low levels of tourists were down 8 percent from the previous year and down 14 percent for the off-peak season. Hotel occupancy stood at only 39 percent.

Qualitative research showed that travel agents were reluctant to recommend (in fact, recommended against) Jamaica to clients and viewed Jamaica as an unfriendly place. Caribbean tourists also had a negative opinion of the people and the political situation in Jamaica. Interest in visiting was low.

In late 1980 a change in government brought a commitment to regain the pre-eminent position in tourism Jamaica once deservedly enjoyed.

The problem advertising had to solve was this: while people were aware of the many virtues of Jamaica, a perception of violence and unrest remained (as perpetrated by the media and travel agents) that kept people from selecting Jamaica as a vacation destination.

The advertising objective was to convince people that Jamaica was entering a new, highly positive era and once again offered more vacation benefits and a warmer welcome than any other Caribbean island. More specifically, the objective was to increase revenue by encouraging visitors to come back to Jamaica, particularly the higher-income, longer-staying, higher-rate-paying tourists who supported the peak winter season. The primary target was previous visitors, with a secondary target of Caribbean tourists who had never visited Jamaica.

The creative strategy was to assure tourists that once again Jamaica was a warm, friendly place offering a uniquely beautiful vacation opportunity. Spectacular television presentations focused on the people of Jamaica, who communicated a new, hospitable feeling, and showed that Jamaica had everything: a diverse, rich heritage, sun and beaches and many sites of natural beauty, enchanting people, and a unique blend of fascinating cultures.

The television advertising was a tapestry of Jamaica, a panoply of the island showing its heritage, ambience, civility, richness, beauty, and tranquility along with the uniqueness

JAMAICA TOURIST BOARD

Continued

of its culture and people. The television camera was used not so much to capture specifics, but to paint impressions of the island's vividness. The language in the commercials was lyrical, to summon up the verbal tone of Jamaica's people. A haunting musical refrain supported the visual images.

The result was tourism advertising that struck an immediate responsive chord with the target audience.

Despite the introduction of the campaign during the off-peak season (June 1981), the goal of maintaining visitor volume was quickly exceeded. In fact, with only four exceptions, every month's volume exceeded its prior year level for the first thirty-seven months of the campaign. Hotel occupancy for 1983 was 63 percent compared to the 1980 level of 39 percent. And the number of higher-paying, peak-season tourists had far more than doubled since 1981.

Awareness of Jamaica's advertising became the highest of any Caribbean destination after only a few months of advertising; Jamaica's advertising is recalled by seven consumers in ten.

Make it Jamaica.
Again.

CASE
HISTORY
PLEDGE

Courtesy of S. C. Johnson & Son, Inc., and its agency, J. Walter Thompson.

While television is a medium that can be used to touch people in many ways, it is unexcelled in *demonstrating* product differences. And a good, dramatic demonstration can pack a ton of conviction.

For years, Pledge had been the leading furniture care brand. As such it was a natural target for Endust and Behold.

Consumers associated Pledge with the heavy, thorough cleaning job. Many no longer believed that *wax* meant good routine furniture care. Competitive advertising indicated that Pledge was undesirable because a spray wax can build up when used frequently. Endust was promoted for day-to-day dusting and cleaning, while Behold was said to clean better than Pledge and to cost less too.

The new advertising for Pledge had to perform a triple task. It had to overcome the wax build-up perception. It had to convince consumers that wood needs Pledge every time they dusted. It had to distinguish Pledge's performance from the competition's.

Research and development substantiated that Pledge does *not* build up, but is self-cleaning in fact. Pledge cleans away the old polish every time it is used, thus *preventing* wax build-up.

Because many consumers did not understand the value of using Pledge, advertising had to communicate that Pledge protects and cares for wood's natural beauty.

In use, Pledge reflects light, highlighting the natural grain of the wood and masking imperfections, while Endust leaves wood dull and dry. Lab photos showing that this difference in end appearance could be visualized became the crux of Pledge advertising.

In a two-day test shoot, three time-lapse cameras shot six different surfaces, demonstrating that "no-wax sprays like Endust evaporate, leaving wood looking dry and defenseless." Pledge's emotionally involving commercial shattered the wax build-up myth and communicated a benefit of beauty and protection.

Results have been more than good. The commercial, "Look! No Build-Up" received high scores in qualitative research tests and has proved to be a valuable marketing tool. Despite accompanying promotional efforts, advertising is getting the major credit for dispelling a negative competitive myth and reinvigorating the brand.

S.C. JOHNSON & SON, INC.
PLEDGE

"Look No Build-Up" :30

WOMAN: Mom and Dad bought this table the year I was born.

Look at it. Beautiful.

And all Mom did was dust every week with Pledge.

And <u>now</u> Endust says "Watch out for buildup".

After 28 years? C'mon.

Pledge is self-cleaning,

for a fresh shine every time you dust.

Compare that to Endust

which just evaporates leaving wood looking dry and defenseless.

A Pledge shine protects and cares for wood.

ANNCR: Pledge. A fresh shine every time.

WOMAN: For 28 years and counting.

J. WALTER THOMPSON CO.

5

Setting the Stage
for Creativity

Chapter Topics

Writer involvement in
    research
Best source of inspiration
Organized research
Research example
Development of a single ad
Inspiration follows
    footwork
Origin of creative ideas
Technique for producing
    ideas

Key Terms

Demonstrable product
    difference
Brainstorming

Case History

O'Keefe & Merritt

There is no question about it: background research precedes creative effort. All forms of research—product, marketing, sales, consumer—feed information to the advertising writer. But perhaps the most rewarding form of research for the copywriter is research that begins at home: personal study of and experience with the product.

In the search for ideas, you live with the product, become the customer, check personal reactions, and listen to family and friends who have used the product. You become immersed in the problem and let your instincts go to work.

Advertising agency chief Leo Burnett once said to a group of aspiring writers, "Your best source of inspiration for ideas, your best copy research, your best test market, your best copy chief is—you."[1]

But from formal research down through the most personal investigation, the key word is "organized." Keeping in mind at all times the specific goals of the advertising, you will find both formal and informal research efforts more meaningful. You will also find that the work you have done on research will comprise a surprisingly large percentage of the work you must do as a writer—for good advertising writing, above all else, must inform.

Other things of great value will flow from the research. And if it is thorough and done with creative perception of the ultimate goal (to sell and motivate), the research can also yield the basic selling idea upon which the whole creative approach can be based.

AN ACTUAL RESEARCH EXAMPLE

The following brief case history illustrates how research can supply the basic advertising theme and all but write the advertising copy.

A number of years ago, one of the authors was involved in the solicitation of a large and prestigious manufacturer of gas stoves. In the process, the manufacturer suggested that a new print advertising theme might be welcome. The writer took the following chronological steps to accumulate necessary background information:

1. He obtained the names of the stove manufacturer's local retail customers at each dollar volume level.

2. He obtained and studied with care copies of the manufacturer's print ads for the previous two years.

3. He located in the public library print ads of *all* gas stove manufacturers that had appeared during the previous year. He analyzed and compared these ads with those of the prospective client.

---

1. Leo Burnett, *Communications of an Advertising Man* (Chicago: Leo Burnett Company, Inc., 1961), p. 27.

4. He made personal calls on the two largest local customers of the client, on two medium-size retail outlets, and on two small dealers who stocked the stoves. In the retail stores he interviewed floor managers, sales personnel, and customers. Part of the questioning was common to each interview. Specifically, he asked the following questions and received these answers:

Q1. Why do you sell (or consider buying) these ranges?

A. Because it's the best range on the market.

or

A. Because it's an old, reliable company that makes an outstanding range.

Q2. Why is it the best range? What makes it outstanding?

A. Because it's a high quality range that does an outstanding job.

Q3. Why does it do an outstanding job? What features make it exceptional?

A. It holds up. It cooks well. It has that reputation.

From this research at the point of sale, it was clear that the stove company had become so entrenched in the market with a good product that everyone accepted its high quality. It had a good image. It was equally apparent, however, that the company had never tried to develop public appreciation of any particular feature of the ranges. At this point, the writer could see that further research was indicated. He pursued it as follows:

1. He examined the stove company's then-current sales literature in search of any claim of product difference. He found none.

2. He made a second visit to the largest retail customer (The May Company) and asked the section manager if there were any old catalogs or sales literature of the stove company available. The section manager searched his files and produced a large folder with outdated reference material. The writer studied it carefully but found only one possible feature that was unique—the fact that the gas was released through holes in a star-shaped gas head and through a ring that surrounded the star.

It now became evident that further research was necessary with the product in use. The writer located by telephone and then visited three homemakers who used the range. He asked them the same question put to the salespeople and potential customers in the retail stores, and the answers of two of the homemakers were similar. However, the third liked the range because it cooked with "an even flame."

After receiving the answer, the writer knelt on the kitchen floor and watched the movement of the gas as the control was turned up and down under a pot. It burned evenly at any level, without flickering.

This provided the key the writer sought to a bona fide and demonstratable product difference.

After further cooking experimentation on the writer's own gas range (a competitive product) and a prolonged discussion with his wife (a gourmet cook), a definite advertising theme was built around a genuine product difference, and the print ad shown here was designed and written to include a slogan ("For Perfect Cooking Control . . . The O'Keefe & Merritt Star Jet Ring of Flame") set above the brief and simple comparative illustrations.

This simple little case history shows in an unglamorous way a fairly typical example of how advertising "inspiration" comes only after some dogged footwork. A few advertising writers will insist that their copy is "intuitive," but you may be sure that the intuition was triggered by preparation.

WHERE DO CREATIVE IDEAS COME FROM?

Many scholars have tried to analyze the generation of copy ideas—but not one of them slights the necessity of preparatory research. One of the great copywriters of all times, James Webb Young, discoursed at some length on his technique for producing ideas.[2] In a simple explanation that follows the classic four-stage creative formula of exposure, incubation, illumination, and execution, Mr. Young says: (1) you gather raw materials, fully exploring the problem and the store of knowledge surrounding it; (2) you work it over in your mind; (3) you let it incubate for a while as your unconscious mind takes over; (4) Eureka!—your idea is born. If you have several ideas you shape and develop the single, most workable idea to practical usefulness.

Another famous advertising agent, Alex Osborn, believed in a massive frontal attack on a problem by a group of people. He called it "brainstorming," and the object was to pile up lots and lots of ideas at one sitting. During this process, no negative judgments were permitted. Later, the many alternative ideas were sifted to find the most suitable.

That noted professor of advertising, George Burton Hotchkiss, always asked himself first: What *response* do I want from the reader? The very last thing he concerned himself with was the literary and artistic form the message would take.[3]

As for ideas for the message itself, different writers try different ways to find inspiration. Some go through a word association process

---

2. James Webb Young, *A Technique for Producing Ideas*, 6th ed. (Chicago Advertising Publications, Inc., 1949), pp. 53–54.
3. George Burton Hotchkiss, *Advertising Copy* (New York: Harper & Bros., 1947), p. 27.

Why Do Great Cooks Prefer Gas?

Ever since man first learned to trap and use natural gas as a fuel, great cooks have preferred it for cooking.

The reason is simplicity itself. There is no other cooking fuel which can be brought from low to high, high to low instantaneously.

The advantage of this is obvious—immediate control of the gas flame provides a high degree of cooking control.

Knowing this, O'Keefe & Merritt analyzed the method of projecting gas through an intake pipe through jets to the point of flame. Finding that the many small jet holes which emitted the gas restricted the upward movement of the fuel, causing a flickering, uneven flame, O'Keefe & Merritt set out to develop a gas jet which would eliminate this flickering and its consequent hot spots.

After much research, a new type of jet was developed. Because it was crowned with a star, O'Keefe & Merritt named it the Star Jet. But its name is not really important. What is important is what the star jet did —for it produced an unobstructed, steady ring of continuous flame.

In cooking tests, it was found that the star jet ring of flame eliminated all uneven hot spots, all fluttering. This, in turn, made it possible to attain a degree of cooking control never before dreamed of.

This is the simple story of the evolution of gas as a cooking fuel. We believe it will tell you why great cooks prefer gas, and how any cook can rise to the heights of greatness with the perfect cooking control of the O'Keefe & Merritt star jet ring of flame.

For Perfect Cooking Control... The O'Keefe & Merritt Star Jet Ring of Flame

O'Keefe & Merritt

Manufacturers of the World's Finest Ranges

which is sometimes referred to as "clustering." Some study *Bartlett's Familiar Quotations*. Some review a thesaurus. Some check a clip file of outstanding ads and editorial features. Some browse through thick photographic annuals in the hope that a dramatic picture will trigger a great idea.

The ideas *do* come. They come when you have your objective clearly in mind. They come when you have done your background study thoroughly. And frequently they come when you least expect them.

As you progress in your own writing career, you will learn that there are two kinds of advertising ideas: (1) ideas about what goes into the story (creative strategy), and (2) ideas about ways to present the story. The former give solid foundation to the latter.

Regardless of its origin, creativity is capable of significant stimulation, and this stimulation can and does flow—in nine cases out of ten—from the inspiration inherent in thorough background research. If you are looking for a mantra to use in your creative meditations, let it be this: "seek and ye shall find." If you seek out every available research fact relating to your creative assignment, you will almost certainly find the answer to every creative problem.

6

Headline and Visual:
Indivisible

Chapter Topics

Copy-art team
Visual/verbal together
Total communication
Illustration and headline in
    combination
Importance of thinking
    visually
What a layout is
Seven basic layout
    categories
The function of an
    illustration
Twelve ways of using
    illustrations
Art or photography?
Responsibilities of the art
    director
Three chief headline
    categories

Key Terms

Art director
Account executive
Print advertising
Layout or format
Copywriter's rough
Trade character
Finished layout
Self-interest headline
"Blind" headline
"How to" headlines
Subheads

Case Histories

The Travelers
Gold'n Plump Poultry
Maker's Mark Bourbon

COPYWRITING IS COOPERATIVE

We interrupt these proceedings to take you on a giant leap from being a student and beginner to being a sophisticated copywriter at a large Madison Avenue agency. We do so to introduce you far ahead of time to the greatest joy in creative advertising. We want to whet your appetite for, and give you some understanding of, the very special working arrangement that is to come.

The Role of the Art Director

In no way will you be a Lone Ranger in the creative world. Once you learn your craft you will become part of a team—a copy-art team, and there is nothing more exhilarating for a copywriter than to work in harness with a first-rate art director. Each sparks the other, each brings out the best in the other, and the result is likely to be superior to what either of you might have created alone. It's a sort of $1 + 1 = 11$ equation; the total is much greater than the sum of its parts.

As this book makes abundantly clear, you, as a copywriter, are far, far more than a wordsmith. You are a thinker-upper of total communications ideas—in print, on radio, in television. You're a writer, yes. But you find yourself communicating with pictures and symbols and "looks."

And what is your teammate, your partner in art doing at this same time? Just as you are no longer merely a wordsmith, your partner is no longer simply a designer. Your art director, too, is thinking of total communication. Your art director is also dealing with *words*—with a writing pencil as well as a drawing pencil.

The two of you work as one. "Never the twain shall meet" was certainly not referring to the copy-art team. This happy combination is standard procedure in the best advertising circles. Copywriting, or making ads, is definitely a cooperative venture involving far more than the copywriter.

In some of the finest agencies, the top creative director is an art director, not a copywriter. Long gone are the days when some smug copywriter thought all an art director had to do was illustrate the copywriter's idea.

The Basic Team + One

The team reigns supreme. It is the backbone of agency creative staffs. In some instances, the basic team of copy and art is joined by an account executive, whose input reflects insights into the possible psychological and emotional aspects of the client's reactions. This troika can start analyzing, planning, and doing strategic thinking at a very early stage.

It is this team that shapes the creative strategy and evaluates proposed advertising tactics.

Occasionally the team of copy-art-account executive is supplemented by a broadcast producer, which might happen if the account in question were a big television user and heavily into visual imagery—a soft-drink advertiser, for example.

Copywriting is a cooperative team activity. But you have to learn and earn your way onto that team and the best way for you to start is with the discipline that is forced on you when you work in print. *Your* choice of picture, *your* choice of headline, *your* choice of words, all carefully combined in a restricted unit of space, must stop, interest, and persuade the casual reader. It's a demanding task.

VISUAL AND VERBAL WORK TOGETHER

The first thing that a beginning ad-maker must learn is to stop thinking in terms of words alone. Words are indeed the essential tools of your trade. But the moment you start making ads you find yourself working with other dimensions. You are no longer involved with words alone, but with a *total communication*. And total communication definitely involves pictures, symbols, shapes, layouts. These elements are as important to advertising communication as words are. Sometimes more so. Ask not merely, "What shall I say?" but, "How shall I show it?" and "How will it look?" The visual and the verbal work together. Even though you are a *writer,* you must begin to *think visually.*

With this basic rule in mind, let's now examine the procedure for making a print ad. When you create an ad for magazines or newspapers, you are dealing with a unit of space that is specific and restrictive. It cannot be stretched or exceeded. It is flat. It does not move. You do not have music or the human voice or sound effects as in radio. There is no dazzling motion as in television. All you have going for you are still pictures, printed words, and an overall look to the message. You are going to jell these three elements in such a way that you attract, inform, and persuade an unseen and largely uninterested audience. The process is neither art nor entertainment but does contain elements of both. As you sally forth to dazzle that unseen audience, put your trust in these two little words: *Headline/Picture. Picture/Headline.* Together, they hold the key to success.

You have the assignment, the strategy, and the background information provided by research. You know who you're going to talk to, you have the germ of an idea buzzing around in your head, and you have pencil and paper in front of you. Now how do you actually start to create an ad? What are the mechanics? Do you jot down a provocative headline? Do you dream up a gripping picture?

The answer is that you do both, at pretty much the same time.

THE IMPORTANCE OF THINKING VISUALLY

Years ago Keith Kimball, a former creative supervisor with the Batten, Barton, Durstine & Osborn agency, defined a headline as simply "a believable promise to the right audience."[1] Obviously, an illustration can fit the same definition.

A couple of generations back, many magazine and newspaper advertisements were composed chiefly of words enclosed in an ornate frame or border. Today's advertisement is far more likely to feature a spectacular photograph supplemented with a comparatively short text. The balance between words and pictures has totally changed over the years. Yet the copywriter is still responsible for the basic advertising idea. You are interested in communicating, and since all human communication involves symbols—whether words, pictures, signs, or gestures—you simply use the best symbolic tools available to do the job.

A Chinese proverb asserts that one picture is worth more than ten thousand words. The ratio may be exaggerated, but the analysis is correct. You are urged to think visually for three very sound reasons:

1. Think visually if you want to get your message across fast. People of varying educational levels and backgrounds can respond without hesitation to a strong picture. A picture involves them emotionally while even the most stirring collection of words may demand some slight mental processing before it is fully understood.

2. Think visually if you want to talk to all kinds of people. Where there are language or cultural barriers, a strong visual symbol dissolves communications differences. A universal message of courage was transmitted by Winston Churchill's upraised hand with two fingers spread in a V.

3. Think visually if you hope to attract even a ripple of attention in this day and age of well-made, visually oriented advertising.

Despite the need for visual impact in advertising, the copywriter is still vitally concerned with words. The first such concern must be with the headline, which will serve as the conduit from eye to brain, explaining, amplifying, or reinforcing the picture.

David Ogilvy, one of the most successful advertising writers, asserts that when you write your headline you have spent eighty cents of your client's dollar.[2] Noted mail-order specialist John Caples insists that the headline is far and away the single most important element in any ad.[3]

1. John Caples, *Making Ads Pay* (New York: Dover, 1966).
2. David Ogilvy, *Confessions of an Advertising Man* (New York: Dell, 1964), p. 130.
3. John Caples, *Tested Advertising Methods* (Englewood Cliffs, NJ: Prentice-Hall, 1974), p. 17.

To borrow from a famous advertising slogan," it's what's up front that counts," and what's up front in most good advertisements is an illustration and headline *in combination*. The wise copywriter is aware that to be effective, to create maximum excitement and reaction, headline and illustration are indivisible—like bow and arrow, like bat and ball. A strong headline makes a great picture work harder. A great picture makes a strong headline even more effective. The two together—headline and visual—are the most important part of an advertisement. If you can pack the crux of your message into the headline/visual element, you will almost surely be a successful communicator.

The Mechanics of Thinking Visually

Having established the indivisibility of headline and visual, let us now examine them separately beginning with the visual element.

While advertising writers are not expected to be artists, photographers, or typographers, they are expected to be concerned with the total look of the advertisement. This element of total appearance is sometimes called "format," but is most often called "layout." It is the organization of all the various facets of an advertisement into a pleasing, unified whole, and usually begins in the form of a copywriter's rough layout.

Copywriter's Rough Layout.   Even if you cannot draw a straight line—and most professional copywriters cannot—you can make an intelligible layout by using stick figures to indicate illustration, squiggly bold strokes to indicate headlines, and horizontal parallel lines to indicate main text, as shown on the following page. The purpose of your copywriter's rough is to relay to an art director what you see in your mind. Its function is simply to get the creative ball rolling. Your original vision may alter many times before the advertisement is finalized, but it is essential to start with a crude rough layout. This is how ad-making professionals begin communicating with one another.

Once you plunge into this strange new world of creating advertisements, you will become aware of basic visual patterns that keep reappearing. The various formats that follow are for labeling purposes only. Each suits a certain advertising purpose, and you should familiarize yourself with all of them. You need not be a slave to form but can devise variations to serve your own special purposes.

Basic Layout Categories

As you work, consider these basic categories of layout as an idea checklist or collection of alternatives. Ask: Suppose we tried it this way? Or that way? Have I considered all the options? New revelations sometimes occur in this process.

"COPYWRITER'S ROUGH" LAYOUT

(On 8 ½ × 11″ sheet of plain typewriter paper indicate as best you can how you see the relative emphasis of all the elements in your ad. If you fear your drawings may not get the idea across, write a brief description alongside layout.)

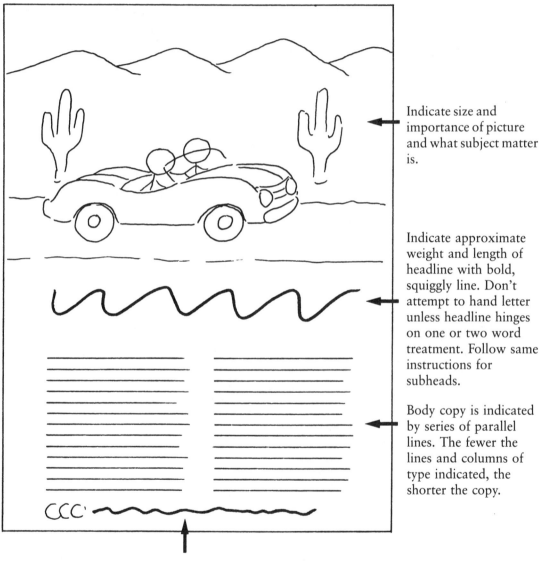

Indicate size and importance of picture and what subject matter is.

Indicate approximate weight and length of headline with bold, squiggly line. Don't attempt to hand letter unless headline hinges on one or two word treatment. Follow same instructions for subheads.

Body copy is indicated by series of parallel lines. The fewer the lines and columns of type indicated, the shorter the copy.

Indicate logotype or signature with crude symbol or squiggly bold line.

For use as a copywriter's guide, here are seven basic layout forms:

1. **Standard layout** (or Layout "A" as it is nicknamed by art directors), the most commonly used format, consists of a dominant illustration, headline, body copy, and signature—generally in that order. The standard layout is the most straightforward manner in which to organize most selling propositions. The accompanying sample of a copywriter's rough layout is a standard format. So are most of those classic, much-admired black and white Volkswagen Beetle ads. If you are stymied or confused over format, you can hardly go wrong by selecting the standard layout.

2. **Editorial layout** takes its name partly from the fact that these advertisements often resemble editorial matter in a publication. Words dominate and illustration is secondary, frequently absent entirely. These are long copy ads, ideally employed when you wish to give a detailed, rational explanation of your sales proposition.

3. **Poster layout** puts almost total emphasis on the visual. The large illustration tells the story at a glance; copy is held to a minimum, perhaps to only one pithy line. The poster technique is especially suitable when the advertising is for familiar, everyday products such as soft drinks, gum, or candy, which do not justify or require a detailed explanation. The poster generally serves the purpose of a gentle, pleasant, recognizable reminder. The poster layout is popular with fashion advertisers because it gives an up-close look at the featured item.

4. **Cartoon layouts** take several forms. The "pure" cartoon (as seen on the editorial pages of *New Yorker* or *Playboy*) is seldom used in advertising. But variations of the format range from the almost pure cartoon to long-copy advertisements that feature a cartoon drawing at the top. The cartoon format can be a sure-fire, attention-getting device, especially helpful when you have an intangible *idea* story or impression to get across. One ad showed a cartoon of sophisticated party-goers admiring a Jacuzzi. It was eye-catching, amusing, and got its snobbism point across. A photograph of the same situation would have looked absurd.

5. **Comicstrip layouts** follow much the same principles as newspaper comics. Ads of this style use a series of drawings or photographs (not always humorous) to tell a developing narrative in which the product or service plays the pivotal, heroic role.

6. **Picture-caption layouts** are extremely useful when you have a multifaceted product or service to present. You can picture many features (of a car, for example) or many vistas (of a vacation spot) with short explanations accompanying each picture. For some rea-

SEVEN SUGGESTED CATEGORIES OF LAYOUT

Standard

Editorial

Poster

Picture-Caption

Cartoon

Comic Strip

Picture-Cluster

son, people who will not even look at a long block of solid text will read every word of picture-caption copy.[4]

7. **Picture-cluster layouts** have a dominant visual element that is not a single item but a fitted set or cluster of several vertical and horizontal rectangles—all in different sizes. Lines separating the rectangles can be of even or varying widths, but always thicker than ordinary newspaper column rules. Generally, the rectangles will be pictures; occasionally a rectangle will contain a copy message. The picture-cluster layout (sometimes referred to as Mondrian because of its resemblance to the design technique for which the Dutch artist is famous) performs much the same function as the picture-caption layout, only without the captions. It, too, is ideal for presenting a multifaceted subject.[5] The picture-cluster layout might be interpreted as indicating quantity and variety of items while the picture-caption layout indicates order and control.

These seven layout categories (illustrated on pp. 90–91) can be augmented by countless variations of your own choosing and shaped to suit your special purposes. Think in terms of the total impact of the message. Keep your layout clean and uncluttered, pleasant to look at (even upside down), and easy for the eye to move through. As a rule, one element should be dominant. And as with most other tools of communication, there is no substitute for simplicity.

Importance of the Illustration

A layout organizes all the elements that go into a single unit of space, such as a magazine page. More often than not, the key feature in a layout is the illustration, which can make or break an advertisement.

A carefully selected illustration has great storytelling powers, showing at a glance what the ad is about and automatically buttonholing the particular audience the advertiser is trying to reach. It touches people emotionally, and in some instances can do almost a complete selling job. But the illustration can produce these miracles of communication only if it logically fits the basic selling idea in the first place. An illustration that is a trick, a come-on, or simply window dressing may catch a few eyes but isn't likely to win many friends. The illustration should be honest, and it should stick to the business at hand.

Not only should your illustration be pertinent to your selling proposition, but you should edit every element of your illustration with extreme care. The situation depicted in the illustration should be one

---

4. S. Watson Dunn, *Advertising Copy and Communication* (New York: McGraw-Hill, 1956), p. 174.
5. Roy Paul Nelson, *The Design of Advertising* (Dubuque, IA: William C. Brown, 1973), p. 81.

to which your prospects can relate. It should be within their range of comprehension and feeling and contain no sour notes. Without a meticulous selection of believable, acceptable photographic models and settings, your entire idea—no matter how valid—may come tumbling down. The woman who looks right serving hot biscuits to her family may look totally out of place serving scotch and soda to a male caller. While the actual selection of models and settings is technically the province of the art director, the copywriter who created the basic idea is usually entitled to veto rights.

Ways of Using Illustrations. Illustrations, like layouts, fall into several category types. Allowing for reasonable overlap, here are several types of illustrations you are likely to identify in thumbing through any magazine. They have been categorized by veteran advertising executive, Otto Kleppner:

1. **Product alone.** This is a favorite visual with manufacturers, but may not thrill readers—unless the product has inherent visual interest. A new car, for instance.

2. **Product in use.** The product shown doing its job, performing a benefit, is likely to be more interesting to look at—and more effective—than a product that just sits there.

3. **Product in a setting with people.** The simple addition of the human element makes it infinitely easier for the reader to relate to the product and its message.

4. **Result of using (or not using) a product.** One use stresses the positive, one the negative. An electric razor message can illustrate a smooth-shaven Adonis being admired (result of using the product), or it can illustrate the painful and embarrassing nick of a blade razor (result of not using the product).

5. **Dramatization of evidence.** A catsup ad may show a tall stack of fresh-cut tomato slices, indicating the raw state of what goes into the jar.

6. **Dramatization of a detail.** This technique has particular value when the detail being dramatized represents product differentiation. Tupperware highlighted the way its tight-fitting lid seals in food flavor by showing a freshly cut fruit or vegetable with a shiny metal lock on it. This type of illustration can also indicate quality, as in the advertising for expensive furniture that pictures, for example, exactly how door hinges are set into the cabinet. The reader does not buy the magnificent cabinet for its door hinges, but *information* about the door hinges helps the customer justify the premium cost of this luxurious piece of furniture.

7. **Comparison or contrast.** Basic selling psychology is applied to illustrations (ours versus theirs; before versus after, old versus new). Comparison or contrast is a compelling visual technique

WAYS OF USING ILLUSTRATION

Product alone

Product in use

Product in setting with people

Result of using product

Dramatization of evidence

Dramatization of detail

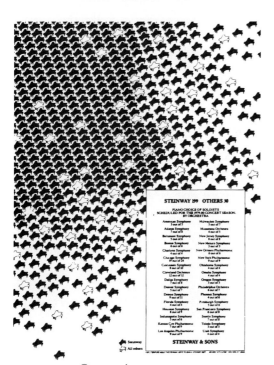

Comparison or contrast

Cartoon or caricature

Trade character

Charts and diagrams

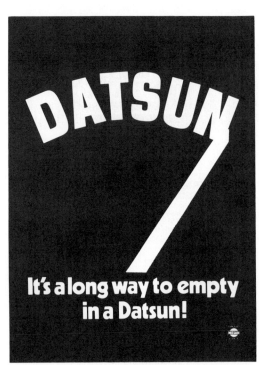

Symbolism

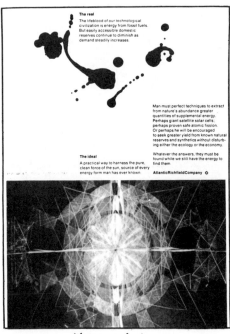

Abstract design

that has found special favor with sellers of tangible merchandise, from small and large household appliances to automobiles.

8. **Cartoon or caricature.** Not only is a cartoon an attention-getting device in its own right, but it can be particularly useful in trying to explain intangible benefits when you don't want to be literal. A life insurance campaign humanized the business by showing ridiculous disasters occurring to cartoon characters. An ad urging people not to ignore the first signs of cancer showed a large cartoon of an ostrich with its head buried in the sand.

9. **Trade character.** A trade character, which may take any one of a number of forms—a person, a symbol, or an object, builds identity, and can be a unifying factor woven through many different phases of an advertising and promotion program. A famous sailing ship is the trade character of Cutty Sark whiskey. Consider also Old Grandad, White Horse, and the Michelin tire man.

10. **Charts and diagrams.** Although they do not sound very artistic or enticing, charts and diagrams can prove fascinating and per- suasive to that small but crucial group of prospects who are in the market right now. Charts and diagrams permit you to organize a clear presentation of varied and detailed information that would be difficult to present in text. Sears has made great use of this technique in advertising color television sets.

11. **Symbolism.** Symbols are frequently employed as surrogates for the product or service being presented. DeBeers Diamonds, for instance, may show a soft-focus sunrise over a flowery meadow as a symbol of the beginnings of young love and romance. Many airlines dramatize one flight attendant as symbolic of their services.

12. **Abstract design.** Although rarely used as illustration for the ob- vious reason that a great many readers don't understand it, ab- stract art may strike a responsive chord with the very narrow market segment you are trying to impress if your proposition is somewhat esoteric. It may also suggest that a high level of creativ- ity is possessed by the advertiser in designing products.[6]

The above list may not be complete but it gives you a fair sampling of many types of illustrations (as shown on pp. 94–96). Often they can be used in combination with one another. Use this series of art possibilities as an option list only and consider other choices before making a final judgment.

Art or Photography?

Many newcomers to advertising ask, "Which is better, photography or hand-drawn art?" The answer is that you select the technique that best

---

6. Otto Kleppner, *Advertising Procedure,* 5th ed. (Englewood Cliffs, NJ: Prentice-Hall, 1966), pp. 113–24.

suits your purpose. The overwhelming majority of advertising illustrations today are photographic, and certainly photography gives a sense of authenticity and accuracy. In the case of foods, it provides a realism and appetite appeal that art can seldom deliver.

Original artwork is ideal for projecting a certain mood or for emphasizing a particular feature (especially in fashions). Hand-created art offers all manner of possibilities, from oil painting to decoupage to woodcuts to pen and ink. But in these areas, you will have the guidance and support of your irreplaceable working mate, the art director.

Layout Stages. Your *copywriter's rough layout* indicates how you think. Your art director shows you how she or he thinks, often in *thumbnail sketches* that would fit on a telephone memo sheet. The two of you explore many variations and finally come up with a workable *rough layout*. A rough layout is crudely drawn but made to the proper size and understandable to people in the business of making ads. The copywriter completes and polishes the copy while the art director prepares *finished layout* for management personnel—company or client—who okay expenditures for the project.

Once the advertisement is approved, the art director has the responsibility for selecting the outside art source, whether individual or studio, and overseeing every step of the technical process until the ad is sent to be published. While the art director is going through this, the advertising writer moves along to the next problem.

The Other Half of Indivisible. Now that we have examined the visual elements of layout and illustration it is only fair to give equal attention to the other partner in that indivisible pair—the headline.

Headlines

When David Ogilvy equated the headline with eighty cents of an advertising dollar, he was speaking from years of experience in advertising research. Survey after survey taken by Gallup & Robinson readership research indicated to Ogilvy that four out of five people do not read beyond the headline of an ad.[7] Much the same conclusion is apparent from examination of Daniel Starch Readership Service studies. Over many years, consumer surveys have shown a sharp drop-off in scores between ads that were merely noticed and those that were associated with a particular advertiser. Both these research findings lend credence to the notion that "it's what's up front that counts." John Caples suggests that you ask yourself what would make *you* buy the product, and then get that important point into your headline and illustration.[8] Noted

---

7. Ogilvy, op. cit., p. 130.
8. Caples, *Tested Advertising Methods*, op. cit., p. 38.

direct marketing advertising oracle Vic Schwab says that the headline must (1) select an interested audience, and (2) promise them a worth-while reward for reading.[9]

Self-Interest Headline.   It is difficult, if not futile, to attempt to cate-gorize headlines except in the most general sense. In almost every case, a headline is determined by the particular marketing situation. You do not set out to write an emotional headline or a gimmick headline; you write what seems logically required. However, in over fifty years of writing advertising, John Caples has found that by far the most effective headline is the one that appeals to the reader's self-interest. "Why should I take the time to read your ad? What's in it for me?" the reader asks—and rightly so.

News Headline.   Second in effectiveness, although well behind self-interest, is the news headline. People are born inquisitive, and anything that offers new information is almost certain to win attention.

Curiosity Headline.   Third in advertising effectiveness—but a distant third—is the curiosity headline, often referred to as a "blind" headline or, algebraically, an "x" headline. It is dependent on the reader's taking the time to go a step farther to unveil what you teased with in your headline. Alas, most readers won't bother. Caples also urges you to avoid the negative and take the positive angle, and try to suggest in your headline that here is a quick and easy way for readers to get something they want.[10]

An Unlovely Example.   To illustrate a number of the principles in-volved in writing a "believable promise to the right audience," John Caples cites an unlovely but successful mail order test headline: "Corns gone in 5 days, or money back."

Note that the first word, "Corns," selects the right audience. A reader who does not have corns won't even see the ad. The reader who does have corns will see it, no matter in what far-off corner of the magazine it may be tucked. Readers with corns exhibit one specific form of self-interest. They want to get rid of the darned things, and the faster the better. "Corns gone" is highly desirable, but somewhat general. The sufferer wants to know how long the process is likely to take. "In 5 days." Can't beat that. But it sounds almost too good to be true. "Or money back." What is there to lose? It's worth a try.[11]

Can a change in headline really make a dramatic difference in re-sponse? You bet it can. Just ask any writer who toils in the direct marketing vineyard, where every appearance of an advertisement is a

---

9. Victor O. Schwab, *How to Write a Good Advertisement* (New York: Harper & Row, 1962), p. 5.
10. Caples, *Tested Advertising Methods*, op. cit., pp. 37–38.
11. Ibid., pp. 22–23.

test. These writers do not have to guess about headline performance; they can tell you about results right down to the last decimal.

The Classic Example. The classic example from the direct marketing field concerns the Sherwin Cody home study course in English. Many years ago, one of that organization's most lucrative ads contained about one thousand words of copy, a small photograph of scholarly Sherwin Cody, and the headline: "The Man Who Simplified English." In the process of continually testing appeals, Maxwell Sackheim took that almost identical Sherwin Cody ad and changed the headline to: "Do You Make These Mistakes in English?" Responses immediately increased, and kept right on increasing. For over twenty years, that company was never able to come up with a test headline that outscored "Do You Make These Mistakes in English?"

Classic Example Analyzed. Why is the second headline so much more effective than its successful predecessor? There appear to be a number of reasons.

"The Man Who Simplified English" is a *statement,* which may or may not have much portent for the reader. "Do You Make These Mistakes in English?" is a *question,* which stops readers, involves them, and pulls them in.

"The Man Who Simplified English" may have an implied benefit, but "Do You Make These Mistakes in English?" talks directly to the reader's problem. There is no guessing about the subject matter.

"The Man Who Simplified English" is general in meaning where "Do You Make These Mistakes in English?" is specific in meaning.

Importance of a Single Word. Just as the right headline can make a difference in readership, the right word in a headline can make a difference in sales results. Suppose the winning Sherwin Cody headline had said simply: "Do You Make Mistakes in English?" It would have been natural for the reader to respond, "Who don't?" and turn the page. But the word "these" intrigues the reader. *Which* mistakes? Do other people make the same mistakes? Perhaps they make even worse mistakes. So the word "these" impels the reader to investigate. The word "these" also implies some free help just from reading the ad—a specific reward for the time the reader will spend.[12]

Question Headlines. The fact that the classic Sherwin Cody headline is written in the form of a question does not mean that a question headline is foolproof. But a sensible question headline quickly involves readers, forcing them to participate in your copy.

Challenge or Quiz Headlines. A challenge or quiz headline will often have the same effect. A famous liquor campaign challenged: "If you

---

12. Caples, *Making Ads Pay,* op. cit. p. 77.

can find a better bourbon, buy it"—a pretty clever way to build instantaneous product credibility. Another ad might ask: "Can you answer these questions about serving wine?"

"How To" Headlines.   "How to" headlines are frequently effective because they make a specific promise of helpful information. "How to give hamburger a new taste"; "How to improve tire wear."

Remember the gas stove ad example in Chapter 5? The headline of that ad ("Why Great Cooks Prefer Gas") was reached as a result of the following chronological thought processes, which virtually dictated its copy:

1. What sort of headline will attract all potential customers and pull them into the body copy?

2. How can the headline reach both users of electric and gas ranges with impact?

3. How can the headline sell gas ranges in a forceful and believable way?

Length of Headlines.   The aspiring copywriter may ask: "How long should a headline be?" The answer: "The headline should be as long as it has to be to get the job done." Brevity is desirable, but not just for its own sake, and never at the expense of clarity or persuasiveness. If you can pack all you want to say in one word, more power to you. A striking ad for house slippers uses the single-word headline: "Tranquilizers." The famous ad that introduced the Plymouth automobile said: "Look at All Three." If your selling idea takes many words, so be it. A great ad for Chesapeake & Ohio said: "A hog can cross the country without changing trains . . . but you can't."

Use of Subheads.   Make every effort to keep your headline short. Learn to use subheads. Subheads are an extension and reinforcement of your headline idea. The subhead should also be as terse as possible, but it does provide for a fuller explanation of the main headline. A subhead for the headline "Hate Winter Driving?" might be "Now a safe way to go on ice and snow."

Quantity of Headlines.   When writing your headline, have plenty of paper handy. Write dozens of headlines, scores of headlines. Don't just attack a problem, surround it. Come at it from every angle. Writing oodles of headlines is not a hateful chore; it is a labor of love, and it bears fruit.

David Ogilvy tried twenty-six headlines for his famous Rolls Royce advertisement before he wrote, "At sixty miles an hour, the loudest noise in this new Rolls Royce comes from the electric clock."[13] George

---

13. Dennis Higgins, *The Art of Writing Advertising* (Chicago: Advertising Publications, 1965), p. 79.

Gribbin, former president of the Young & Rubicam agency, said his organization would practically ostracize a copywriter who submitted only one headline with an advertisement.[14] In addition, leftover headline attempts often make great copy lines for the main text of the ad.

But no matter how you construct it, a good headline—Vic Schwab advises—must get *immediate attention* from an *interested audience,* must be *persuasive,* and must offer a *reward* for reading.[15] Combine such a headline with dramatic visual interpretation of the same message, and your advertisement will achieve instant impact. The other details of your advertisement are important but secondary. *It's what's up front that counts.* And what's up front is the headline and the visual—indivisible.

14. Ibid., p. 61.
15. Schwab, op. cit, p. 4.

CASE HISTORY
THE TRAVELERS

Courtesy of The Travelers and its agency, William Esty Company, Inc.

A favorite umbrella can do a lot more than just keep you dry. The Travelers found that out. They took their favorite umbrella, revitalized it, and made a bit of advertising history.

In recent years, deregulation of the financial services field provided new opportunities but resulted in a blurring of the distinction between companies and their product/service offerings. The Travelers had a solid reputation as an old-line, traditional insurance company but was not as well known for the broad range of financial services products it offered. Research studies in the mid-'80s indicated that overall awareness of the company was low, and that lack of awareness was the major deterrent to future growth.

The task of marketing/advertising effort was to increase awareness of The Travelers and document the company's extensive experience and expertise in a wide range of insurance, financial, and health-care services. The messages were to be targeted to upscale consumers, college-educated adults aged twenty-five to sixty-four, with annual household incomes of over $30,000. Particularly important as a target market were corporate decision-makers and small business owners/managers.

Much could be done (and was done) with repetition, continuity, and highly selective media use. But the key to success was the establishment of an overall creative theme. It was right at hand.

For many years, the symbol of The Travelers had been an opened red umbrella—the ideal indicator of coverage for a rainy day. But the red umbrella, while ever-present, had been simply a quiet symbol, a design element in the advertising.

In December 1985 The Travelers revitalized their red umbrella, brought it to life, and made it the focal point of their advertising. In a memorable television commercial, they put it in with a moving sea of black umbrellas. It popped right out at the viewer, while the copy line made the point that "In the Lookalike World of Financial Services, One Stands Out." Utterly simple, the umbrella treatment had instant impact and was instantly understandable.

The red umbrella became the "hero" of subsequent advertising on television, in newspapers, in consumer magazines, and in precisely targeted trade/professional magazines. A reassuring theme line was added: "You're Better Off Under the Umbrella."

The results of this multi-million dollar national corporate campaign have been outstanding. Unaided company awareness increased 44 percent in one year, the largest

THE TRAVELERS

Continued

percentage gain in the category. The Travelers is now the eighth most well-known insurance and financial services company in America, outdistancing the higher-spending Shearson/American Express and John Hancock. Almost 90 percent of the target audience now state that The Travelers has experience and expertise in a broad range of financial products and services. Unaided advertising awareness more than doubled in one year, representing the largest percentage increase in the category. After a year of advertising, of those recalling The Travelers advertising, the umbrella symbol is now more frequently recalled than any competitor's symbol/logo/mnemonic, including Prudential's "rock," John Hancock's "signature," and Aetna's "Glad I met ya!"

Next time you hear people in advertising ask about the value of an "umbrella theme," refer them to The Travelers!

IN THE LOOKALIKE WORLD
OF FINANCIAL SERVICES, ONE STANDS OUT.

Everywhere you look, there's another one.
Another financial network. Another financial service.
Which one's for you?
Look for the one with the long record—more than
120 years of financial success.
The one who *never* missed a dividend in all
those years.
The one with a solid foundation—over $46 billion
in assets.
The one with the diversity that protects against
adversity.
The one who knows when to fund ventures and
when to buy Treasury notes.
The one that America's most demanding
corporations count on for pension plans, employee benefits,
risk management and leadership in comprehensive
health services.
Look for The Travelers.
One of the most respected financial experts
in the world.

The Travelers Insurance Company and its Affiliates, Hartford, CT 06183.

TheTravelers
You're better off under the Umbrella.

105

CASE HISTORY
GOLD'N PLUMP POULTRY

Courtesy Gold'n Plump Poultry and its agency, Clarity Coverdale Rueff.

One of the most difficult products to advertise is a generic product, or a product that people *perceive* to be generic. Like chicken. All chicken is alike, some say. Not so, not so, say folks in Minnesota. *They* have chicken that's different—Gold'n Plump Chicken.

Competition for Gold'n Plump has mostly been unbranded chicken or store-brand chicken. Against these products Gold'n Plump chicken offered better quality and value, not for any singular difference, but for a variety of reasons.

Gold'n Plump chickens eat a special diet of corn, vitamins, and minerals. They receive no hormones and nothing artificial. Gold'n Plump chickens are super clean. They have over thirty inspections, five times as many as the government requires. Gold'n Plump Chickens have a healthy, golden yellow color, and have 25 percent less fat per bird than regular chickens.

Consumers were aware of the brand name but many did not have perceptions that Gold'n Plump chicken was better than the competition, nor *why* it was better.

The marketing/advertising need was to increase the un- aided brand awareness levels among consumers and especially to make them aware of the specific points of difference mentioned above, points of difference that would help prove the superiority of Gold'n Plump chickens.

A number of messages were used over time—on television, radio, and in newspapers—to create the overall perception of quality and superiority over other chicken. Each message was based on and highlighted one specified quality feature. The messages were friendly, even slightly humorous, but they were totally factual. Every good word for Gold'n Plump was supported by a solid reason and underscored with a touch of regional pride in the theme line: "Raised by Minnesotans. The Best Way We Know How."

By the conclusion of the advertising schedule, unaided brand awareness for Gold'n Plump jumped over 50 percent in the primary market. And consumers were able to provide unaided mentions of specific points of differences about Gold'n Plump: that it is cleaner than regular chicken, inspected more often, fed better, is bigger, has less fat, is tastier and of higher overall quality.

Results that are something to cluck about.

To Us, Cleanliness Is Next To Godliness.

CASE HISTORY

MAKER'S MARK BOURBON

Courtesy of Maker's Mark Distillery and its agency, Doe-Anderson.

Scattered throughout this book are examples of how a company can differentiate itself with its advertising. Here is a most delightful and unusual campaign from—of all places—the liquor business.

The campaign stemmed from a firmly held belief of Bill Samuels, Jr., a seventh-generation distiller and current president of Maker's Mark Distillery. While he was convinced of the need for advertising to communicate the Maker's Mark story to the marketplace, he was also convinced that no one reads liquor advertising. Further, interest in bourbon whisky had dropped considerably. It was considered the drink of an earlier generation and somewhat out of step with current tastes toward lighter, less rugged beverages.

Bill Samuels and Maker's Mark thus chose to do non-whisky ads. Gone is the traditional glamour shot of the bottle. Missing is any reference to lifestyle or social acceptance.

Instead, there is what appears to be a series of anecdotes about the whisky told by its maker, Bill Samuels. In one, he relates how people thought his father was doing something crazy by substituting mild winter wheat instead of rye as the flavor grain in the whisky. In another ad, he talks about some of his ancestors: Frank and Jesse James. In still another, he relates a whimsical letter from a Canadian man who presented his prospective father-in-law with a bottle of Maker's Mark. In yet another, there is a Christmas message from Bill's nine-year-old son.

The important point is that each Maker's Mark advertisement is a very real communication from the head guy that is designed to be both entertaining and informative. And those communications are beautifully executed by the Doe-Anderson Advertising Agency of Louisville.

Along the way, the ads have also worked to position Maker's Mark apart from other bourbons. In one ad, James Bacon (the *Los Angeles Herald Examiner* columnist and Hollywood's official Scribe to the Stars) was quoted as saying: "I'm not a bourbon drinker ordinarily, but Maker's Mark is the best I've ever drunk by far, one of those rare bourbons only connoisseurs know about."

It is interesting to note that all the bourbons on the market are currently experiencing declining sales—except Maker's Mark. It is the only bourbon that continues to show sales increases year after year.

Naturally, Bill Samuels is pleased with the Maker's Mark sales growth. But he's more pleased with how the *reputation* of the brand has grown. And he'd be the first to tell you that his somewhat different advertising approach has played a major role in building that reputation.

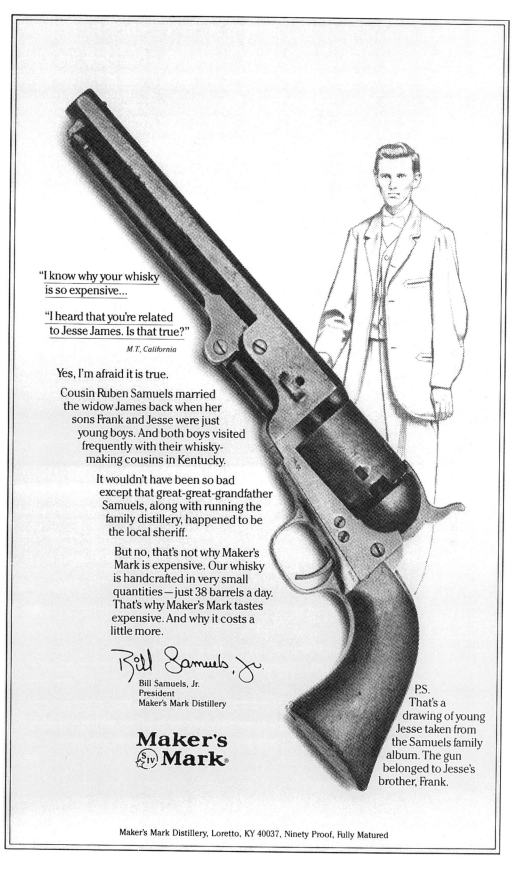

7

Completing the Writing Assignment

Chapter Topics

Function of body copy
Forms of body copy
Length of body copy
Specifics versus generalities
Claims versus facts
Ways of building belief
Suggested format for
    typing copy
Crude creed for
    copywriters
Emphasis on basic selling
    idea
Strive for the unexpected
Magazine ads versus
    newspaper ads
Creating folders and
    brochures

Key Terms

Body copy
"Reason why" copy
Testimonial
Basic selling idea
Unexpected quality
Recurring theme
Page domination
"Dummy"

Case Histories

The Wall Street Journal
Carnival Cruises
Michelin Tires

Once the creative team has visualized the concept, once the headline and subhead are stated, the rest of the advertisement—generally referred to as the "body copy" or "main text"—should follow naturally.

Body copy stems directly from the headline. It must explain the headline, speak in the same tone as the headline, and present evidence in support of the headline. And body copy must do these things with dispatch. If the headline says, "Fur Coat Sale Wednesday," the body copy will not start by saying, "Back in 1897, when the Acme Store was founded by Joshua Jones. . . ." A warning light should flash in your brain if a headline talks one way and the lead-in copy line talks another.

The visual-headline combination pulls the prospect in the door of the store, so to speak, while the body copy closes the sale. The headline-visual gets attention with an interesting proposition; the body copy fills in the details.

Body copy explains the attraction of the headline-visual proposition. Body copy gives facts and figures and makes the benefit perfectly clear. Body copy convinces. It persuades. And it tells the reader how to respond.

Body Copy Must Flow in a Straight Line.   Body copy must flow from the headline in logical progression. It must not go off on tangents, confuse the prospect, or introduce extraneous material that might be better handled in another ad. This precise focus begins with the single benefit featured in your creative strategy. The much-admired Volkswagen campaign provides numerous examples of the principle of body copy hewing to the line established by the headline-visual. One such ad shows a dramatic photograph of a solitary VW "bug" splashing toward you over a desolate muddy road. The provocative headline says, "Every new one comes slightly used." The body copy reads:

> The road to becoming a Volkswagen is a rough one. The obstacles are many.
> Some make it.
> Some crack.
> Those who make it are scrutinized by 8,397 inspectors. . . .
> They're subjected to 16,000 different inspections.
> They're driven the equivalent of 3 miles on a special test stand.
> Every engine is broken in.
> Every transmission.
> Many bugs are then plucked from the production lines. Their sole function in life is to be tested and not to be sold.
> We put them through water to make sure they don't leak.
> We put them through mud and salt to make sure they won't rust.
> They climb hills to test handbrakes and clutches.
> Then comes the dreaded wind tunnel and a trip over 8 different road surfaces to check out the ride.
> Torsion bars are twisted 100,000 times to make sure they torsion properly.

Keys are turned on 25,000 times to make sure they don't break off in the keylocks.
And so it goes on.
200 Volkswagens are rejected every day.
It's a tough league.

That particular advertisement was written to register the single impression of stringent quality control in manufacture. Notice that the body copy does *not* talk about styling, purchase price, gas mileage, location of engine, cooling system—all legitimate topics for VW selling. Instead, the text talks only about factory tests, reaches a conclusion, and stops.

WHAT FORM SHOULD BODY COPY TAKE?

Just as the headline is determined by the particular marketing problem you're trying to solve, the form of the body copy is determined by the headline. Body copy is written to match the headline. If the headline says, "Quick Quiz for Home Owners," it's almost certain that the text will follow a question-and-answer format. If the headline is brash and breezy, the text will be brash and breezy. If the headline is humorous, the body copy will sport humorous touches. (A Keebler Cookie trade ad interspersed cartoon sketches with text to prove the headline that "It Pays to Believe in Elves.") If the ad headline resembles a newspaper headline, the body copy is likely to be written in the style of a news bulletin.

All Body Copy Is "Reason Why."   The function of the body copy is always to substantiate the headline proposition. *All* body copy is *reason why*—regardless of the particular form it takes. Even when the dominant appeal is emotional rather than rational, the psychological benefits should still be persuasively detailed in the text.

HOW LONG SHOULD BODY COPY BE?

The length of body copy is determined in great degree by the public's familiarity with the product. Coca-Cola can show a big picture of a gorgeous creature sloshing down a cool soft drink. The ad may say only, "Have a Coke and a smile," or say nothing and simply emphasize the shape of the bottle. This is a poster ad, a reminder ad, jogging our awareness of an old acquaintance. The ad doesn't *have* to say any more because (a) practically the entire human race has been brought up knowing about Coke and (b) the product distinction is based on taste, a quality difficult to express in words. Compare such a Coke ad with the VW ad just quoted. That Volkswagen body copy was 175 words long, and it was tightly written.

Eliminate Non-Essentials.   All advertising copy should be as brief as you can make it and still complete the sales story. For one thing, the prospect's time is precious. For another thing, no prospect is ever as interested in a product or service as the copywriter may be. Every ad should be determinedly stripped of nonessentials by ruthless, repeated rewriting. The copy may be five words long or five hundred words long. In either case, *there should not be one word too many.* For instance, when selling diamonds for sentiment, DeBeers has shown a lovely female fist clutching several rings and saying, "No Woman Should Go Empty-Handed." When selling gems rationally, DeBeers may show stark diagrams of diamond-cutting along with hundreds of words of explanation.

Be Brief, But. . . .   The majority of national ads seen in the United States have relatively short copy. There is either little need for explanation or the illustration in the ad does the lion's share of the storytelling. Nevertheless, prospects will read long, detailed copy if they are not too knowledgeable about a product they find interesting. A good example of this was a twenty-six page newspaper insert once run by the New York Stock Exchange, which pulled over 20,000 requests for reprints. A person actively in the market for a car will digest every word of a lengthy automobile ad that might repel a casual reader. Strive for brevity and crispness, but don't forget the detail and the conviction.

Make It Memorable.   Packing conviction into brief copy requires writing discipline, editing skills, cutting and rewriting, and more cutting and rewriting. It is a rare copywriter who can afford to be satisfied with a first draft. In advertising you seek distinctive phrasing, and it is almost a sin to say the obvious and the ordinary because, while truthful, it does not jolt people and is not memorable. A certain ad might have said, "You really should try this refreshing soft drink with the distinctive flavor." Instead it said, "Be a Pepper!" It is not enough to be right in advertising copy; you must avoid being dull.

Avoid Generalities.   To carry conviction your copy must avoid being general. This habit of using generalities is one of the biggest (and most natural) traps for beginning copywriters. Generalities have little meaning whereas specifics and details are believable—as in the VW ad quoted. A restaurant that advertised its fried chicken as "delicious" would hardly raise an eyebrow. That over-used generality simply has no wallop.

At one major university, the initial assignment in the advertising creative course is the preparation of an advertisement for any restaurant in the college community. Beginning writers have a tendency to show the picture, name, and location of the spot along with the phrase, "Good food at fair prices." This short sentence contains two generalities. "Good food" does not tell us what kind of food it is, why it is good, or what the specialty of the house is. Nor can we imagine any restaurant not boasting that it had "good food." As for "fair prices," what exactly is meant? (One carmaker blandly referred to a luxury hard-top as "surprisingly affordable.") Generalities simply don't communicate. They are so ordinary and so expected that the public ignores them. To say that a restaurant offers "good food at fair prices" may be honest, but it is meaningless. To say "Cheese-and-mushroom hamburger on an onion roll, with potato chips, only $3.25"—*that* communicates. Even such a sophisticated copy line as "Superb Cuisine" (a glittering generality) hasn't nearly the impact of "Which would you rather enjoy tonight— Oysters Rockefeller or Beef Wellington?"

Use Facts, Not Claims.   Guarding against the use of generalities and clichés in copy is a lifelong battle, even for the most seasoned writers. The use of generalities is often a matter of laziness. It is easier to write "snappy take-offs" than it is to ferret out and reveal that the car goes "from 0 to 50 m.p.h. in 60 seconds"—but it isn't nearly as convincing. The most stirring *claim* doesn't pack nearly the conviction of a simple *fact*. For an illustration of this point, re-read the copy in the gas stove example in Chapter 5.

WHAT MAKES READERS BELIEVE WHAT A COPYWRITER SAYS?

Advertising copy may be beautifully conceived and written but will have absolutely no value unless it is believed. Because advertising is by its very nature a biased source of information, even a straightforward statement of absolute fact may be looked upon with skepticism by some readers. The wise copywriter does not try to buck human nature but instead uses forms of available evidence in a manner to build belief and conviction.

Guarantees.   The most basic evidence of good faith in selling is the guarantee—an official and public statement of responsibility on the part of the advertiser. Although advertising guarantees take a lot of kidding in and out of the profession, that does not make them less attractive to the prospective customer. The more expensive the product, the more important the guarantee becomes as a selling inducement. American Motors sold its "Buyer Protection Plan" with as much vigor as it ever promoted individual cars. Victor Kiam of Remington Razors promises on TV a shave as close as a blade shave or your money back.

Customer Examination.   Consumer examination is a proven way of convincing prospects. This method enables them to see for themselves, and can be used in a number of ways—through a free trial, through the gift of a sample, through an on-the-spot demonstration, or through a functioning scale model of the product.

A leading direct marketing clothing manufacturer says, "Wear these lightweight poplin slacks for two weeks, free." To add even more conviction to the advertiser's highly descriptive pictures and copy, a swatch of the material is included so that the prospect can see the color, feel the texture, and test the lightness of the material. That swatch may be small, but it is *real,* and thus far more convincing than words.

Third-Person Endorsements. What a third party says about you is more impressive than what you say about yourself, particularly when the third party is an authority. A loving mother saying her child is a brilliant student is very different from the principal of the school saying the same child is a brilliant student. (An exception to this principle is Lee Ioccoca of Chrysler, who has done an outstanding job of speaking for himself and his company.) It is important that the authority be germane to the subject, however. Many testimonial advertisements have featured celebrities who have little or no connection with the product, and although there is nothing deceitful in this approach, it doesn't make good sense. For example, a famous heart-throb athlete is much more convincing when he models boots than when he pushes a popcorn popper.

A testimonial does not always have to feature a well-known person, but the endorser should be believable, an honest-to-goodness consumer of the product. The homeowner who tells what happened to the clogged sink should *be* and *look like* a frustrated sink-unclogger—not like a professional television model.

Outstanding Success Stories. A product that has been judged outstanding in its field provides ideal grist for the copywriter. Notice the amount of movie advertising that boasts, with justifiable pride, "Winner of three Academy Awards." One margarine tastefully revealed that it had been specified on the official dinner menu for the annual meeting of the American Society of Cardiologists. Implication: If heart specialists choose it, the cholesterol level must be satisfactory for normal consumption.

Highly Respected Names. Sometimes you may have the pleasure of being associated with a company or store so prestigious that its very name wins customers. Chanel No. 5, for example, will often simply show a picture of the bottle with no copy, as if to proclaim: "What more is there to say?" Notice how many product ads will point out, "Available at Marshall Field & Company in Chicago, and other fine stores." The implication, of course, is that a store of Field's reputation would not handle the product unless it were of unquestioned quality. Advertising will occasionally call attention to the media in which it appears. For example, the words, "As advertised in *Good Housekeeping*" have a reassuring effect on some consumers.

Use the manufacturer's name liberally in the copy *only* when the company's reputation has made it almost a household word. Otherwise, extensive use of the name borders on bragging and can act as a sedative.

Performance Tests.   Performance tests can carry conviction, as they did in the Volkswagen copy. You might be able to detail some internal quality control test in the manufacturing process, or describe some use tests after the manufacturing process is completed—for instance, what happened at the automakers' test track. Even more convincing is a test performed by some independent service—like the taxicab fleet test of Motorcraft auto parts.

Record-Setting Sales.   If the product has an exceptional sales record, it is just good psychology to call attention to it. If a certain car is "America's fastest-selling slant six," this means it has performed well and has won over a lot of folks. Some advertisers will use sales figures in ingenious ways. For example, Pabst boasted that it was "Milwaukee's favorite beer," that it outsold all other brands in the beer capital of America, that it was top dog in the city that Schlitz made famous— certainly a statistic to give a beer drinker pause!

SUGGESTED FORMAT FOR COPY

Every agency and every company will probably have its own guidelines for typing copy, and you will want to conform to your employer's rules. However, those rules are not likely to vary a great deal from the general suggestions that follow.

When an ad is ready for presentation to management, it is typed in a rather simple and straightforward format, as you can see from the accompanying sample.

The identifying information about company, product, media, unit of space, and ad title goes in the upper left-hand corner. The headline is always typed in capital letters. Subheads, if any, are typed in capital and small letters and are underscored. The copy should be typed to approximate the arrangement of elements in the layout—by sequence and by the area allowed for it. *All* the words in an advertisement should appear on the typed copy, regardless of what words may be lettered on the layout.

A COPYWRITING CREED

Years ago one of the authors developed a simple checklist for students called the "Crude Creed for Copywriters." Notice how closely this creed applies the principles of your creative strategy.

Suggested Format for Copy

Client or Corporate Name

Name of Product
Name of Media
Unit of Space
Title of Ad

Illus: (Enclose in parentheses a short description of your major illustra-
tion, if you have one.)

Headline: WRITE YOUR HEADLINE IN ALL CAPS

Sub-head: <u>If you have a subhead, it should be
underscored.</u>

Copy: Your body copy should be double-
spaced with triple-spacing between
paragraphs. The amount of copy depends on your ad, but what is written here should correspond to your
layout. In other words, if you've
ruled eighty-five lines on your layout and write fifty words of copy
your layout isn't accurate.

If you want bold lead-ins, you can
underline them.

Illus: (Maybe you have another smaller
illustration.)

Caption: Perhaps you have some words to put
under or alongside the smaller
illustration.

Logo: SIGNATURE OF ADVERTISER

Start with a
      BASIC SELLING IDEA OR CONCEPT
      that succeeds at
      LINKING CONSUMER BENEFIT
      and PRODUCT EXCLUSIVE . . .
      then
      THINK VISUALLY
      TALK FRIENDLY
      KEEP IT SIMPLE
      PROVE YOUR POINT
      STAY ON TRACK
      STRIVE FOR THE UNEXPECTED
      SEEK A RECURRING THEME
      BE YOURSELF

The emphasis on basic selling idea or concept is a reminder to concentrate on substance rather than on technique. Positioning Maytag as the long-lasting washing machine with fewer repairs was a basic selling stance; the use of the lonely repairer was a matter of technique. Using national shrines to demonstrate the quality of Sears house paints is a great basic selling idea that overshadows even the magnificent production given each commercial.

The basic selling idea should link a consumer benefit with a product exclusive—or, at least, a strong product advantage. The benefit outranks the feature, that is, the prospect's self-interest comes first. A diamond isn't just a brilliant stone; a diamond is forever. Coffee crystals are not just flash-frozen; the customer is assured fresher flavor.

The admonition to *think visually* is a matter of common sense today when the visual is such a dominant element in communications. To get the primary message across with both speed and impact, the illustration and headline must be thought of as indivisible. The more of the story the visual can tell, the more effective the communication.

Talk friendly. Here's where the personal profile is so helpful. Adopt a conversational tone, as though talking to somebody across the table or across the back fence. Say "you" oftener than "we." More important, show genuine interest and concern; indicate an understanding of the problem and an eagerness to help.

Keep it simple. Concentrating on your strategy's principal benefit, build each ad around one basic idea and only one idea. It is especially crucial to plant a single overriding impression in the mind of the prospect when working with radio and television, where the message is fleeting.

Prove your point. Prove you can deliver your promised benefit. Be specific, detailed, and credible. Avoid overstatements and generalities; they lack conviction.

Stay on track. Once a creative strategy is established and a selling proposition is stated, the presentation should follow through in a straight line to a logical conclusion. To prevent you (or your prospect) from becoming sidetracked with other considerations, begin by stating a truism with which your reader can agree. It is a good idea to throw in a summary line at the end of the copy that refers back to the headline appeal and that ties up the whole story in one neat knot.

Strive for the unexpected. Most of the advertising we see today is good; some of it is great. The key to superior work and the quality that sets some advertising apart is the unexpected: a visual or verbal surprise, a twist, an odd combination of two previously unrelated elements that makes the prospect snap to and pay attention. You want to make the reader say, "By golly, I never thought of it that way before." This quality of the unexpected is what Andy Armstrong of the Leo Burnett agency once called "the break in the terrain." It is what Batten, Barton, Durstine & Osborn refers to as "Breaking the Boredom Barrier," the most crucial step in communicating through the mass media. There is no formula for coming up with the unexpected in copy, but you have to try for it or you will be condemned to eternal dullness.

A *recurring theme* contributes cohesiveness—a common thread—to an entire advertising and promotion campaign. Often called a "tag-line," it can be a repeated copy line like AT&T's "The Right Choice" or American Express Card's "Don't leave home without it." This is what people pick up and remember. This is how they identify an advertiser. A good recurring theme gives mileage to a promotion far beyond the total of its separate physical parts.

Be yourself. We all have our own ways of seeing the world and talking about it, and each of us should encourage this spark of individuality in ourselves. The most sought-after writers are those who do their own thing, who have their own inimitable styles, who have their own special flair. Writers who succeed are the writers who—within the rules (or most of them)—do it in a unique way.

MAGAZINE ADS VERSUS NEWSPAPER ADS: WHAT ARE THE DIFFERENCES?

We have been using the term print advertising in a broad sense to mean any advertisement that is not broadcast. We do not offer separate chapters on newspaper advertising and magazine advertising because the basic procedures of making ads for these two media are extremely similar and the differences are few.

Although most of the advice you have read up to now covers both magazines and newspapers, there are some ways in which newspaper advertising differs from magazine advertising.

You'll probably be dealing with only a fraction of the newspaper page so choose a size that dominates it. You may want to use some kind of a border or a judicious measure of white space to set the heart of your message off from competing messages on the same page.

Color printing is common in magazines, whereas newspaper advertising is predominantly black-and-white. Therefore, color in newspapers can really make your ad stand out.

The size of your headline should probably be somewhat larger in a newspaper ad than in a magazine ad.

Layouts for newspaper ads should be kept extremely simple and strong in order to combat competition on the same page.

Other than these few points of difference, making a newspaper ad is just like making a magazine ad.

CREATING FOLDERS AND BROCHURES

Parallel to the making of print ads is the making of printed advertising pieces such as folders and brochures. Certainly the creative strategy procedure is the same: you arrive at a principal benefit and a principal target audience.

Once you know what you want to say, and to whom, you tackle the organization of a folder by making a layout or "dummy." In a simple single fold, you number the pages 1, 2, 3, and 4. On page 1, the first outside page, belongs the headline-visual that would normally lead off an ad. This is the element that stops a reader, arouses interest, and impels the reader to look inside the folder. Here we have pages 2 and 3, which can be treated either as a two-page spread or as two distinct pages (that is, the reader reads all the way down page 2 before moving to the top of page 3). The outside back page, page 4, features the signature and the "mechanics" that might go with your particular selling proposition: the price list, the map of your location, the order blank, and so on.

If you'd like to experiment, make believe you are the Chamber of Commerce and create a simple folder extolling the virtues of your favorite vacation area. Would you try to attract single adults or families with children? Be sure to get the chief benefit on page 1. How would you handle a mixture of pictures and words on pages 2 and 3? On page 4, how would you ask an interested reader to follow through?

The process of creating print advertising messages does not vary greatly according to the medium. Before you move on to broadcast advertising, the next chapter gives you a quick peek at an exciting modern development in print advertising.

CASE HISTORY
THE WALL STREET JOURNAL

Courtesy of The Wall Street Journal *and the Fallon McElligott, agency.*

When the advertising client is a superbly-edited newspaper, the advertising copy had better measure up. Which it most certainly does for *The Wall Street Journal*.

With an average daily circulation of approximately two million, *The Wall Street Journal* is the nation's most widely circulated newspaper, recognized for its high editorial standards and product quality. But following a trend of steady circulation growth for several years through 1983, *The Wall Street Journal* was beset by a circulation decline in 1984.

The Journal had neither a credibility nor an awareness problem. But it was facing increased competition from enhanced business coverage in national and local newspapers, and from television and radio news broadcasts.

Research indicated that people held the following perceptions about *The Journal:* 1) Virtually universal recognition of *The Journal* as a premier *financial* newspaper, but 2) Lesser recognition of *The Journal* as a source of *general business* information. 3) Acknowledged importance to others (i.e. "my boss"), but questionable importance to the individual surveyed (i.e. "someone like me").

The Journal's marketing goal was to regain circulation losses and increase subscription levels by converting non-subscribing readers to subscribers, by encouraging trial readership among qualified non-readers and by maintaining acceptable renewal rates among current subscribers.

Needed was an image that attracted new readers without endangering the current franchise. Through advertising, *The Journal's* goal was to expand the perception of the publication as a source of relevant personal business information. The result was the tag line, "The daily diary of the American dream."

The Journal was advertised, primarily on television, through an image-enhancing campaign. Supporting print ads ran in *The Journal* itself, and in complementary publications. Subsequent television efforts featured a spokesperson who informed about the product, with a separate voice making the offer to subscribe. While the spokesperson could not be considered "impartial," he did lend a measure of credibility.

Results have been very satisfying. During the first two years of the campaign, circulation from trial subscriptions improved. Newsstand sales also grew, suggesting that new readers tried the paper. *The Journal* continues to attract new readers.

In each message, the copy is carefully chiseled, right down to the last punctuation mark. One ad features a dollar bill with the headline, "Unfortu-

THE WALL STREET JOURNAL

Continued

nately, it doesn't come with instructions." Another headline reaches out to super-Yuppies: "The fast track has a passing lane." And in an ad featuring immigrants we find this section of body copy that broadens the market: "At *The Wall Street Journal*, we think the American dream is still coming true.

It's happening in the mailroom and in the boardroom. In tiny office cubicles and plush executive suites. In the Mom-and-Pop food market and in the New York stock market."

And this final truism—"In the pages of *The Journal*, you'll find the fuel that dreams run on: information."

They didn't bring riches. They brought something better.

They arrived with little but their families, their clothes, and the dream of a better life.

It was called the American dream. Not because it was invented here. But because, for so many, it came true here.

At The Wall Street Journal, we think the American dream is still coming true.

It's happening in the mailroom and in the boardroom. In tiny office cubicles and in plush executive suites. In the Mom-and-Pop food market and in the New York stock market.

Wherever there are people driven by ideas, talent, and a determination to succeed, the American dream flourishes. As you might suspect, so does The Wall Street Journal.

In the pages of The Journal, you'll find the fuel that dreams run on: information.

Broad-ranging, accurate information about everything in the world that could influence the course of your career.

The Journal leaves you better prepared. Better informed. And better equipped to pursue your own personal American dream.

To subscribe, call **800·872·5466**. We can't promise you riches right away. But a wealth of information is a pretty good head start.

The Wall Street Journal.
The daily diary of the American dream.

CASE HISTORY
CARNIVAL CRUISES

Courtesy of Carnival Cruise Lines.

Ahoy, mates. Harken to the story of the family-owned company that revolutionized cruising. Some fifteen years ago there was a certain stigma to cruising as far as the general public was concerned. Most people had no first-hand knowledge of cruising but held certain negative attitudes on the subject. They thought cruises were (a) expensive, (b) for old folks, and (c) generally boring.

Enter farsighted entrepreneur Ted Arison of Carnival Cruise Lines. He borrowed money, bought a veteran ocean liner, renamed it *MardiGras,* and started a new enterprise aimed at expanding the cruise market from the Port of Miami.

From an advertising point of view he completely changed the principal benefit of his product. Cruising suddenly became *fun, fun, fun.*

Destroying class distinctions and pretensions of formality with a vengeance, the Carnival line turned traditional passenger cruising topsy-turvy, making the shipboard experience so vibrant that voyaging between ports turned into total recreation, rather than just a relaxing mode of travel. It was the beginning of the "Fun Ship" concept that has become Carnival's basic selling theme.

After three years of near-bankruptcy struggle, the Carnival idea caught on with a bang.

Additional ships have been added to the line, including three fabulous brand-new superliners. Cruises from Los Angeles to Mexico were begun, as well as cruises originating in San Juan, Puerto Rico. In 1984, Carnival deviated from its highly-successful seven-day service by adding three-day and four-day Bahamas sailings to its schedule.

This move gave tremendous impetus to cruise travel among younger people and people who lived reasonably nearby. The basic seven-day schedule had always appealed to the folks who split their annual two-week vacation into a week at one time and a week at another.

Carnival made cruising a big value, well within financial reach. People who tried Carnival early on were impressed. Their word-of-mouth comments were highly favorable and highly influential. In addition, Carnival has been an aggressive marketer over the years, with the largest advertising budget in the cruise business. A heavy user of national network television, Carnival backs up its TV effort with weekly and biweekly newspaper ads in 190 markets.

In 1983 Carnival Cruises highlighted its "Fun Ship" television advertising with a happy combination of an engaging representative and a catchy old tune from the Twenties. The representative was Kathy Lee

125

CARNIVAL
CRUISES
Continued

Gifford, a talented singer and talk-show host who had appeared frequently on network television programs. Charming and natural rather than glamorous and artificial, Kathy is the kind of woman with whom Mr. and Mrs. America would feel comfortable. In a clever stroke of programming, Carnival's advertising people resurrected a great old favorite tune from the flapper era entitled "Ain't We Got Fun." It was a natural for the Carnival message; even the original lyrics adapted almost perfectly. For several years, Kathy and "Ain't We Got Fun" became an instantly recognizable signature in television homes.

Carnival advertising has recently featured Kathy Lee Gifford with a newer and wonderfully pertinent song, "If My Friends Could See Me Now" from the Broadway show, "Sweet Charity." It is not only a great song, it is a terrific bit of psychological selling.

127

CASE HISTORY
MICHELIN TIRES

Americans love pictures of babies. If you were to study Starch Readership Reports from their beginnings in the early 1930s, you would realize that no ad illustration is as appealing as a picture of a baby. But in all those years, no advertiser has shown us babies with more symbolic meaning and more impact than has the Michelin Tire Corporation.

In 1985, Michelin confronted major obstacles of their own in addition to a somewhat declining passenger tire replacement market: (1) Michelin tires were, on average, more expensive than those of the primary competition, Goodyear, and a growing number of lower-cost imports; (2) Michelin was outspent an estimated three to one in advertising by the category leader, Goodyear; (3) Michelin had no new major passenger tire introductions scheduled for 1985.

Michelin marketing and advertising efforts had to acknowledge their high-price image while competing with a minimum ad budget compared to Goodyear. Michelin advertising was charged with achieving high levels of awareness among consumers while communicating the key sales points of quality and value. Among dealers, the advertising had to create high levels of awareness as well as excitement and pos-itive response. With a relatively modest budget, the campaign had to cut through television clutter, have impact, and maintain the high image of Michelin.

The creative solution was to single out and concentrate on every tire-owner's most precious possession: children and family. Taken a step further, children and family were symbolized by an innocent baby. Michelin enclosed that baby inside the ring of the tire. To this universally recognized visual, Michelin added the down-to-earth reminder in its theme line: "Because so much is riding on your tires." In the clearest and simplest of human terms, the advertising said protection, quality, and value in a manner that was remarkably fresh and novel for tire advertising.

The results exceeded expectations. Instead of simply maintaining the previous year's sales levels, replacement passenger tire sales increased significantly. As for the advertising itself, research showed unaided awareness of the "Baby" campaign was high: 34 percent of the respondents recalled the Michelin campaign versus 45 percent for Goodyear (despite Goodyear's ad spending advantage). Registration of Michelin's advertising slogan was high: 32 percent versus 18 percent for Goodyear. An independent research firm concluded that the Michelin "Baby" campaign was extremely effective. It was highly memorable, generated

MICHELIN
TIRES
Continued

excellent recall, and was considered unique and a pleasant change from typical tire category advertising. The commercials communicated what they intended to communicate, with no confusion, and compatibly reinforced Michelin's quality image.

Michelin dealers responded just as positively as did consumers.

And so the Michelin "Baby" campaign has continued. Variations have been used, some ingenious situations have been dreamed up, and certain baby roles have been expanded. But the advertising never departs from its basic message: protect what you love most with the finest quality tires available regardless of price. In 1987, Michelin replacement tire sales were up sharply, well ahead of industry levels—which says a lot for presenting a high-quality product in a strong emotional light.

MICHELIN. BECAUSE SO MUCH IS RIDING ON YOUR TIRES.

Who consistently makes the finest tires? Ask most people in the tire business and chances are they'll say Michelin.

Ask most of your customers and they'll agree.

Unfortunately, many of these same customers aren't willing to spend the difference to get the best.

In 1985, Michelin's advertising is going to be very single-minded in convincing people that, when it comes to tires, it's worth paying more to get the best.

This year our slogan, "Michelin. Because so much is riding on your tires." is going to be more than a slogan. We're going to drive that message home in the kind of advertising the tire industry's never seen before. Unique, fresh advertising, that preliminary tests tell us is going to get customers into your stores ready to pay the difference for Michelin.

Of course, even the best advertising isn't effective if nobody sees it. So we've bought time on some of the biggest sporting events of the year. In 1985, we'll be where your customers are.

Advertising isn't all that's new at Michelin. Joining last year's spectacularly successful XA4 All-Season Radial is our new Michelin XH all-purpose passenger radial. It's computer designed to enhance the ride and performance characteristics of most American cars.

For light trucks and recreational vehicles, we're introducing the Michelin XCH4. This is the tire that's going to offer buyers fuel savings over conventional tires, plus long tread life, a quieter ride, and reduced incidence of punctures.

If history is any indication, your customers will recognize these new tires as the best in their category.

And if our new advertising has anything to say about it, they'll be willing to spend the extra money to buy them. From you.

MICHELIN.

8

Modern Miracle:
Desk-Top Ad Making

Chapter Topics

Do-it-yourself ads
Creative software
High-resolution
    reproduction

Key Terms

Laser printer
Camera-ready

Case History

David Shih—Hunger,
    Literacy Campaigns

Before we leave the world of print temporarily and enter the world of broadcast, let's briefly examine a modern miracle of ad-making.

How would you like to think up an ad, lay it out, write it, do the artwork for it, and produce it--all at the same time?

Yes, do-it-yourself has come to advertising. Computers now make it possible to create and produce ads right at your own desk.

With certain sophisticated software, you can do incredible things at lightning speed. You have a choice of several type faces, in several styles such as bold, outline, and italic, and in a wide range of sizes. With a small electronic hand indicator you can create your own illustrations and logotypes. You can enlarge them or reduce them. You can install all kinds of patterns of dots. You can draw lines, thin to thick, as you wish. You can call up borders, frames, shapes. You can erase. You can lasso objects on the screen and move them to another location. You can "cut" an item from the page and store it in an electronic scrapbook. You can use a computer catalog of clip art from which to select appropriate illustrations.

Most wonderful of all, you can experiment and improvise and "play" with all these elements until you get your page ad exactly the way you want it. What you see on your computer screen is what you'll get on the printed page. Then you can store it until you're ready to call it back again.

If you have a laser writer you'll get high-resolution reproduction with 300 dots per inch. Using a digitizer or scanner, the laser writer will reproduce photographs and drawings with remarkable sharpness and clarity. The result is camera-ready advertising that can save a bundle in art and production costs.

On the assumption that one picture is worth a thousand words, shown here are two sets of award-winning ads created by David Shih of Young & Rubicam when he was a student in 1987. The Literacy Campaign won a national contest co-sponsored by the International Newspaper Advertising & Marketing Executives and the American Academy of Advertising. The Hunger ads won a Gold Medal and a Bronze Medal in New York's prestigious "One Show" for advertising. Not only are these outstanding ads in themselves, but they were totally, completely, 100 percent prepared on an Apple Macintosh computer at David Shih's own desk.

We are not suggesting that you use desk-top publishing to turn out finished ads, but what a miraculous way to experiment with ideas!

If nothing else, think of all the paper you would save.

YOU CAN'T FEED SYMPATHY TO A STARVING CHILD.

There are millions of children all over the world who are starving to death.

In fact, 13 million children under the age of five die each year as a result of hunger.

It's sad, but true.

But just feeling sorry for them isn't going to solve anything.

There *are* solutions to the hunger problem.

But we can't do it without help.

If you would like to give more than just your sympathy, please fill out this coupon.

And maybe someday, there won't be anything to feel sorry for.

The Hunger Project
P.O. Box 789, San Francisco, CA 94101

☐ Enclosed is my tax-deductable contribution of $_____ .

☐ I would like to participate with The Hunger Project in my area.

Name_____

Address_____

City_____ State____ Zip_____

Phone H(___)_____ W(___)_____

The Hunger Project
The time has come to end world hunger.

UNFORTUNATELY, EATING ALL THE FOOD ON YOUR PLATE WON'T HELP THEM A BIT.

Has anyone ever told you,"Eat all your food. There are kids starving in Africa"?

Well, that person was right.

There are thousands of children who are starving to death in Africa.

And thousands more in Asia. And Latin America. And the Middle East.

The sad fact is, 13 million children under the age of five die each year as a result of hunger.

But eating all your food isn't going to solve their problem.

It takes more than just sympathy.

It takes individual support. World hunger *can* be ended.

We have solutions which *have been proven* and *are affordable.*

In fact, 41 countries have already solved their food problems since 1960 alone.

So go ahead and leave a little food on your plate.

But please help to put a little more on theirs.

Illiteracy can really make a person feel unwanted.

HELP WANTED

Various full-time and part-time positions available. Good salary and benefits. Call 328-6805 for an interview. Ask for Sue.

Consider the idea of going through life not being able to read. Sound like a tough job?

Today, there are 27 million adults in America who have the terrible misfortune of being functionally illiterate. 2 million in Illinois alone.

These people really have their work cut out for them. Because they can't do a lot of basic tasks like read a job ad or fill out an application.

If you know someone who cannot read, encourage him or her to enroll in a local adult literacy program. Bring them in yourself if you have the time.

For more information, call the **Illinois Literacy Hotline** toll-free at **1-800-321-9511**.

Remember, an illiterate person can't read *this* ad either.

The Illinois Literacy Council
Linking Students with Tutors.

9

Writing Advertising for Radio

Chapter Topics

How radio has changed
Stations rather than
    programs
The tools of radio writing
Creating pictures in the
    mind's eye
The fleeting message
Concentration on one
    theme
Example of repeated key
    elements
The medium of the
    imagination
Eighteen rules for writing
    radio copy
Suggested script form
Identifying scene and
    characters
Basic broadcast terms
Use of music and sound
    effects
Timing the commercial
Importance of writing it
    "short"
Reading copy aloud
Types of radio
    commercials
Writing for local AM and
    FM stations

Key Terms

Pictures in the mind's eye
Fleeting message
Fact sheet
Segue
"Straight" copy
"Production" copy

Case Histories

Kelly Services
Radio Advertising Bureau

Radio was invented little more than sixty years ago. Within a few years of its birth, it had become the universal medium. Fast as the flick of a switch, widely separated families in every part of the United States were instantly sharing the excitement of an event or the enjoyment of a performance. Overnight, radio phrases became part of everyone's language.

Radio quickly became the dominant medium for national advertising. Millions of dollars were switched from magazines into coast-to-coast radio hookups. Every major advertiser (and many a minor advertiser) seemed to be the sole sponsor of a network show with corporate names attached. Radio ended up with most of the advertising dollars and all of the glamour.

THEN ALONG CAME TELEVISION

When television burst upon the scene right after World War II, it might have appeared that radio was finished. Instead of dying, radio changed almost completely. There are far more radio sets in use now than in radio's heyday, but the usage is totally different. Gone is the family glued to the set in the living room. Now we listen to radio while we do something else. Gone also are the giant network entertainment programs, with their coast-to-coast broadcasts, and the star-spangled sponsored shows.

Today, Americans listen to *stations* rather than to *programs*. Into the network void have rushed many small local stations, each with its own specialty, each with its own audience. The listener turns on a favorite station and leaves it on. If the listener likes talk, a talk station is turned on. For sports, classical music, rock and roll, or country and western, the listener just turns to the appropriate number on the dial. Little wonder Hanley Norins refers to radio today as "The Segmented Medium."

Even though the glamorous advertising medium is currently television, advertisers are spending huge sums in radio, simply distributing the expenditures in smaller units. Today they buy "spots." But, as far as the copywriter is concerned, the creative delights of writing for this versatile medium remain the same. Your imagination can really take wings in radio!

However, if you want to write successfully in radio, you are first going to have to break a lifelong habit. From your first day of school, you have been writing prose—compositions, book reports, examinations, essays, letters—for a second person to read and comprehend. Now you are going to write for the ear instead of for the eye. There is a big difference.

In radio, there is no visual—no striking layout, no handsome type setting, no colorful illustration. But radio has delightful compensations that print messages cannot equal: the warmth and persuasiveness of the human voice, the many moods of music, the dramatic excitement of sound effects. All these combine to let the copywriter conduct a sort of "symphony of persuasion" on that most miraculous of all instruments—the imagination of the listener. While writing for radio may be quite different from any writing you have done in the past, it offers you absolutely limitless effects.

Throughout this book, we have repeatedly urged you to think visually. Now you may well ask, "How can I think visually in a non-visual medium?" The answer is that you are creating *pictures in the mind's eye*. The wonderful part is that the listener does all the work for you.

Where print is a space medium, ruled by inches, radio is a *time* medium, ruled by seconds. A page ad in *National Geographic* is fixed in position forever. It does not move or change in any way. But the radio message is fleeting; it does not remain in one place where it can be carefully studied and absorbed. It moves, and it does so quickly. Thus it is crucial in writing for radio that you stress one principal idea. You must keep your advertising message simple, simple, simple. Concentrate on one theme. And repeat key elements.

In a classic Burger King radio commercial, the principal benefit to be stressed was the large size of the burgers. Among other things, one musical radio spot said:

> It takes two hands to handle a Whopper.
> You have to put it down to sip your shake,
> To munch your fries, to take a break.
> It takes two hands to handle a Whopper
> 'Cause the burgers are bigger at Burger King.

Notice how many ways the writer tells you that the burger is big. First off, with the very name "Whopper." The product is so big that it "takes two hands" to hold it. You can't hold it in one hand while you grasp your milkshake or eat your french fries with the other. No, you have to "put it down" because it keeps two hands busy. The writer reminds you of that again, and again uses the name "Whopper." Finally, the writer tells you right out that the "burgers are bigger." You cannot come away with any other impression after hearing this commercial. One theme has been stressed and reinforced in several ways.

Remember that selective attention is a small factor in radio listening. People are doing other things—driving, eating, working, sunbathing—and radio simply provides background. The radio is *on*, all right, but the prospect is not really listening, not attentively at any rate.

The first thing your commercial must do is capture and hold the listener's attention with entertainment of some form. You may employ humor, music, or drama. You may be hilarious, solemn, or startling. But whatever your opening gambit, it must hook the listener and pull the listener in.

One Oldsmobile commercial opened with crowd and traffic noises immediately followed by the sirens of an approaching caravan of police motorcycles. What's going on? A news announcer reveals that a stunt driver is about to drive a new Olds straight up the side of the Sears Tower, the world's tallest building. Wouldn't *you* stop to listen?

It is amazing how deeply listeners can become involved once their attention has been captured. The greatest historical evidence of listener involvement occurred during the famous "War of the Worlds" broadcast by Orson Welles and his Mercury Theatre of the Air on Halloween Eve in 1938. The program spread panic across the nation; there were even reports of a woman who considered suicide rather than face being ravaged by a Martian.

Records and tapes of the classic "War of the Worlds" broadcast abound at most schools. If you have never heard it, you may want to listen to it now. It is as gripping today as when it was first aired—a superb example of how realistic a radio drama can be.

Thanks to the imagination of the listener, the effects you can evoke in radio copy are boundless. There are no restrictions on travel or time, for example. If you open your message with a stentorian announcer stating "Moscow, 1917," the listener is transported there instantly. The listener can *feel* the cold, *see* the Cossack cavalry charging. In the next five seconds your speaker can announce, "London, today," and the listener instantly bridges time and space. In the mind's eye, the listener sees the monarch and the changing of the guard at Buckingham Palace.

This is an effect that television, for all its marvels, cannot achieve. Television is a *literal* medium. What you see is what you get. Radio is truly the medium of the imagination, and there is no end to what your listener can see in the mind's eye. All you have to do is give the hint.

Consider, too, that radio has a quality of timeliness unequaled in the print media, even in newspapers. You can keep messages current, adapting to events of the day. Radio is flexible enough to permit eleventh-hour copy changes, when necessary.

HOW TO WRITE RADIO COPY

When composing your radio copy, it is a good idea to make believe you are talking across the coffee table to an acquaintance or chatting across the back fence to someone representative of your personal profile. Write the way you talk. The chief advantage of radio is the human voice, and the best way to employ the human voice is to be conversational. Here are some suggestions to help your radio writing succeed:

1. Keep your copy conversational.

2. Forget perfect, polished language. (People just don't talk that way.)

3. Use contractions. ("We do not care" sounds stilted; "We don't care" sounds natural.)

4. Use short sentences. Use sentences fragments. Use one-word sentences. (Not even professors of English converse in complete and perfect sentences.)

5. Use the grunts and gasps and pauses that are so expressive in person-to-person chatter. (Do not try to out-do famed British playwright Noel Coward. You waste precious seconds and you may sound un-American. When somebody in the United States receives an unexpected gift, the response is likely to be a whistle or a "Wow!" rather than "My, what a delightfully charming surprise!")

6. Use short words.

7. Use easy-to-pronounce words.

8. Use clear, simple words.

9. Be colloquial, even slangy, but tasteful.

10. Repeat the key elements of your appeal.

11. When you want the announcer to "punch" a word, underscore it.

12. When you want the announcer or actor to pause, use a double dash or write (PAUSE).

13. Hyphenate modifiers, so the announcer won't mis-read or pause before the connection is complete.

14. Remember, the listener can't see your product on radio. Be specific about visual and mechanical features that differentiate your product. (If it comes in a red squeeze bottle, be sure to tip off your listeners so they'll recognize it faster when they get to the supermarket.)

15. Beware of jamming too many "s" words close together. (That's all right in prose; in radio, it sounds snakelike.)

16. Alliteration must be handled with care. (Repetition of the same or similar sounds can sometimes be pleasant and memorable, sometimes childish and offensive.)

17. Internal rhymes can contribute to memorability—if not overdone.

18. A certain rhythm or beat to the writing is desirable, although this is an almost-unconscious knack that the good writer develops over time.

All the little bits and pieces of advice come back to the one overriding rule for the radio copywriter: be conversational. Just relax and talk friend-to-friend. Don't think about speaking into a microphone. Visit across the table with the customer in your personal profile.

MAKING A START

If you have never written for radio before, you may feel a bit apprehensive at first. The most sensible way to begin is with straight copy—words only. Pick a topic and write twenty-five seconds' worth of copy about it—your wrist watch, for example. Why did you buy it? Or why did somebody choose it for you? Describe it. Tell what you like about it. What makes it different from other watches? Re-read your copy. Is it relaxed and conversational? Or is it still a little stiff and formal?

Try role-playing this time, still using words only: you're the mother of a famous person from the past, present, or future, from history or fiction. Tell how your famous offspring feels about a certain product. Re-read what you've written. Does your copy sound like a sure-enough person talking? Is there definite character in the way she talks? Have you given her a few distinctive, authentic phrases to say?

Try something a little more elaborate. Re-tell the famous poem of Paul Revere's ride in radio form. Invent your own characters and dialogue. You can even have a talking horse. Add some music, some sounds. Now you're beginning to get into the spirit of the thing, to realize what a joy it is to write for radio.

A famous advertising writer and teacher, Walter Weir, believes that studying playwriting sharpens copywriters' ability to write believable, natural dialogue (of which there is a great lack on the airwaves today). His advice is worth following. If you can't study playwriting, study drama, or at least read several contemporary plays. Note how the author uses dialogue to build character and propel the plot along.

The script of a radio commercial is not unlike the script of a stage play. The sample radio script on the opposite page contains, not a commercial, but several nuggets of advice on how to rough out a commercial.

Identifying the Scene or Situation

Radio listeners cannot see what's going on so you must quickly plant signals to help them. Is this dramatic scene of yours taking place in a schoolyard? Then let's hear playground noises in the background. Do we have people arguing in the kitchen? Then let's hear the rattle of pots and pans and dishes. Are two people talking in a car? Establish the hum of the motor. Are they standing on the city sidewalk? Let's hear the sounds of traffic. These are sketchy examples, but you can see that to play fair with your listener you need to give hints right away telling where the listener is and what's going on. Mueller's Macaroni commercial began with the sound of a fog horn, followed by the rattle of an anchor chain. These sounds said *sea*. They were followed by a distinctively accented voice saying, "Up here in Boston, etc.," and the setting of the scene was completed.

Suggested Script Form - Radio

Client Name

00-sec. Radio

1st ANNCR: You are about to see (*STAGE WHIS-
                 PER*) that only the words the lis-
                 tener hears are typed in upper
                 and lower case.

2nd ANNCR   That's absolutely right. All in-
(JOVIALLY):   structions to the producer or di-
                 rector or talent are typed in
                 capital letters. (MUSIC: "STARS
                 AND STRIPES FOREVER" IN AND
                 UNDER)

1st ANNCR: That's true not only of music but
                 of. . . (SOUND: DOOR SLAMS. HUR-
                 RIED FOOTSTEPS. SCREAM. BODY
                 FALLING DOWN LONG FLIGHT OF
                 STAIRS.)

2nd ANNCR: Writers are safe if they first
                 remember that only the words the
                 listener hears are typed in upper
                 and lower case.

1st ANNCR: We might remind them also to time
                 commercials with a stop watch
                 . . . or with the sweep-second
                 hand of a dress watch.

2nd ANNCR: Good point. And they must allow
                 time as they read for any special
                 effects required, such as music,
                 sound, pauses, etc.

1st ANNCR: Announcers are grateful when the
                 copywriter's commercial runs a
                 few seconds short—say twenty-
                 seven seconds for a thirty-second
                 spot. Those few seconds give us
                 announcers time to put dramatic
                 selling effects into the copy.
                 (MUSIC: UP AND OUT)

NOTE: The above is not a commercial and is no prescribed length. It
       simply gives some idea of script form that is reasonably stan-
       dard throughout the business.

Identifying Characters

When you prepare your script you must indicate for the benefit of your producer or director who says what when and how it is said. Don't overdo it, but try to be reasonably specific about what you want.

If, for example, your idea involves the use of two announcers, you simply say, in capital letters, 1st ANNCR: and 2nd ANNCR:. An announcer is a professional seller, and your listener accepts this. Announcers are not actors, not characters in a playlet; they are salespeople.

If you want a particular character in your script, use a specific name or title or role: HUSBAND and WIFE, CROOK and COP, JOHN and MARCIA. Identify them for the listener with such dialogue as: "Tell me, Officer." "Marcia, pay attention!" "But you're the only husband I've got!"

How Characters Speak

Your actors and announcers will speak in a normal tone of voice, at a normal pace, unless you instruct them differently, for example: MADGE (SLEEPILY); HUSBAND (SHOUTING); COED (SOUTHERN ACCENT). You can even ask for a voice change in mid-sentence and the performer must give it to you.

Some Basic Broadcast Terms

You don't have to know many technical terms to get along in radio. In referring to volume or loudness, use the word UP to make it louder and the word DOWN to make it quieter or softer. When you want something held in the background, use the word UNDER to indicate activity going on *underneath* what's playing up front, center stage, so to speak. When you want conversation, music, or sound to stop, you use OUT. MUSIC OUT means get rid of it, end it, take it out. For a gradual effect say FADE OUT MUSIC.

How to Call for Music

Music is a marvelous tool for the radio writer because anyone not built of stone responds to it. It definitely expresses mood and feeling, it can express time, and it can express place.

The musical jingle has long been a fixture in radio and probably always will be. The music *is* the commercial. But when using music only as background, you ask for it in various ways: by broad category (MUSIC: WALTZ), by narrow category (MUSIC: STRAUSS WALTZ), or by specific title (MUSIC: "TALES FROM THE VIENNA WOODS"). Unless a particular song is of vital importance to your idea, it is probably best to give your director some leeway in making a choice.

To begin your commercial with music, just write that instruction down as the first element in your script.

One ingenious way of using music in radio is the *segue* (pronounced seg-way). This is a musical transition or medley from one tune to another, generally to indicate a change in mood, time, or place. The segue can be a great story-telling device, compressing much dramatic action into a very short interval of broadcast time without dialogue. For example, you can easily follow the story told in these three popular George M. Cohan songs: "I'M A YANKEE DOODLE DANDY" SEGUE TO "OVER THERE" SEGUE TO "GIVE MY REGARDS TO BROADWAY."

How to Call for Sound Effects

Sound, too, can be almost as expressive and dramatic as the human voice or music. Most often it is used to set the stage or to intensify the drama. The Mueller's Macaroni commercial previously mentioned set the scene with a fog horn and rattling anchor chain. A gripping, thematic sound is the "thump, thump, thump" that underlies the "Heartbeat of America" commercials for Chevrolet.

When you want to indicate sound in your script, use the word SOUND or SFX, which is a short, snappy way of abbreviating "sound effects." Be terse in your instruction, but be specific enough to help your director (SFX: TRAIN APPROACHING).

Timing the Commercial

In the matter of timing radio copy, the clock is preferred over the word count. (Even in straight copy, not all words are the same length, nor meant to be read at the same pace.) Use a stopwatch or the sweep-second hand on an ordinary watch. If you prefer a word count, aim for sixty to seventy words per half-minute.

But no matter how you time your copy, write it short. A few seconds' leeway will permit carefully selected professional talent—announcers, actors, musicians, sound controllers—to put far more feeling into your message than you ever realized was there. Instead of writing a thirty-second script, write for twenty-five or twenty-seven seconds. Take full advantage of the skills of your talent by leaving room for the performers to contribute. Every second counts. You cannot be casual about one or two seconds; a thirty-one-second spot is simply not acceptable.

READ YOUR OWN COPY OUT LOUD

The most important factor to remember about writing radio copy is that you are writing to be heard. It is not at all satisfactory to scan a few typewritten lines with your eyes when you are finished. *The copy must be read aloud* to be evaluated sensibly. This is a different kind of English. Get your spouse, roommate, or classmate to read it out loud to you. If there is nobody else available, read it out loud to yourself. Don't just move your lips, but speak up and speak out. You may want to tape record it and play it back. Your own ear will relay reactions to your brain in mid-sentence. It will quickly tell you how your copy sounds—whether it makes sense, whether it rings true, whether it contains tongue-twisters or word-blocks over which your announcer will stumble. (Today's job-seeking writer is likely to bring a small audiotape rather than typewritten copy to an interview.) If it is at all possible, be present in the studio when your radio copy is recorded. Listen to the actors reading your words as they warm up their talented voices. If they hit a false note, it's probably the fault of your copy. Try to smooth it out for them before they start recording.

TYPES OF RADIO COMMERCIALS

There are several types of commercials, from straight copy read by a single announcer, to musical productions with a full orchestra and vocalists.

Straight copy (typewritten words only sent to each station on the media list) done imaginatively and persuasively, can be just as effective as a super-colossal musical treatment. A company called Verbal Advantage offers a series of tapes designed to increase your word power and language facility. Using words only, their announcer talks so beautifully that he is a living example of the benefit of the course. No commercial is better than its basic selling idea. Put punch and personality into those precious words because that's all you have working for you. You don't even know what kind of announcer is going to step up to the mike and read them when the time comes—unless, of course, your commercial is recorded. In this case, you or somebody from the agency will have selected one particular announcer for the unique timbre in her or his voice that you believe matches the precise needs of your script. Any time you are writing straight copy, ask yourself: Would I say this, face-to-face, with the audience representative in my personal profile?

A *production spot* is any commercial—from words only to super dramatic or musical treatment—that is produced or recorded in a studio under strict control. Duplicates of that recording are then sent to all the stations on the media list.

Dialogue commercials, or any treatment using the contrast between two or more voices, offers a greater dimension of interest (but only if the dialogue is interesting to begin with). Bob and Ray excel at verbal byplay. And commercials for Kelly Girls secretarial service feature totally natural, believable conversations.

Dramatized commercials, vignettes of a real-life problem, are quite common. Some are very gripping, but most are slightly nauseating. Why? Because the writer often puts phony or commercial words into the mouth of a supposedly average citizen. The listener mentally says "uh-oh" and tunes out. All it takes is one wrong word spoken by one of the dramatic characters. The shrewdest way to use the dramatized commercial format is to set up the problem with the little dramatization, but bring in a professional announcer to handle the selling copy. The Stiller and Meara commercials for United Van Lines are real-life situations with a smile.

Musical commercials can be very infectious, or just ho-hum. Properly composed and produced, a musical spot can win quick identification for your product. Ford Motor Company has used a catchy musical message for a public service announcement about seat belts called "People Who Do." A commercial based on a popular song (or "standard") has a lot going for it because the listener responds as though to an old friend. In introducing its then-revolutionary "Pepsi Generation" campaign, Pepsi-Cola borrowed that great old Eddie Cantor tune from the Twenties, "Making Whoopee." Wesson Oil has used a bubbly favorite, "Personality"; United Airlines adapted George Gershwin's famous "Rhapsody in Blue"; Campbell Soup has long used a charming oldie, "Give Me the Simple Life."

In the golden days of radio programming, elaborate "cast commercials" were prepared that were almost as entertaining as the show itself. Jack Benny and his entire troupe were particularly adept at integrating such commercials into the program—both for Jello and for Lucky Strike. No more, however; the species has vanished.

Yet radio remains the most fertile of fields for the imaginative writer. Great spots have been done with distinctive voices (the Oscar Mayer Kid), with famous, recognizable voices (Lloyd Bridges, Burgess Meredith, Mason Adams), with comedy voices (Bob and Ray, Stiller and Meara, Jonathan Winters), with authoritative voices (Alex Dreier, John Cameron Swayze, Tom Bosley). Ingenious spots have sprung from product sound effects (Mazda cars and Maxwell House coffee). Inventive variations have been evolved for long-running musical themes (Coca-Cola, Pepsi-Cola).

WRITING FOR LOCAL AM AND FM STATIONS

The big-time stations and studios can make almost any effect available to a writer. The writer for a local AM or FM station is going to have to be inventive, ingenious, and—on occasion—a little bit daft.

Because production facilities are so limited at local AM and FM stations, the greatest number of spots aired will be straight copy—words only—read by a station announcer. Variations are available, however, at little or no cost.

Many small stations run live copy (a straight announcement) over theme music. The music is available on a number of rental broadcast albums (ASCAP, BMI). A particular musical selection may be chosen for a local advertiser and reserved for use under that advertiser's copy only.

In addition to rental albums of sound effects, there are small, inexpensive production libraries available—special records from The Producers and Sounds of Broadcasting that offer everything from sound effects to stingers to generalized jingles to seasonal music.

Sometimes the advertiser can be used to deliver copy over the air. Occasionally a locally known personality (such as a popular athlete) might deliver an announcement. At times a local resident speaks up as a satisfied customer. Sometimes the station's disc jockey may be given a fact sheet and asked to ad lib in that performer's inimitable style. For special effect an impressive echo or reverb can be achieved with a straight announcement if the engineer loops the audio tape for playback. Some stations will use two voices to give more punch to copy; other small stations haven't the staff to do even that.

The chief writer at one small FM station in Illinois has proved highly inventive. She has gone into an advertiser's restaurant and taped interviews with actual diners. She has used a stairwell for an echo chamber. To duplicate the effect of a background airport announcement she has had the sound controller tape the message in the men's room. To duplicate the sound of a smash-up she had all the station's wastebaskets and folding chairs piled up in the hallway and had a child run into them.

No question about it, writing advertising for a local AM or FM station can make strange demands!

CASE HISTORY
KELLY SERVICES

Courtesy of Kelly Services, Inc.

The medium of radio offers the warmth and persuasiveness of the human voice, but the magic works only if the writer gives that radio voice believable words delivered in a convincing way. It sounds simple, but truly believable copy is so rare in radio commercials that it stands out. A superb example is the dialogue in the network radio commercials for Kelly Services—the Kelly Girls.

Kelly Services, Inc., is a comprehensive temporary help service that provides customers with temporary employees with skills in the following areas: office clerical, automated office, light industrial, technical support, and marketing support.

For the first thirty-five years of its history, Kelly Services was able to meet the market demand for qualified temporary employees by recruiting skilled individuals and testing to ensure their skill levels. But as office automation—word processing and new personal computers at secretarial workstations—took over, it became apparent Kelly would have to expand its services. In addition to testing, Kelly began offering computer training and on-the-job support to its temporary employees.

In January 1987, Kelly Services introduced the Kelly PC-Pro System, a personal computer training, testing, and on-the-job support program for eleven leading word processing software packages. Support included simplified software reference guides and a toll-free hotline number where temporary employees' questions could be answered immediately by an office automation expert.

Kelly introduced this new program with an advertising campaign on network radio, as well as in business and trade publications. The key to the radio copy lies in the fact that Kelly *interviewed its own customers for their reactions.* As a matter of fact, the voices you hear in Kelly radio commercials are *actual customer voices.* A professional interviewer talks with the Kelly customers and all conversations are recorded in their entirely. From the verbatims, Kelly selects a few of the best interviews to be edited into sixty-second commercials. During the editing process, Kelly occasionally re-writes and re-records the interviewer segments, *but the customer portion is never scripted.*

Prior to air date, each customer is given the opportunity to read a script of the commercial as it is to run, and approves it as accurately representing his or her opinions, attitudes, feelings and experiences with Kelly Services. If a Kelly customer were to object to any portion of the commercial, it would not run. This has not happened in a single instance.

The Kelly PC-Pro System program has produced a sig-

149

KELLY SERVICES
Continued

nificant increase in sales for temporary personal computer word processing skills. Customers appreciated having qualified temporary operators who could meet their assignment requirements with little of the customer's time wasted answering simple questions and solving problems.

One problem for Kelly Services, however, was the concern that their customers might begin thinking of Kelly as a "specialty" automated office service and turn to the competition with their orders for traditional office skills. Again, Kelly turned to an advertising campaign on network radio as well as in general business and trade publications. Again, Kelly interviewed satisfied Kelly customers who regularly requested clerks, typists, receptionists, and secretaries. Kelly's share of business in traditional office skills was retained and new customers were attracted. Kelly's reputation was maintained as the best service to call for *all* temporary help.

Even though radio copy should be *heard* rather than *read*, the honesty and believability of the dialogue shines through all the Kelly Services commercials. As you read through the accompanying Kelly radio copy, try to imagine their unhurried, low-key delivery.

150

Chuck Blore & Don Richman Incorporated

1606 North Argyle, Hollywood, California 90028 • (213) 462-0944

RADIO SCRIPT

Agency: CAMPBELL EWALD CO.

Client: KELLY SERVICES

Title: "Temporary Risk" - McKee - Rev.

Date: 3-24-87

Page 1 of 1

Length: 60" sec.

McKEE:	1	I have used another temporary service in the past and they just
	2	didn't meet up to my standards and now I only use Kelly.
DAVID:	3	And you have high standards?
McKEE:	4	Oh, yes. Definitely.
DAVID:	5	And Kelly meets those standards?
McKEE:	6	Very much so. With Kelly Services, I get my money's worth.
DAVID:	7	Why?
McKEE:	8	Because they match you with people that you need.
DAVID:	9	Really?
McKEE:	10	They always call me up, too, after an assignment, and ask me how
	11	the person worked out.
DAVID:	12	Typists? Receptionists? Secretaries?
McKEE:	13	Yes. We've not only had people work up in the front offices but
	14	we've had people doing clerical-type duties. And they always send
	15	a very good match to us.
DAVID:	16	Is that a way of eliminating temporary risk?
McKEE:	17	It does eliminate a lot of risk for me.
DAVID:	18	How?
McKEE:	19	Well, (LAUGH) if I don't get someone in here that's going to do
	20	the job then I'm wasting a lot of money.
DAVID:	21	So nobody tries as hard to make sure you get your job done as
	22	Kelly Services, the Kelly Girl People?
McKEE:	23	Nobody does try as hard as Kelly. (LAUGH)
DAVID:	24	The first and the best?
McKEE:	25	Definitely.
	26	

151

CASE HISTORY
RADIO ADVERTISING BUREAU

Courtesy of Radio Advertising Bureau.

Copywriting students who have been urged since day one to "think visually" often ask how they can do that on radio. They can learn a lesson from the experience of the Radio Advertising Bureau whose members face that question many times a day as they attempt to sell advertisers on using radio as a medium.

The single biggest objection to using radio advertising, according to a variety of RAB-sponsored research studies among clients and advertising agencies, is the perceived lack of visuals.

In 1987, the Radio Advertising Bureau adopted a new creative approach in its continuing effort to address the number-one objection to radio advertising: the absence of visuals. Using the tag line, "I Saw It on the Radio," the RAB campaign was designed to demonstrate radio's ability not only to create visual images, but to draw on images and impressions stored in the minds of consumers to sell goods and services. Commercials were created to bring forth visual imagery that would directly relate to those businesses that are a radio station's most likely prospects.

The 1987 radio commercials were written and produced by the American Comedy Network and were honored as the best radio campaign of 1987 in the International Broadcasting Awards Competition co-sponsored by the Hollywood Radio and TV Society. Of the ten spots produced, five make radio's sales points humorously and five are straight voices. Working with the basic visualization concept, these commercials discuss target marketing, radio's efficiency, radio's popularity, and radio's selling power and strengths in comparison to television and newspapers. But all ended with the musical jingle, "I Saw It on the Radio."

Results have been most encouraging. Radio revenues on the local level posted a 5.5 percent increase in 1987. Member radio stations responded favorably to the campaign (which also has secondary applications for client presentations and internal sales training).

Each of the humorous situations uses radio's great assets—sound effects, varying human voices, music—to bring the listener right into the scene. Who says there are no pictures in radio? When you write for radio you are creating pictures in the mind's eye.

THE POPULAR RESTAURANT   (:60)

ANNCR.:   [SFX: Restaurant ambience] We're here today with . . .

AP: Al Popular.

ANNCR.:   . . . of . . .

AP: The Popular Restaurant!

ANNCR.:   Now you haven't tried advertising on the radio yet because . . . ?

AP: People just can't see my delicious food on the radio.

ANNCR.:   Uh-huh. [Pause] Do you have any specials today?

AP: Sure! Let me tell you about 'em!

ANNCR.:   No, uh—just show me your TV commercials.

AP: Oh, I can't afford those . . .

ANNCR.:   Well, show me your newspaper ad?

AP: Nobody reads the papers much anymore . . .

ANNCR.:   Well gee—how do you sell your specials?

AP: I just describe 'em . . . [SFX: behind] like my succulent, juicy baby back ribs. I grill 'em slow over a mesquite flame, and then I slather 'em all over with my mouth-watering honey-mustard sauce. It's to die!

ANNCR.:   Mmmmm! Sounds great . . .

AP: Right! I just used the right words and your imagination did the rest.

ANNCR.:   No pictures, just words: sounds kinda like radio . . . don't you think?

AP: [Laughing] Oh, no . . . no . . . no . . . no—this kinda thing is completely . . .

ANNCR./AP: [Together] . . . the same!

ANNCR.:   Radio can work for you too. [Music up and under] Call this station or the Radio Advertising Bureau and say . . . [Jingle].

SYLVIA'S SOPHISTICATED SPORTSWEAR   (:60)

ANNCR.:   [SFX: Store interior ambience] I'm here today with . . .

Syl: Sylvia.

ANNCR.:   . . .of . . .

Syl: Sylvia's Sophisticated Sportswear.

ANNCR.:   . . .and you spend more of your advertising dollars on . . .?

Syl: TV, darling. On television my sophisticated clientele can see my sophisticated clothes.

ANNCR.:   Sounds. . .Sophisticated. But I've never seen your commercials.

Syl: Yeah. Don't you watch the "Mr. Ed" reruns at 3 AM?

ANNCR.:   Mr. Ed?

Syl: It's all I could afford, love. TV production costs and air time are real expensive.

ANNCR.:   I know, but advertising on TV doesn't necessarily mean you'll be seen by your sophisticated customers.

Syl: It doesn't?

ANNCR.:   No. In fact, with all the money you spent producing your TV commercial, you could be reaching your sophisticated customers more often on the radio.

Syl: Look shorty, I like the way the horse talks, aw-right?

ANNCR.:   [Chuckling, coming in over scene] No matter what you're selling, you can reach more people more often with affordable radio advertising. And your customers will have a better chance of seeing you . . .on the radio!

Syl: Come on short stuff, sing with me [Fading up, singing] "A horse is a horse, of course, of course—come on, sing along!—and no one can talk [etc., fading under].

ANNCR.:   Find out how radio can work for you. [Jingle theme up and under] Call this station or the Radio Advertising Bureau and say. . .[Jingle].

10

Writing Advertising for Television

Chapter Topics

Achieving one total impression
What TV does best
Expressing your TV idea
Suggested TV script form
Camera terms for script writer
Indicating distances
Transition methods
Various effects
Use of voice-over
Importance of writing it "short"
The storyboard and its uses
Importance of pre-production meeting
Basic forms of television production

Key Terms

Videotape
Audio
Video
Cut
Establishing shot
Zoomar lens
Super
Voice-over
Storyboard
Key visual
Animatics
Photomatics

Case Histories

French's Mustard
Mercury
Dannon Yogurt
Bud Light
Raid

Magazines offer the copywriter pictures, type, color. Radio offers the writer voices, sound, music. Television offers the copywriter all those advantages, plus one more: movement. Although television exceeds all other advertising media in impact, it also exceeds them in irritation. When critics decry the excesses of advertising, they almost invariably give examples from television.

To the uninitiated, television advertising may seem to be outrageously expensive. A single "participation" in the Super Bowl game can cost an advertiser half a million dollars. But television advertising can be tremendously effective, and for this reason it now receives the giant's share of the United States' total advertising budget for national advertising. Because television is so highly visible and so very intrusive, it may turn out to be the worst enemy advertising ever had. Meanwhile, however, the television medium is a copywriter's best friend. Writing copy for television can be demanding and nerve-wracking, but it is never dull; it is, after all, advertising and show business combined.

Historically, television did comparatively little evolving, bursting almost full-blown upon the scene right after World War II. Home receiving sets were quickly manufactured in abundance, and the geographical network was completed at remarkable speed.

In the earliest days of television, much of the program production and TV commercials were "live," that is, you saw them at the precise moment they happened. However, most commercials were filmed, as they still are today.

Television grew in form and structure patterned after radio and, some critics aver, making the same mistakes. This was true of the writing as well. Television copywriters did not exist, so the assignments went first to radio writers. Radio writers had certain basic difficulties with the new medium since they were used to thinking in terms of sound rather than pictures. Print writers *were* used to dealing with pictures, albeit still pictures, but were leery of the show-business aspects of television. However, there is no substitute for enthusiasm in any enterprise, and advertising people who were wild about television's possibilities ended up in charge.

The greatest contribution to the sanity and skill of everyone connected with television production was the early development of videotape. Its one central electronic switching control panel records picture, sound, and special effects all at the same time, then quickly plays it back for review. Consequently, there is now somewhat less of the guesswork, anxiety, and fingernail biting that goes with television production.

In much less than the span of one generation, television totally replaced radio as America's dominant entertainment medium. Today, radio and television play two quite different roles. In radio people listen to *stations;* in television, people watch *programs.* In radio, the audience is segmented by various interests; in television, entertainment generally leans to an all-family appeal. With television, people still get up from their chairs and change the dial or press the remote control button.

Most of today's advertising writers have been brought up with television. It is second nature to them, and first in importance as a medium. Many writers have become so adept at the technicalities of writing for television that they have evolved into writer-producers.

While Hanley Norins refers to radio in *The Compleat Copywriter* as "The Segmented Medium," he calls television the "Fast, Fast Medium."[1] There seems little doubt today that television is the advertising medium of greatest involvement and greatest impact. But, like radio, television is fleeting, and the ticking of the seconds is inexorable. At best, the audience receives a moving impression (which does not make television the ideal medium for recipes, dress patterns, or craft instructions). The copywriter must strive to register *one total impression*.

THE IMPORTANCE OF THE OVERRIDING IMPRESSION

Total impression is achieved by what might be called *simple unity of idea*. If you analyze the television commercials you enjoy personally, you will find that each revolves around one simple, memorable idea and does not stray from it. In fact, great television commercials rarely vary from the opening situation or setting.

Popular with certain advertisers today are frantically jolly family or group activities that are almost exhausting to watch. Some of these adventures take place in rather exotic settings and employ a cast of hundreds. Yet the one overriding impression—the sales message—is so simple it is almost ridiculous: this particular soft drink, for example, is a pleasant break and very much a part of the fun.

One recent oil company television spot opened with a businessman scrambling out of a cab and rushing into one of the towers of the International Trade Center in New York City. You see only his legs and feet as he hurries through the lobby. Instead of taking the elevator, he starts up the stairs. We see him climbing to the tenth floor, the twentieth floor, the thirtieth floor. His pace gets slower. He takes off his jacket and tie as he continues to climb. Higher. Higher. We almost lose track of the numbers. *Finally* he reaches the top, opens the door to the roof, and signals a waiting helicopter. The viewer's impression is up, up, up— how far does this poor fellow have to go? At the end, the advertiser makes the point that that's how far down into the earth oil rigs have to drill before they can even hope to strike oil. A simple, memorable, understandable way of impressing on you the idea of great depth by showing great height. A single overriding impression.

---

1. Hanley Norins, *The Compleat Copywriter* (New York: McGraw-Hill, 1966), pp. 149, 192.

Dr. Pepper reproduces, with elaborate settings, costumes and cast, the heartrending story of the "Hunchback of Notre Dame." We see poor Quasimodo, physically beaten, dying of thirst. Will nobody in the cruel crowd take pity on him? At last, the brave and pretty little gypsy girl offers him water. He pleads with her in his garbled speech for something even better than water. Dr. Pepper, of course. The crowd goes wild and joins in. Dr. Pepper is consumed in a score of novel ways, with surging musical background. The overriding impression? Dr. Pepper is probably a wild and crazy drink. Different. Worth a try.

Pepsi Cola is highly inventive in its manner of presentation. One of their television commercials has a spaceship hovering over two soft-drink vending machines. A beam of light comes down and draws up a can of Coke. A second beam comes down and draws up a can of Pepsi. After a slight delay, the magical beam comes down once more and draws up the entire Pepsi vending machine. The commercial has novelty and memorability. The overriding impression? Pepsi tastes better.

Miller Lite Beer has done a marvelous job of concocting amusing story situations with a big cast made up mostly of ex-jocks—the golf outing, the bowling tournament, the camping trip. Although there are lots of cleverly-written gags and lots of sparkling by-play, the basic message never changes. In fact, the exact words don't change. "Less filling! Tastes great! It's everything a beer should be—and less."

Bartles & Jaymes commercials feature two homespun hicks who are so square and honest that their product must have honest quality, too.

Bud Light shows and tells us in a hundred inventive and entertaining ways that we had better order that particular product by name. Not just light beer, but *Bud* Light. Regardless of the special technique involved, the overriding impression comes through loud and clear.

The television camera can capture and relay any impression you wish to convey. It can display any emotion from joy to shock to sorrow. But the one thing television does best of any medium is *demonstrate*. You can show the car moving, the golf ball rolling, the egg frying, the soap washing. Very few arguments are as persuasive as a good demonstration. This is not the only way to use television, of course, but it's a method that ranks at or near the top.

PREPARATION OF TELEVISION COPY

The element of creative genius aside, there are certain steps to be followed in preparing copy for television. The most important principle to remember is that television is a *picture* medium; it is not a word medium. *If you are not telling the story in pictures, you are in the wrong medium.* No matter how often you see somebody recite radio copy into a television camera, it is still not good practice. An audience member would have every right to insist, "Don't tell me, show me!"

THE TELEVISION CONCEPT

How do you express your television commercial idea? Eventually you're going to end up with a script in a form unlike any other you may have worked with, but first try the following exercise to organize your thoughts.

On a sheet of typewriter paper turned sideways roughly pencil in four widely spaced oblongs with a fair amount of space under each. Do not write a word on the paper. Think, think, think of your product and its benefits. You are now a dramatist thinking in terms of story, action, *picture*. Sketch a picture of your opening scene in the first oblong. The crudest kind of stick figure drawing is fine. What is the second important picture your viewer will see as your story unfolds? Sketch it in the next oblong. No words yet. Sketch the crucial action in oblong three. Go on to oblong four, drawing mere stick figures. On another sheet of paper draw four more oblongs. Perhaps you'll use six oblongs to complete your idea, perhaps eight. Use as many or as few oblongs as it takes to get your idea across. The important thing is that you are *forcing yourself to think in pictures*. Only after you have gone through this crude process will you begin to put down words. By then the words are probably already on the tip of your tongue. When you have all your crude hieroglyphics organized, you are ready to tackle a formal script.

Below are some of the new terms you may have to deal with (which will be explained as we go along):

Audio	Video
CU	MS
LS	ECU
Pan	Tilt
Zoom	Dolly
Boom	Truck
Cut	Dissolve
Wipe	Super
Freeze Frame	Voice Over

Begin organizing your script by dividing your page in half vertically. All the *video*, or picture instructions, go on the left side of the sheet; all the *audio*, or sound instructions, go on the right side. On the video side of the script you are describing pictures as you wish them to appear on the home TV screen. When you indicate a new instruction, it means that viewers will see something noteworthy happening on their television receivers—not just action per se, but significant action that propels your commercial story along. Your script describes *only significant action*. Television is primarily a close-up medium, and you move in tight for the crucial action. Watch a few commercials and count how many close-up shots you see.

TELEVISION SCRIPT FORM

To get a taste of this fascinating new medium, let's examine a sample of television writing.

Suggested Script Form—TV

Video	Audio
1. OPEN ON LS COLLEGE QUADRANGLE	MUSIC: THEME FROM "HALLS OF IVY." IN AND UNDER
2. CUT TO MLS MEN & WOMEN STUDENTS HURRYING TO CLASSES	
3. CUT TO MS STUDENTS ENTERING DOORWAY OF GEORGIAN-STYLE COLLEGE BUILDING	
4. CUT TO MS STUDENTS ENTERING DOOR OF SEMINAR CLASSROOM	SOUND: INDISTIN-GUISHABLE STUDENT CHATTER
5. CUT TO LS STUDENTS SEATING SELVES AROUND LARGE OVAL TABLE	
6. CUT TO MS OF YOUNG WOMAN FLANKED BY TWO YOUNG MEN	
7. CUT TO CU WOMAN. SHAKES HEAD, PUTS FINGERS TO LIPS	GIRL: Shush! Not now!

This is what we are asking for here, step by step:

1. We open on an *establishing* shot, which immediately identifies the setting as a university even to a person who has never set foot on a campus; we set the stage. (A playwright would begin by saying, "Curtain rises to reveal, etc.") To back up the identification in the picture element, recognizable college-type music is introduced as background music to the scenes that follow. The particular music

continues to play until instructions are given to take it out or change it in some way.

2. Having established in our LS (Long Shot) that this script is about a college, the picture changes rapidly as we move in a little closer to a MLS (Medium Long Shot), which reveals it as a coeducational institution.

3. The picture changes (in a flash) and we are now in even closer, to a Medium Shot. We can expect something dramatic to happen on the other side of that doorway.

4. Instantly we are on the other side of that doorway, as students come inside a classroom. The audio direction tells us that we are now close enough to hear the students talking without being able to distinguish what they are saying.

5. Instantly, we are further from the doorway, showing the entire room. We see that it is a special kind of classroom.

6. Now we concentrate on three particular students. Note that we specify that a young woman has a young man on each side of her.

7. Quickly we change to a CU (Close Up) of the woman. She shakes her head and puts her finger to her lips—both significant actions. She says, "Shush! Not now!" This is the first line of recognizable dialogue that the home viewer hears.

This is not really a script of anything, but it gives you a rough idea of how one is put together. When you write a television commercial script, you are simply trying to make your basic idea understandable to others in the most primitive way. Delicate nuances and shadings can come later. Give as few video directions as are necessary to get your idea across, and indicate only those scene changes crucial to the comprehension of your story line. Keep your instructions telegraphic, and use abbreviations as much as possible. In most cases, music can contribute to your commercial—even if it simply plays unobtrusively in the background, so make sure that music is on your checklist of elements to consider.

To be a good writer of television copy, you do not have to be skilled in, or even very conversant with, the demanding mechanics of film and videotape production. It is even possible that attempting to acquire and apply too deep a knowledge of film production might inhibit your creative juices at first. Let experts steer you through the production channels.

You are responsible for the *idea* that gets the ball rolling, the skeleton upon which everything else is built. Although there is no substitute for plain, old-fashioned English for making yourself understood and technical terms do not automatically make you a creative genius in television, it's nevertheless easier if you know a little of the language.

CAMERA TERMS FOR SCRIPT

The television camera is a formidable-looking but most versatile instrument, which you can control with a number of simple directions. While stationary, the camera can PAN, i.e., the camera head can move horizontally left or right from a fixed pivot—the way your old grammar school class pictures were taken. It can also TILT, i.e., the camera head can be pointed DOWN to look at the floor or UP to look at the ceiling. Through the use of a Zoomar lens, the camera can almost instantly ZOOM IN from a long shot to a close-up, or ZOOM OUT from a close-up to a long shot. The entire camera base is also movable because it is mounted on dolly wheels. So you can DOLLY IN or DOLLY BACK (DOLLY OUT). A DOLLY movement will be slower than a ZOOM movement. The camera can also BOOM UP or BOOM DOWN when mounted on an electrically operated or manually operated crane. (This gives the effect of a low-level aerial view, as when you pull back from a close shot of a couple dining, and move up and away to show an entire banquet hall with many guests.) When your camera moves parallel to and along with a moving object or actor, this is called a TRUCK-ING shot. (TRUCK shots are widely used in automotive commercials, to ride along the highway with a bright new-model car.)

Distances

Distances must be indicated, but since there are no precise rules of terminology you will have to depend upon your own judgment to a very great extent. The distances are not measurable, mathematical distances, but relative distances as you see them in your imagination. Abbreviate instructions about distances as follows: ELS (Extreme Long Shot); LS (Long Shot); MLS (Medium Long Shot); MS (Medium Shot); MCU (Medium Close-Up); CU (Close-Up); and ECU (Extreme Close-UP) or TCU (Tight Close-Up). For example, an MS might show a stand-up announcer from the waist up, an MCU might give the view from the shoulders up, while an ECU might focus first on the eyes. You will have to live with such imprecision, because the distances are dependent on what you are photographing. (In the sample script, for example, the LS of a college quadrangle and the LS of a classroom involved very different distances, yet each LS request was legitimate.)

Basic Transitions

Shot transitions, the movement from one picture to another, are accomplished in two ways: CUT and DISSOLVE. When you specify CUT, you are asking for an instantaneous change of picture. (The cinema CUT changes a picture faster than the human eye would, but it is a storytelling practice we have long accepted in motion pictures.) When you specify DISSOLVE, you are asking for the fading out of one picture with replacement by a new picture. The DISSOLVE is often used to indicate some passage of time. The CUT is the most frequently used transition, particularly where there is continuous story action in one locale. For instance, a protracted quarrel might use frequent cuts back and forth showing close-ups of the two combatants, interspersed with medium shots and longer shots of the room in which the battle raged. A good rule of thumb, when hurriedly roughing out an idea, is stick to CUT; refinements can always be made later.

Other Transition Methods

The MATCH CUT (cutting from one particular object to a similarly-shaped object in a different location) is sometimes employed to bridge a time-location gap. For example, cutting from a Medium Close-Up of the speedometer of a speeding car to a Medium Close-Up of a roulette wheel—is a graphic storytelling device. A MATCH DISSOLVE offers the same effect, more beautifully, more dramatically, but also more slowly. Commercial flashbacks often involve the use of a RIPPLE (or SHIMMER) DISSOLVE. For example, as the Supreme Court Justice recalls his college days, the screen goes watery (it ripples); when it clears, we see him as a bell-bottomed collegian of the Roaring Twenties. The RIPPLE DISSOLVE is frequently used in "before and after," "cause and effect," or "problem and solution" demonstrations. And it is almost invariably used to introduce a dream sequence. The SWISH PAN or ZIP PAN, a technique that would have been frowned on just a few years back because it is fast and indistinct, does an arresting job of bridging time and distance. For example, A baseball pitcher winds up and releases the ball; suddenly the camera pans so fast that it completely streaks or blurs the image; the camera comes to rest focused on a surprised batter missing his swing.

Effects

The most common effect is a transition that goes by an inelegant but descriptive term. The WIPE does just what its name implies: the picture is wiped off the screen as though with a sponge, revealing a different picture. The WIPE, which is a fast way of introducing a new thought in your commercial, comes in several self-descriptive varieties: the clock wipe, the barndoor wipe, the flip wipe, and the venetian-blind wipe, to name a few. The WIPE is achieved electronically in videotape production with variation possibilities that are almost staggering.

For years, the term SUPER (meaning the superimposition of an object, a name, a slogan, a benefit, over another picture) was common usage in television commercial writing. Recent technology has developed a videotape process called KEYING that allows the *inset* of another image rather than just an overlap. In film, this is called MATTING. Regardless of the particular technical process used, the effect is to give visual emphasis and reinforcement. It is not uncommon to SUPER (or KEY or MATTE) all important selling points in a consumer packaged-goods commercial to reinforce the spoken word with the printed word. However, an overabundance of supered messages can impair the visual quality and make your commercial downright irritating. Caution: When you use a SUPER be sure the words in the SUPER are exactly the same as the words spoken by the announcer or actor.

Other Visual Devices

Most film writers and television writers are familiar with the PROCESS SHOT (or PROCESS SCREEN), which involves placing your actors or product in front of a blank movie screen on which a "location" image is thrown by a projector in back of the screen. This money-saving technique is also referred to as REAR SCREEN PROJECTION or as a TRANSPARENCY SHOT. Example: We see the honeymoon couple riding in the rear seat of a French taxicab. Over their shoulders, through the rear window, we see traffic passing by on the Champs Élysées. Actually, the honeymooners may be seated on a bench in a studio mock-up of a cab. On a screen behind them is projected a movie of busy Paris traffic.

A fashionable new device in picture-making is the FREEZE FRAME, in which picture motion is suddenly stopped in order to emphasize or study a particular detail. In recent years, SLOW MOTION photography has had a great vogue, again with the object of emphasizing or dramatically lengthening one crucial action. Rarely used in television commercials is another interesting effect known as the SUBJECTIVE CAMERA. All action is photographed solely from the audience point of view; the spectator, in effect, becomes actor. It is as though the television viewer drives the car, opens the door, and climbs the stairs.

Audio

Television offers you the same audio effects you find in radio—voice, music, sound effects—and the terminology is the same: (IN and OUT) for beginning and ending, (UP and DOWN) for volumn control, and (UNDER) for background use.

Off-camera narration comprises the bulk of filmed commercials. It is referred to as VOICE-OVER, and is indicated in the script by the abbreviation VO, as in ANNCR (VO), followed by a colon. If you want a particular type of voice, indicate in your script: STERN DAD (VO): or SHY COP (VO):. The more specific you can be, the more help you provide to your director.

Remember to use MUSIC when it will aid your selling story; more often than not, it can contribute.

Although you will learn scores of other television terms as you progress in the business, the few given here will help get you started in a reasonably professional manner. If you never use any additional terms, you need not feel embarrassed; correctness of terminology is not nearly as important as making your idea understood to a producer.

Timing

The timing of television scripts is a problem. The stopwatch seems preferable to word count for a picture medium. But the only person who can time the rough script intelligently is the writer, because only the writer has an image of what the viewer will ultimately see. Only the writer knows which scenes or which copy lines gallop, and which are lingered over. The script of one thirty-second spot may be completely typed on less than a single sheet of paper; the script of another thirty-second spot may run to a page and a half. It all depends on the idea.

Guesswork? To a degree. But timing becomes highly educated guess-work after a few go-arounds. Even in the matter of the length and number of scenes, advice givers cannot be very specific. In the early days of television, some said a scene had to be on for a minimum of three seconds in order for the viewer to comprehend it. But the recent use of quick cuts certainly appears to have voided that rule. One research company suggests that a picture of less than seven seconds' duration is poor, that a picture of thirteen seconds' duration is good. Yet another research organization suggests that too many scenes, too many voices, cut down on remembrance.

Ignore these details at first and concentrate instead on getting a great *idea*. When you think you have it, we suggest a double dose of advice we gave for radio: *write it short*. If your boss needs a thirty-second commercial, write a twenty-five-second commercial script. You can't go far wrong, and may even be hailed as a genius, because your basic idea, your rough script, is essential, but it is only a beginning, only the bare bones of an outstanding television commercial. Your basic idea takes on life, form, substance, and shading in the process of production. Those precious extra seconds give the production professionals breathing space in which to flesh out the bare bones you have provided.

IMPORTANCE OF OUTSIDE TALENT

Above everything else, the writer of television commercials must be aware of and appreciate the importance of outside talent. Even after the most accomplished copywriter finishes typing a script, a great deal of the creativity has yet to appear on the scene. This additional measure of creativity is contributed by the producer, the director, the actors, announcers and performers, the lighting crew, the stage crew, the lab people, the film editor. These people are artists with a highly trained instinct for creativity. All these professionals will add their own special spark that can propel your basic idea to greater heights of charm, inventiveness, and effectiveness. Respect their contributions and make them feel like co-creators, not just hired hands. Properly used, outside talent can make you look like a star. Improperly handled, outside talent can make you look like a bum. There's no end of wonderful insights to be learned from show business professionals. If you have ever watched an Academy Awards telecast, you've seen that the glamour figures of Hollywood are well aware of the creative contributions to their craft by people unknown to the general public.

Several years ago, the Screen Editors Guild prepared a remarkable demonstration of their craft. Three of Hollywood's top editors were given every scrap of the footage shot for one episode of the long-running television program "Gunsmoke." As you may know, moviemakers shoot far more footage than will finally be shown on the air. Working with the identical footage—the identical settings, action, and dialogue—each of the three famous editors produced a regular-length "Gunsmoke" episode markedly different from the others in pacing, emphasis, atmosphere, and "feeling." Each version bore that particular film editor's distinctive stamp of creativity.

It's a long trail that leads from your script to the film editor's touches, but nothing starts without your idea.

If at this point you want to experiment with television script writing just to get the hang of it, take the famous old American poem "Casey at the Bat" and see if you can tell that story in television script form. Decide on your establishing shot. Maybe it's an aerial view of the country village of Mudville, or perhaps you zoom in to see all the villagers trooping expectantly to the baseball diamond on the edge of town.

Once the copywriter's thoughts are on paper, the writer teams up with a TV art director who is not only a good advertising person, but who is thoroughly grounded in theatrical production. The art director knows set design, costume design, stage movements, camera movement, lighting. The TV art director offers suggestions or revisions, and together art director and copywriter work out a rough storyboard that is sent to the TV art department for finished rendering.

The Storyboard

A *storyboard* is a series of artist's sketches that highlight the significant actions in your idea—not unlike a comic strip. It is a generally-used method for presenting motion picture commercial ideas. Under each sketch is a panel of typed copy that gives video or picture instructions, then audio or sound instructions. There is no standard size for these sketches. The copywriter usually makes the presentation to management, describing the sequence of picture action first, then going back and delivering the audio portion.

Storyboards are only reasonable facsimiles of the real thing, but they are helpful in performing two essential steps: (1) presentations to management (the boss who likes the idea will budget money for its production) and (2) getting job bids from several selected production companies. Storyboards can create special problems, however. A roughly sketched storyboard runs the risk of being vague and indistinct, of not quite getting the idea across. A finely sketched storyboard runs the risk of being taken too literally, of locking-in the production people.

When preparing a sample book, many copywriters will not include bulky storyboards but will show a script accompanied by a rough sketch of the commercial's key visual, the most memorable and recognizable feature of the commercial—the white hot sword of the Marine officer, for example, or the Kemper cavalry riding to the rescue.

Another recent expansion of storyboard use is in pretesting commercial ideas with the public. The problem is to show an approximation of the finished commercial while avoiding the tremendous expense of finished production. This is done by taking the storyboard sketches (or some specially made still photographs) and filming or videotaping them. Movement is achieved by tricks of the camera—zooming in and out, panning, wipes, dissolves, etc. The resulting commercials, for test use only, are called *animatics*.

You might prepare your own amateur storyboard by taking a series of photographs covering the story action of your idea. Mount them in proper sequence with the typed instructions under each picture. When agencies prepare storyboards in a similar manner they are called *photomatics*.

Production: The Vital Step

Once the job has been awarded to a certain production company, a date is set for a preproduction meeting. Most veterans consider the preproduction meeting the most vital step in smooth production. Here the writer, the art director, the producer, the director, the set designer, the costume designer, and the talent director ask and answer a thousand questions before being committed to expensive studio time. Perhaps the writer has indicated in the script some key action involving a "young girl." The producer wants to know how young a girl the writer had in mind. Eight years old, ten years old, twelve years old? Blonde, brunette, redhead? Quiet or vivacious? How should she be dressed? Decisions are made, guidelines are set down. After a carefully arranged preproduction meeting, every key person involved will enter the studio with assurance. Questions and problems will still arise during the shooting, but the preproduction meeting may already have saved thousands of dollars in studio time and talent costs.

THE BASIC FORMS OF PRODUCTION

From the day your original script is okayed by management until the finished commercial goes on the air, some eight to ten weeks (or more) may elapse if your commercial is being produced on film. Videotape production is likely to take less time and live production is fastest of all.

Live, film, and videotape are the three kinds of television commercial production with which you should have some familiarity. Each has certain advantages, each has certain disadvantages, and each has its own set of considerations for a copywriter.

Live Production

Live production, which involves action as it actually takes place, has become extremely rare. Live production is a one-time-only happening, not recorded for posterity, and not available for playback. A modest amount of local advertising may be live, usually consisting of a stand-up announcer delivering a straight spiel. As the production crew has only one chance, the mechanics are kept extremely simple—one set, simple props, limited action. Because of the emphasis on simplicity, live production is the least expensive production. For the same reason, it is also the quickest. The picture quality is excellent because it is pure electronic television, with no intervening variables. Live production offers the writer the opportunity to make last-minute copy changes right up until the cameras start to roll. In live commercials mistakes do happen: the announcer blows a line, a stagehand misses a cue, or a product or a prop fails to operate properly during a demonstration. Oddly enough, the audience is very sympathetic to these human failures. The occasional fluff evidently has an element of humanity, of warmth, of folksiness lacking in more polished productions.

Film Production

Since television's infancy, the bulk of all commercial production has been on film. These are "movies," just as at your local movie theater. A picture image is recorded on a strip of celluloid; when you hold a reel of developed film up to the light you see a small picture of what will be projected on the screen in giant size. Motion picture footage is shot and produced all over the world, but the overwhelming share of U.S. television film production is done in Hollywood and New York.

Film is the most expensive kind of television production, principally because of the time involved. Film shot on one day has to be sent out to a lab to be developed; rarely can it be viewed until the following day. Often the picture is shot in one location while the sound and music are recorded at another location, to be "mixed" at yet another location at a still later time. Effects like dissolves, wipes, and montages are done at a film laboratory after all the shooting is completed. The master step of editing—selecting and blending precisely what footage will go into the finished product—comes later in the game. All these technical stages call for separate timetables, separate facilities, and separate experts. And then, when the semi-finished product is shown to management for an okay, these worthies may have to journey to a rented projection room with special interlock equipment to play the picture track and the sound track in synchronization. No question about it, under the best of conditions and in the most skilled hands, film production is a highly involved process.

But film is unequaled for big productions—for spectacles, for unique locations, for vast expanses (showing a fleet of cars racing across the Great Salt Flats, for example). Film is limitless. You can have live action (regular movies), animation (Disney-type cartoons), or a combination of animation and live action (as in most Jolly Green Giant commercials). Film production assures perfect lighting effects (so important, for example, with a jewelry store product). Film production means complete control of lab and editing effects. (You name it, they'll give it to you.) Film production allows great freedom in making talent arrangements; shooting schedules can be tailored to accommodate certain actors, directors, camera operators. (If a great star says, "I can spare forty minutes between planes in Cleveland," you can have a film crew ready at the airport.)

Economy-minded producers know that good film footage can be adapted for several different commercials. A big advantage of film production is the reuse that can be made of the completed product. Film is easily and fairly inexpensively duplicated. It is handily packaged. Commercial film can be shown time and time again—at sales meetings, at trade shows, at dealer presentations, in classrooms, for special audiences anywhere. All that is required is a sixteen millimeter sound-on-film projector (practically standard equipment in most schools, clubs, offices). If there is no silver screen, a blank wall will do.

Videotape Production

Videotape may be the copywriter's best friend for a number of reasons. To put it unscientifically, it is a fantastic miracle. Instead of a little picture you can see clearly, there is an electronic impulse pattern recorded on magnetic tape that has a shiny finish on one side and a dull finish on the other. The electronic impulse pattern is recorded on the dull-finished side. You cannot see it with the naked eye, and even if you could see with the aid of some kind of technical booster, you would not be looking at a recognizable picture.

There is no such thing as inexpensive television production, but videotape production is only moderately expensive compared to film. This is true, to a great extent, because videotape production can be done all in one operation: picture and sound are recorded simultaneously; film inserts can be transferred easily to videotape; editing is electronic and instant, done with the flick of a lever on the control panel. It is possible to walk out of the videotape studio the same day you went in (or even just a couple of hours after you went in), with the commercial completed exactly as it will appear over the air.

With the rapid advances in portable cameras and equipment, videotape can now offer almost as extensive a scope as film. Even in animation, where film has long held a decided edge, the videotape industry makes new strides daily in electronic animation.

Far and away the greatest asset videotape offers is *immediate playback*. You see at once whether a scene has been played as you wanted it. If you like it, you keep it. If you don't like it, you can have the crew redo it then and there. If the weakness in the scene arises from your concept, you can make on-the-spot alterations. If a representative of management is in the studio during the shooting, an okay or approval also can be immediate. A completed commercial on a videotape cassette is reasonably compact to carry and handle, and videotape cassettes are certainly now in common usage.

For television production in general, it helps the writer to have as firm an estimate as possible of money available. It is a fact of advertising life that the money allocated will often determine the scope of the creative approach.

Television production of any kind—live, film, or videotape—is truly fascinating, and your knowledge of it will expand as you pursue your career. But you need not be an expert; the technicians will be there to guide you.

The most important lesson is that production is secondary to concept. Your *idea* comes first. Realizing that television is basically a picture medium, review mentally the checklist suggested to you for the different ways of using illustration. Just as in print advertising, the picture idea must be relevant to the basic selling idea. It must help attract the right audience; it must be pertinent to the self-interest of the viewer; it must tie in a product benefit. If your television script idea embraces those points, you will have done the crucial part of your job. The production professionals will see you through the rest.

Three Kinds of Television Production

Live	Film	Videotape
(Action as it takes place)	(Picture image recorded on celluloid; same as "movies")	(Electronic impulse pattern recorded on magnetic tape)
Least expensive	Most expensive	Moderately expensive
Quick production	Long, involved production	Fast production
Simple production	Big production (outdoor spectacles; locations)	Extensive production (almost as good as film)
Excellent picture quality	Good picture quality for TV	Excellent picture quality
Restricted movement	Limitless (live action or animation or both)	Simple animation
Immediate result	Sound often recorded separately; "mixed" with picture later	Immediate electronic editing
Mistakes are a hazard—but audience sympathetic to "fluffs"	Complete control of lab and editing effects	Picture and sound recorded simultaneously
Only one result	Don't see results right away	Immediate playback (mistakes caught at once)
Client approves in advance	Client okay delayed	Fast client approval
Last minute copy changes	Changes delayed and costly	On-the-spot changes (updated copy)
No film involved	Good footage adapts to several commercials	Can use film inserts
One shot only	Ideal for talent arrangements	Easier on nerves
Upon Completion	**Upon Completion**	**Upon Completion**
Gone forever!	Easily duplicated for sales meetings, trade shows, special audiences	Videotape cassettes have become commonplace

CASE HISTORY
FRENCH'S MUSTARD

Courtesy of R. T. French Company and J. Walter Thompson.

The most magical dimension television brings to advertising is *movement*. The ultimate movement occurred in 1985 when French's Mustard unexpectedly brought sandwiches to life. Also brought to life was a somewhat eroding sales curve for French's Yellow Mustard.

The mustard business is made up of several categories, of which the largest by far is yellow. French's had historically been the leader of this yellow mustard segment with approximately a 47 percent share of market. But in the late 1970s and early 1980s French's experienced long-term share erosion from controlled and generic brands. With French's mustard at least 30 percent more expensive than the controlled and generic brands, customers were trading off the brand quality of French's in favor of price savings.

As a consequence, French's first advertising campaign in two or three years had two objectives. It had to accelerate the sales and market share of French's yellow 16 oz. squeeze package. It had to stabilize and/or reverse the declining share trend by regaining share from the non-branded products and by communicating that French's was the best yellow mustard.

With a modest national budget of $2 million, the job called for a television commercial that was attention-getting and entertaining. French's got just that in a highly inventive, highly intrusive thirty-second commercial entitled "Be Good to Your Food." In it, various sandwiches and assorted food items come to life and cringe in terror at the thought of being inundated with a cheap, low-quality mustard.

The terror-stricken sandwiches found a sympathetic and responsive public. The French's squeeze package featured in the commercial showed a significant share gain over the previous year. French's yellow mustard category showed a modest share increase while non-branded products showed an equivalent amount of share erosion.

In advertising tests, the cringing sandwiches did remarkably well. The *entertainment* value and *impression of advertiser* ratings were the highest attained in the history of Burke Clucas Testing Techniques. The *entertainment* value measures the consumer's desire to watch the commercial many times to almost indefinitely. The norm is 23 percent; French's obtained 68 percent. The *impression of the advertiser* measures degrees of favorability. French's obtained a very to extremely favorable rating of 79 percent versus the norm of 38 percent.

Chalk up another triumph for the unexpected.

CASE
HISTORY
MERCURY

Courtesy of Lincoln-Mercury Division of Ford Motor Company and its agency, Young & Rubicam.

Music not only hath charms to soothe the savage breast, music also hath charms to woo a certain segment of the buying public and to help change the image of a car. That's what Lincoln-Mercury and its agency, Young & Rubicam, discovered in 1984.

They believed then that a real opportunity existed in the marketplace to attract younger, more affluent, and better educated buyers with greater volume potential and the ability to buy more expensive cars. Persuading these people to buy a Mercury at a younger age could establish them as loyal Lincoln-Mercury buyers for a longer period of time.

Mercury was introducing new, more contemporary aerodynamic styling in two models, the kind of cars that would attract these desired new buyers. The chief problem was Mercury's then-existing image as either "non-existent" or just a "jazzed up" version of a Ford. Further research revealed that consumers first considered a car purchase on an emotional level before they studied the practical side, and the Mercury advertising at that time wasn't generating emotional feelings.

The new approach that was needed in order to improve Mercury's image had its basis in music from the 1960s. The agency felt that the use of '60s music and a relevant copy platform would create the necessary emotional appeal among the target market of Baby Boomers. These people had grown up listening to rock and roll, and the use of this music told them instantly that these commercials (and, of course, the new Mercury automobiles) were meant for them. The voice-over copy focused on shape, which referred to the individual's shape as well as to that of Mercury cars—a good idea in a fitness-oriented society.

The campaign debuted using songs like "Born to Be Wild" for Cougar, "Wouldn't It Be Nice" for Topaz, and "Ain't No Mountain High Enough" for the full line of cars. The ads were an immediate success and the use of rock music continued for two more years with such songs as "Help," "Heatwave," "Reach Out," and many others. During the next two years the median age of Mercury buyers dropped by four years, median income rose by more than 13 percent, and the percentage of college graduates buying Mercurys increased. The idea of using rock music proved so popular that many other advertisers followed suit. Products like beer, soap, even dog food were advertised in similar fashion. In 1987, still believing in the charms of music, Mercury turned to synthesized New Age music in order to once again stand out from the crowd.

YOUNG & RUBICAM INTERNATIONAL, INC.

CLIENT: LINCOLN-MERCURY DIV. OF FORD MOTOR CO.
PRODUCT: COUGAR
TITLE: "BORN TO BE WILD"

LENGTH: 60 SECONDS (DIV.)
COMM. NO: FMCO 4429
DATE: 10/1/84

1. (SFX: CLOCK)

2. (MUSIC UP)

3. (MUSIC)

4. (MUSIC AND LYRIC)

5. (MUSIC AND LYRIC)

6. (MUSIC AND LYRIC)

7. (MUSIC AND LYRIC)

8. (MUSIC AND LYRIC)

9. (MUSIC AND LYRIC)

10. (MUSIC AND LYRIC)

11. (MUSIC AND LYRIC)

12. (MUSIC AND LYRIC)

13. (MUSIC UNDER)
ANNCR: (VO) You've come too far for a car that's shaped just for show.

14. We shaped the Mercury Cougar to use the wind...

15. to help the car hug the highway.

16. It's a shape you'll feel good in for years to come,

17. like that old leather jacket. (MUSIC AND LYRIC)

18. Cougar...

19. (MUSIC)

20. From Mercury.

175

CASE HISTORY
DANNON YOGURT

Courtesy of The Dannon Company, Inc., and its agency, HCM.

When you have a good reputation, build on it. That was the recent selling strategy of Dannon Yogurt.

For some forty years Dannon built and led the yogurt category. Then in the early 1980s Dannon came under pressure from new competitive brands that were backed by major packaged goods companies.

On the surface, research results seemed to indicate that "health" was a benefit generic to the yogurt category and that "taste" was the primary basis for differentiating brands, which is why Dannon's competition was focusing so heavily on "taste" in their advertising.

However, by listening extensively to consumers during the qualitative research conducted, Dannon realized that the real underlying motivation for eating yogurt was the *overall sense of well-being* customers feel when they do something good for themselves.

Although Dannon had no superiority over the competition on a physical attribute level, the brand did have a forty-year heritage in the field, and was recognized by consumers as the brand most closely associated with basic yogurt benefits. The creative opportunity was there to co-opt the category benefit of "well-being" using the Dannon forty-year heritage as support.

This strategy was followed in a series of human-interest television commercials. The settings, situations, and people were natural: a young woman getting into a car after running; surrounded by the uproar of city life, a young businessman sitting in a park at lunchtime; a typical family about to dive into a traditional heavy American breakfast when they realize one member is missing. Each thirty-second commercial used low-key copy to make its point and ended with the positive tag line: "Dannon *is* yogurt."

The yogurt-eating public responded. After only six months of this advertising, Dannon had regained its original share of market position and was maintaining leadership in the category.

DANNON IS YOGURT

AVO: It's been 42 years since. . .

Dannon introduced its yogurt to America.

And since that time, more than one hundred twenty-five brands have followed.

But to anyone who knows how good. . .

a natural tasting yogurt can make you feel

There is still only one

DANNON

IS

YOGURT

CASE HISTORY
BUD LIGHT

Courtesy of Anheuser-Busch, Inc., and its agency, DDB Needham Worldwide.

What's in a name? Plenty, if you're in the highly competitive beer business. Take the generic term "light." Walk into a bar, call out that word, and get ready to have the most incredible things happen to you. Especially if you've been watching Bud Light commercials.

Miller introduced the light beer category in 1974. There had been a few low-calorie beers before then, but nothing of import. Backed by heavy advertising and promotional spending, Miller Lite grew rapidly to where, by 1982, it held a 58 percent share of the light beer market.

In that same year, Budweiser Light was successfully introduced, with the advertising theme "Bring Out Your Best." However, in 1983 Budweiser Light sales began to soften. Consumers were asking for a light beer simply by using the generic term "light." But Miller had ingrained the term "Lite" into people's minds, which particularly hurt Budweiser Light at bars and restaurants where it is critical to have success early in a beer brand's life cycle. If people have a favorable experience with a beer at a tavern or restaurant, they will make package purchases at a store. Hence, the challenge to Budweiser was how to educate the consumer to ask for a *specific* brand of light beer.

In March 1984, the Budweiser Light brand was relaunched with a shorter, more memorable name—Bud Light—and a totally new advertising campaign was developed to register the Bud Light name in a dramatic way. The "Gimme a Light" campaign was designed to get people to ask for Bud Light by name. The first series of messages were ten-second spots saying simply, "Don't Just Ask for a Light, Ask for a Bud Light." The tag line was: "Everything Else Is Just a Light." In each case, the poor soul who ordered "Gimme a Light" was bedeviled with lights in the most bizarre form, from railroad crossing lights to laser beams. When the customer made it clear that the brand wanted was "*Bud* Light," harmony was restored to the scene.

Almost immediately consumer research showed dramatic increases in advertising awareness and encouraging sales trends.

The "Gimme a Light" bar call campaign evolved from single-situation ten-second spots to thirty-second spots featuring three ten-second vignettes. As time went on, the campaign was freshened with single-situation thirty-second spots, each being even more innovative and unexpected than the previous messages.

Regardless of how wild any given situation might be, the

BUD LIGHT
Continued

basic message remained the same—register the name, the name, the name. It is difficult to remember any other advertising campaign that has registered a name with such flair, with such good humor, and with such success.

BUD LIGHT®

"DOGS/DMCC" :30

(MUSIC UNDER) ANNCR (VO): If you just ask for a light beer,... MAN 1: Gimme a light.

ANNCR (VO): ...you never know what you'll get.

(SFX: DRUM ROLL, DOGS BARKING)

MAN 1: Dogs. No, actually, Bud Light.

(MUSIC)

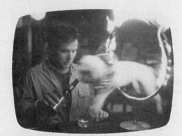
(SFX: DOGS BARKING)

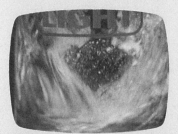
ANNCR (VO): So, if you want the less-filling light beer

with the first name in taste, ask for Bud Light.

MAN 2: Yours? MAN 1: No. ANNCR (VO): 'Cause everything else...

MAN 2: Gimme a light.

(SFX: DRUM ROLL, DOGS BARKING) MAN 1: Show time.

ANNCR (VO): ...is just a light.

ANHEUSER-BUSCH INC., ST. LOUIS, MO.
AUBL-3587
NEEDHAM HARPER WORLDWIDE, INC.

CASE HISTORY
RAID

Courtesy of S. C. Johnson & Son, Inc., and its agency, Foote, Cone & Belding.

You may recall that in the text's discussion of ways of using illustrations it is pointed out that cartoons are not only attention-getting in themselves, they are a sugar-coated way of getting across an *idea,* particularly when you don't want to be too literal.

That's exactly the principle behind what is perhaps the longest-running, unchanged campaign on television today. Celebrating more than thirty years on the television tube, the cartoon Raid bugs have been doing a bang-up selling job for S. C. Johnson. These animated insects have spent years being zapped, smashed, and blown to bits by Raid, and still new bugs are created to star in this gripping series.

The agency creative director says, "All commercials should be entertaining. No exceptions. Our task is to make it FUN to watch these ugly critters go to their eternal reward." It would *not* be fun to see this happen literally. Animation is what makes the difference. As the animation director explains, "Animation allows you to draw to extremes. When you take a frightened expression and exaggerate the eyes and the mouth, they become humorous." Another creative director on the account adds, "Animation lets you see things that you couldn't see with live action, for example, a penetrating mist. With live action, an insect repellent spray would be just a wet spritz. With animation, it becomes sticks of dynamite and lions and alligators and whatever else we want it to turn into to symbolize its power and strength."

In one of the most popular of the fairly recent spots, the creative team turned its imagination loose on the word *afraid.* A tough, arrogant bug rearranges some of the letters, but when he forms the word *Raid,* his fate is sealed.

The Raid creative people have even reinvented Latin and put it in commercials. You may recall seeing how Raid, described as Insectus Deadicus, caused the demise of Roachus Disgustus and Fleabitus Germspreadum.

Over the years, the Raid commercials have proved inventive and amusing. The unvarying theme line is brutally simple and direct: "Raid kills bugs dead." That is what customers remember.

FCB

DATE: April, 1983
PRODUCER: Coast Productions

CLIENT: S. C. Johnson & Son, Inc. (CP82-1319)
PRODUCT: Raid Line
FILM NO.: JSRD3130
FILM TITLE: "Bug Slides"

FILM LENGTH: :30

1. (MUSIC UNDER)
INSTRUCTOR (VO): Roachus Disgustus.

2. Waspi Dangerosa.

3. Flyus Germspreadum.

4. Fleahopita Biteus...

5. ANNCR (VO): You could spend years learning about bugs,...

6. INSTRUCTOR (VO): Plantium Devourum.

7. ANNCR (VO): ...but all you really need to know...
INSTRUCTOR (VO): Antlovem Picnicia.

8. ANNCR (VO): ...is Raid.
INSTRUCTOR (VO): Insectus Deadicus.

9. BUGS: Insectus Deadicus?!?

10. Raaaiiiddd!!!

11. (SFX: KA-BLOOEY)...

12. ...

13. ANNCR (VO): Raid kills bugs...

14. (SFX: POW!)

15. ...dead.

11

The Direct Approach

Chapter Topics

Direct marketing
Famous examples
Reasons for recent boom
Thoroughly tested copy
Direct marketing via direct
    mail
Advantages of direct mail
Typical direct mail
    package
Copywriter as salesperson
Direct marketing catalogs
Other direct marketing
    media
Constant testing
Long copy versus short
    copy
Ways to increase selling
    power
Other uses of direct mail

Key Terms

Selectivity
Feedback
Pinpoint targeting
Scientific advertising
Response devices
The direct marketing
    "must"
Full-line catalog
Bangtail envelope

Case Histories

Black, Gillock & Langberg
Urge Magazine

Now that you understand the mechanics of preparing a print ad, a radio spot, and a television commercial, we are going to explore certain types of advertising that have their own special characteristics. The first of these is direct marketing, a process that sells goods directly from producer to customer without benefit of retailer or middleman. Direct marketing has long been with us in the United States but has had a tremendous boom in recent years.

Famous Examples.   The history of U.S. advertising and selling is studded with outstanding direct marketing advertisements upon which great copywriting reputations were built. Bruce Barton wrote inspired Horatio Alger-type copy for such self-improvement enterprises as the Alexander Hamilton Extension Institute ("A Wonderful Two Years Trip at Full Pay") and Dr. Elliott's Five-Foot Shelf ("This is Marie Antoinette Riding to Her Death"). The legendary John Caples, who is virtually the patron saint of direct marketing copywriting, authored two memorable direct marketing advertisements in his first year on the job back in 1925 ("They Laughed When I Sat Down at the Piano" and "They Grinned When the Waiter Spoke to Me in French"). Both were for home study courses, as were three other famous appeals by other copywriters: "Do You Have a Grasshopper Mind?" and "Again She Ordered Chicken Salad" and, for a memory course, "Of Course I Remember You. You're Mr. Addison Sims of Seattle." Of slightly more recent vintage is the spectacularly successful Dale Carnegie book title and ad headline "How to Win Friends and Influence People."

As U.S. transportation, distribution, and retailing systems expanded and changed, direct marketing lost the preeminence it held on the advertising and selling scene in the days before supermarkets. While it never approached eclipse, direct marketing dwindled in the 1950s and 1960s to a rather modest percentage of the nation's total advertising budget. However, in very recent years, direct marketing has experienced a remarkable expansion—an explosion, some say. There are a number of reasons behind this spectacular resurgence.

Reasons for Direct Marketing Boom.   Computers have revolutionized direct marketing in two ways. First, the lifeblood of direct marketing is the ability to reach highly specific prospects, and computers enable direct marketers to build, to scan, and to edit prospect lists with a speed and accuracy never known before. They give a superb measure of control over the entire direct marketing process. Second, computerized letters—through such technological processes as laser beam printing—enable advertising messages to be highly personalized, not just in the salutation but at several places throughout the message. These letters can be produced at incredible speed and in great quantities. An outstanding example is the Publisher's Clearing House sweepstakes letter.

In addition to computers, the now almost universal use of credit cards has positively affected direct marketing. The credit card makes it so very simple for the customer to complete the transaction in one sitting. And the ability in recent years to call a toll-free 800 number has made the ordering process even easier.

At the same time, the cost-per-call figures have been skyrocketing to the point that the personal salesperson is fast becoming a vanishing breed in America. Direct marketing is helping to fill this void.

One societal factor that has favored direct marketing is the increasing number of women in the nation's workforce. Between handling a career and running a home, these women have less time for in-store shopping and find shopping by way of catalog or mailing piece a great time-saving service. More and more of the country's finest firms are offering superb merchandise through direct marketing advertising. Current copywriting ace Joseph Sugarman composed a direct marketing ad selling a $2,000,000 home in Malibu, California. The ad ran in an in-flight airline magazine.

All U.S. marketing is putting greater emphasis on selectivity, a selling strategy to which direct marketing lends itself beautifully. The universal, built-in advantage for skilled managers is that direct marketing advertising is scientific because it is measurable.

Most Thoroughly Tested Copy. Of all forms of advertising copy, direct marketing copy is the most thoroughly tested. In fact, every single direct marketing advertisement is a test that elicits direct feedback from its audience. Direct marketing advertising relies on no intervening variables, no go-betweens, no sales clerk. Nor can it hide or strut behind an Advertising Awards Jury gold medal or blue ribbon. If the direct marketing advertisement pulls in sales or inquiries, it passes the test. If the direct marketing advertisement does not pull in sales or inquiries, it is a flop, and unlikely to be repeated. As in the case of "Do You Make These Mistakes in English?" a winning appeal may be used time and again as long as it keeps winning in competition with newer copy appeals that are regularly being written and tested. In direct marketing advertising, the "feedback" is measurable and inescapable.

Direct Marketing Media Use. Direct marketing advertising uses a wide range of media that includes practically everything but outdoor billboards: newspapers, free-standing inserts in newspapers, magazines, direct mail, and increasingly, radio and television. It is most visible, however, in the medium of direct mail.

DIRECT MARKETING VIA DIRECT MAIL

"Direct Mail" is a bit of a misnomer. The communication itself is delivered *direct* to the prospect—but not always though the use of the United States Postal Service. A simple printed bulletin slipped under your windshield wiper in a parking lot is direct mail advertising. A free tube of toothpaste tucked inside your screen door is a form of direct mail advertising called door-to-door sampling. A gag object, such as a bird cage delivered by messenger to an executive's office, is direct mail advertising. So while the traditional descriptive term is "direct mail," it may include nonmailed advertising. In any event, direct mail is quite accurately described as "the straight-line medium" by Hanley Norins, creative vice-president at the Young & Rubicam advertising agency.

Advantage: Pinpoint Targeting.   To a direct marketer, the overwhelming advantage of direct mail lies in pinpoint targeting of specific individuals and specific markets. It flies straight as an arrow to only the best prospects. Consequently, direct mail avoids the waste circulation that accompanies use of the mass media. And no matter how elaborate each mailing piece, a direct mail campaign tends to be less costly than a campaign paying for the huge circulation of the mass media. Commercial mailing companies like Reuben H. Donnelly have the mechanics down to such a science that they can control mailings to certain neighborhoods, to one side of a particular street, to particular homes on one side of a particular street. Mailing lists can be purchased covering almost all conceivable categories, large or small, from all registered car owners to all registered nurses to all licensed pilots.

Personalized Message.   Not only does direct mail go to a very select list of prospects, it has the selling advantage of being highly personalized in its presentation. It is, in effect, person-to-person communication. It can flatter a reader by generous use of that prospect's name: "Dear Mrs. White, you can be sure that no other family in Champaign will have bright spring duds like the Whites." Or it can personalize a letter by sympathetic understanding of the reader's job: "Dear Dr. White, few people in the outside world know how many hours a professor must spend in preparing lecture notes." At the time the prospect opens it, a direct mail appeal is not competing for the prospect's attention with other advertisements or editorial matter or program content.

Tight Controls.   The marketer has the tightest control over both timing and format in direct mail. The advertiser does not have to adapt selling strategy to a magazine issue date, a television broadcast date, or the page size detailed in Standard Rate and Data.

Creative Freedom.   Because there are no limitations on space or format with direct mail, the medium is a paradise for creative people. The direct mail piece can be a single sheet envelope stuffer or it can be a wall-filling broadside. It can be a picture postcard or a die-cut multi-page book. It can be a typewritten sales letter or the corporation's annual report. It can be printed on wafer-thin paper, on wrapping paper, or on metallic paper. It can be reproduced via letterpress, offset, or silk-screen. If a writer can come up with an intriguing idea, direct mail can deliver the goods. And direct mail has no equal as a medium for introducing novelty and realism. If your product is an automobile, for example, magazine and television advertising will limit you to a picture in showing it. But in direct mail, you can send a toy-sized working model. If your product is clothing, you can send a swatch of fabric, or even construct your entire mailing out of that fabric. When plastic packaging was first coming into prominence, one imaginative processor sent a mailing of dry martinis!

Response Devices.   Unlike other media, direct mail advertising has made an art of cultivating response. Direct mail offers a thorough means for the reader to say "Yes," based primarily on the self-addressed, stamped envelope or reply card enhanced with call-to-action devices to make answering almost irresistible. What other media can enclose a tiny pen or pencil for use in signing the orders?

The Direct Mail Package.   The classic use of the direct mail medium is the rather elaborate direct marketing message known as the direct mail package.

The package is likely to consist of an outside envelope; a long letter of perhaps two or four pages or even more; a full-color brochure replete with pictures, descriptive captions, and detailed copy; a note-sized "publisher's" letter advocating a second thought before refusal of the offer; an order form that is practically an ad in itself, repeating details of the offer; and a self-addressed, postage-paid return envelope. Often the package will include a separate printed piece detailing a premium offer for prompt response. The outside envelope is sure to carry a provocative message that compels the recipient to look inside.

Such an individual package can be quite expensive, but the production expense is offset by the fact that the mailing piece is going to a highly specific prospect, a likely buyer. To create such a package makes stringent demands on a copywriter.

Writing Copy for the Package.   It begins, as does all intelligent copy, with a thorough knowledge of the benefit and the prospect. The benefit is stated quickly and clearly. The body copy in the letter addresses the prospect as specifically and as personally as possible. The letter proceeds on a straight line from the opening benefit to the close, which asks for the order. The letter is studded with details and specifics rather than generalities, and it uses subheads and indented paragraphs for easy reading. It tells a full and complete sales story. It uses typographical "bullets" (large dots) and occasional boldfaced type to emphasize certain aspects. It includes testimonials from satisfied users as well as some guarantee of satisfaction—a "must" in all direct marketing ads. It offers a special inducement for prompt response and features some kind of involvement device (a tag or token) to facilitate answering.

The brochure tells the same sales story in even greater detail, making great use of headlines and subheads, of pictures and captions, of lists and of feature boxes. To heighten believability, there will be more testimonials, with names and photos of the respondents.

The order form also functions as a selling piece, repeating the essential sales proposition. It is likely to include an involvement device such as a punch-out tag or token that the respondent inserts in a special slot.

The "publisher's" letter is a second letter in the mailing package, generally a short note on very formal note paper. Its purpose is to nudge those readers who may be wavering. It reiterates, in the publisher's or president's lofty words, why this proposition is such a splendid value.

An Actual Example.   At this writing we have in hand a very impressive direct mail package from Bon Appétit Books.

The outside envelope is full-color bleed on slick paper stock showing photographs of scrumptiously mouth-watering food dishes. On one side of the envelope are the words, "Superb cookbooks from the editors of *Bon Appétit*." On the envelope flap is the copy line, "When only the best will do, turn to *Bon Appétit*." Next to the mailing address slot is the inducement, "Now a fabulous cookbook, yours FREE!"

Inside is a four-page letter from the president, printed in two colors, basic black typewriter type with blue accents.

Accompanying the letter is a full-color bleed folded broadside, the equivalent of eight single pages. It shows more appetizing food as well as pictures of the various cookbooks in the series.

The order blank, which is very large and printed in full color on heavy coated paper stock, is not called an order form but a "Free Gift Certificate." If you send it in you receive one book free and a second book for a fifteen-day examination period. If you don't care for the second book you return it and your subscription is canceled. There is a token, a picture of the free book, that you punch out and insert in a slot in the order form.

In addition, there is a folded note from the Senior Food Editor, printed in three colors, which does a bit more selling and includes a free recipe for a delicious appetizer.

Lastly, there is a large business reply envelope, self-addressed, postage-paid.

The entire package is every bit as appetizing as one of Bon Appétit's prize recipes. To whom was it mailed? To a highly likely prospect, a current, long-time subscriber to *Bon Appétit* magazine.

Copywriter as Salesperson.   Every step of the way, the copywriter is a salesperson. You are the only salesperson. You must write as though this were *the only sales message* the prospect will ever hear. You must not only sell the *positive benefits* of your product, you must overcome the *basic negatives* that accompany buying by mail. When you buy in a store, you can see and touch the merchandise. Not so when you buy by mail. When you buy in a store you can take the product home with you right away. No waiting for mail delivery. When you buy in a store you know the company you're dealing with and see little risk. Not so by mail. The direct marketing copywriter has to do a super selling job.

Direct Marketing Catalogs.   The most familiar symbol of direct marketing is that great American institution that comes by mail, the catalog. (Bruce Barton once quipped that the Sears Roebuck catalog had more to do with opening up the West than the Pony Express.) These catalogs can be huge tomes like the full-line volume published regularly by Sears. More often the direct marketing catalog represents a company that specializes in a certain marketing area, like L. L. Bean and Eddie Bauer with their appeals to the lovers of the outdoors. Some catalogs, like Spencer Gifts, cover a wide range of inexpensive items. Others, like Horchow, cover a wide range of expensive items. Many catalogs cover fashion items exclusively, each catalog focusing on a particular sphere— from avant garde to sporty to traditional to preppy.

When you write for the Sears full-line catalog, you have built-in prospects, people already actively in the market and looking for a certain item. You don't have to flag down and pull in that prospect. This may not be as true with the specialized catalog. But in either case, you give full and detailed information about each item you're promoting. Even high-fashion clothing, beautifully pictured, has essential information that must be conveyed to the prospect before you can hope to make a sale.

Whether the direct marketing direct mail piece is an elaborate package of several items or a simple bill enclosure or a bangtail envelope with its extra, removable flap, or a colorful catalog, the chances are it is delivered to a legitimate prospect. And the writer has a certain amount of creative leeway in the tools used to appeal.

Writing for Other Direct Marketing Media.   Those media other than direct mail, which reach a broad, general audience, impose great demands on the writer of direct marketing advertising. With the exception of the multi-page, free-standing newspaper insert in glorious full color, there are severe space or time limitations and no allowance for gimmicks. In a magazine or newspaper advertisement you must tell a full and complete sales story each time. You cannot afford the luxury of feeding the reader bits and pieces of your story over a period of time. You have to stop the reader and close the order, all in one fell swoop. In a single advertisement, you must capture attention, generate interest, activate desire, overcome objections, and get the prospect's signature on the dotted line. It is not an easy task to persuade a prospect to simply think well of you; it is far more demanding to persuade a prospect to sit down right then and send you a check.

Like Face-to-Face Selling.   Good direct marketing writing operates in a manner not unlike that of a dynamic face-to-face salesperson. It takes a direct approach, flagging down prospects via their special interests, such as car owners or home owners. No time here for subtleties or beating around the bush. (Remember "Corns gone, etc." and "Do You Make These Mistakes in English?") The direct marketing copy will state its benefit openly in the headline, then proceed through explanatory subheads and long explanatory copy that leaves no stone unturned. Good direct marketing writing takes the reader through the full sales story, step by step, anticipating the reader's questions, revealing successive surprises and inducements. It builds believability and conviction through the use of product details and specifics, and through the use of testimonials from satisfied users. It guarantees satisfaction in some manner, perhaps a free trial period. And, finally, good direct marketing writing makes it easy for the prospect to respond, using such inducements as pop-up coupons, self-mailing order blanks, and other devices designed to trigger action.

When used as a basic advertising tool, direct marketing logically follows that fundamental principle of learning theory: repetition. The wise direct marketer plans the selling effort as a campaign of several pieces, carefully spaced, and counts on the cumulative effect producing the ultimate sale. Each piece in a direct marketing series contains a full selling story.

Constant Testing.   Remember that all direct marketing copy is tested. Frequently this is done in a split run. *TV Guide,* for instance, can run many versions of an ad in the same space in the same edition. Appeals are constantly being tested, sometimes with amazing results. John Caples reports seeing one advertisement sell over nineteen times as much as another for the same product. Both ads occupied the same space, ran in the same publication, had photographic illustrations and carefully written copy. The difference was that one used the right appeal and the other used the wrong appeal.

Direct marketers test everything. They test basic appeals. They test headlines. They test words within headlines. They test every element in a direct mail package. They've been testing direct mail and print ads for generations. Now they are also testing television. As in print, they've learned that long copy works better than short copy. Consequently you won't find direct marketers running 30-second commercials. They want a minimum of 60 seconds and widely use 120 seconds. They concentrate on selling the product, and they repeat at least twice the information the viewer needs in order to respond.

Results Are Measurable.   Whether they use television, newspapers, radio, or direct mail, experienced direct marketers can tell you to the penny what it costs them to generate a response.

Because other forms of advertising are not measurable in such a precise dollars-and-cents way, direct marketing copywriters may consider most other forms of advertising undisciplined. There is some truth in this, but what they seem to ignore is that most advertised products are sold in quite a different way than by mail.

WAYS TO INCREASE SELLING POWER

The skilled direct marketing advertisement must stand on its own feet and do the full selling job. Since direct marketing writing is and always has been entirely tested copy, certain truths or copywriting principles have emerged over time. A number of successful mail order practitioners have developed rules of thumb for increasing selling power. One of the best known and most respected is John Caples, who offers this advice:[1]

1. Make every ad a complete sales talk.
2. Write in the present tense, second person. (Take the "you" and "now" approach.)
3. Use subheads. (They break up long copy, capture the eye, accentuate key points for a "skimmer," lead the reader through the text.)
4. Put captions under illustrations. (People look for them and will read them.)
5. Use a simple style of writing. (Leave literary techniques for the poets and novelists.)
6. Choose everyday words rather than pompous words. (You can learn about life *and* copywriting from the Ten Commandments.)
7. Give free information.
8. Concentrate on "*selling* copy" as opposed to "*style* copy." (You want to win customers, not advertising awards.)
9. Arouse curiosity.
10. Make your copy specific. (Generalities don't sell, no matter how glittering; there is great strength in the specific.)
11. Don't hesitate to use long copy. (An interested prospect is eager for all obtainable information.)
12. Write more copy than necessary to fit the space. (Cutting and pruning always sharpens copy.)
13. Use understatement rather than overstatement; avoid even the appearance of overstatement. (It's no help to have a proposition that's too good to be believed.)
14. Avoid trick slogans and catch lines that don't stand up under close scrutiny.
15. Study the selling copy in direct marketing catalogs. (Strictly no-nonsense.)

---

1. John Caples, *Tested Advertising Methods* (Englewood Cliffs, NJ: Prentice-Hall, 1974), pp. 129-150.

16. Urge the reader to *act*. (The prospect may even appreciate not being left hanging.)

Not all these and other copywriting hints apply to every direct marketing advertising assignment. Different products have different space requirements. A handmade Christmas ornament does not demand the explanation due to a homestudy course in Yoga. If the basic function or benefit of a product is clear-cut and understandable at a glance, it can be advertised in a small space with short copy. A proposition that is intangible or involved or expensive is likely to call for the full treatment.

John Caples also urges that the writing methods applied in direct marketing publication ads be followed just as faithfully for preparing direct mail advertising letters and brochures.[2]

A Challenging Assignment.   To allow you to try your hand at a direct marketing magazine ad, let's take a product or subject with which by now you are quite familiar—this very course in copywriting. Let's say your school is going to offer it as a correspondence course. To whom would you address your appeal? Housewives with grown families? Recent high school graduates? Independent retailers? People already employed in advertising, but in clerical-type jobs? How would you appeal to each? What benefit or advantage would you stress to each?

A Direct Mail Letter Assignment.   Once you've gotten initiated into direct marketing with that assignment, you might try your hand at a direct marketing direct mail letter. The subject: a book you've enjoyed reading recently. Think of a logical prospect (you might want to compose a personal profile). Then think of the chief benefit for that prospect. After creating an irresistible opening promise, proceed with the full sales story. Include: subheads and indented paragraphs; details and specifics; testimonials; an added inducement for prompt response; the guarantee; the response device. Enjoy yourself!

SOME RULES FOR DIRECT MAIL USE

Edward N. Mayer, Jr.,[3] the late Educational Director of the Direct Marketing Association, offered seven cardinal rules for direct mail success, which are paraphrased for you here.

1. Clearly identify your objective. Do you want a *quantity* of inquires? Is your objective inquiries of a *quality* that results in a high percentage of sales? Or do you want not only more sales, but sales that are profitable?

---

2. Ibid., p. 143.
3. Educational Director, Direct Mail/Marketing Assoc., November, 1974.

2. Be sure your address is correct, and that the list you are using is the right one for your product or service.

3. Be sure your copy promises a product or service benefit.

4. Conform your layout and copy to your precise market. If they don't fit, response will be critically affected.

5. Make it easy for the prospect to take action. Direct mail is an *action* medium.

6. Tell your story over and over again. Many sales are made after the fifth call. If your first mailing doesn't produce desired results but you know it contained the right message for a market that matches the profile of your best customers, try again. Faint-hearted selling, by direct mail or any other medium, seldom succeeds.

7. Research every aspect of your direct mail. Keep testing. When you get a winning combination, don't relax. Keep trying to find one that's even better. Be sure to test the products or services you offer to make certain that they live up to the promises you make. If they don't, modify your offer or improve your product.

To make sure the money you invest in direct mail produces the greatest return, Dr. Ernest Dichter[4] offers this advice:

> Fashion direct mail to suit the personality of the recipient and the personality of your product or service.

To do this, you need to know the *psychographic profile* of your prospect. And you also need to know the profile of your product—not as you the maker see it, but as the customer sees it. That brings us again to that recurring canon of successful advertising: before you decide to take the direct approach, be sure you have done your homework in the form of research that leads to a sound creative strategy.

To learn more about direct marketing copy, read *Tested Advertising Methods* by John Caples, and read what David Ogilvy has to say on the subject in his *Confessions of an Advertising Man* and *Ogilvy on Advertising*. For a full discussion of all the mechanics of direct marketing, read *Successful Direct Marketing Methods* by Bob Stone.

OTHER USES OF DIRECT MAIL

Although direct mail is probably used most often for direct selling, it has scores of other uses: a company can build the morale of employees through bulletins or an in-house magazine; stockholders and employees can be sold on the company's products by way of enclosures with

---

4. President, Institute for Motivational Research.

dividend checks and pay envelopes; company salespeople can feel stimulated to greater efforts through use of letter and bulletins relaying sales success stories of colleagues; personal salespeople can get a start through persistent contact with a group of prospective buyers; actual inquiries can be routed to salespeople; customers can be kept in contact between salespeople's calls.

Direct mail has proved profitable in securing direct orders for merchandise; it has sometimes been used to help win back inactive customers; it can do a remarkable job of selling other items in a company's line—particularly accessories—through use of letters, package inserts, or handout folders. Direct mail is especially efficient in reaching a comparatively small group, such as dealers. It has been used to bring prospects to the dealer's showroom via printed announcements. It can be of tremendous help, through booklets and charts and checklists, in educating retail clerks about how to sell the product.

Certainly direct mail is a natural for merchandising a company's promotion plans to the dealer through advertising pre-prints and display material. In communicating with the consumer, direct mail has proved successful in opening up new charge accounts, capitalizing on special personal events such as promotions and graduations, and amplifying the company's mass media advertising. Booklets, folders, and manuals can explain in detail what cannot be handled in a magazine page or in a thirty-second television spot. Direct mail has also proved invaluable in researching and pretesting new product ideas via sampling.

Direct mail is used to a very great extent in pure consumer research—product preferences, buying habits, opinions, and attitudes. Direct mail is popular with researchers because it offers tight control through precise timing, scheduling, and sampling. Any scientific investigator has to appreciate the mechanics that direct mail makes available.

The use of direct mail for political purposes has long been part of the Washington scene, with free franking privileges accorded to all members of Congress. The use of this medium has expanded noticeably in the last few national elections.

As for the specific forms a direct mail piece may take, they are almost limitless: letters, folders, broadsides, booklets, brochures, self-mailers, postcards, greeting cards, catalogs, annual reports, house organs, posters, calendars, advertising reprints. Truly a communications smorgasboard!

Consider these real-life examples of direct mail offerings: a college exam book with student answers and instructor comments, used as an alumni money-raising device; a miniature outdoor billboard mounted in an outdoor panel frame, promoting a new textbook on advertising; a jigsaw puzzle of a farm scene, promoting the use of a chemical fertilizer; a pleasant, pertinent cartoon greeting card to a retail customer whose account was delinquent; a hanging calendar printed on a dish towel, sent to customers of a popular homestyle restaurant. Ingenuity abounds!

Because direct mail offers so much opportunity, so much freedom, and so much challenge to the creative person, there is an occasional tendency to go overboard on gadget mailings. We caution you to use judgment, especially in the face of constantly rising mailing and production costs for a medium that, even in the beginning, was never the cheapest way to deliver a single message to a single prospect.

CASE HISTORY

BLACK, GILLOCK & LANGBERG

Courtesy of Black, Gillock & Langberg and Specialty Advertising Association International.

Do advertising agencies believe in advertising their own services? Many do, and as you would expect, some of their efforts are amazingly inventive. Witness the campaign of an agency in Houston, Texas, which turned to specialty advertising to make an impact.

The agency of Black, Gillock & Langberg was anxious to secure new accounts. In order to increase awareness of its name among potential new accounts, the Houston ad agency targeted the senior executives of seventy-five major south Texas companies that had been added recently to *Inc.* magazine's list of top 500 companies. Since these companies were new to *Inc.'s* list, the theme "Welcome to the Big Leagues" was used. This theme line was imprinted on the outside of a large mailing tube. Inside the tube was a regulation baseball bat imprinted with the ad agency logo. Attached to the bat by a name-imprinted shoestring was a pennant-designed reply card stating, "We'd like to take a swing at your advertising." Scorecard graphics and baseball language in the copy explained the agency's capabilities in hopes that recipients of the bat would check the reply box that said, "Give me your best pitch."

The idea was a hit. Black, Gillock & Langberg's production manager called the promotion a "smashing success. We can directly attribute pitching (and later picking up) a $1.75 million account to the mailer"—which proves you can have a major league advertising idea without depending on the major media.

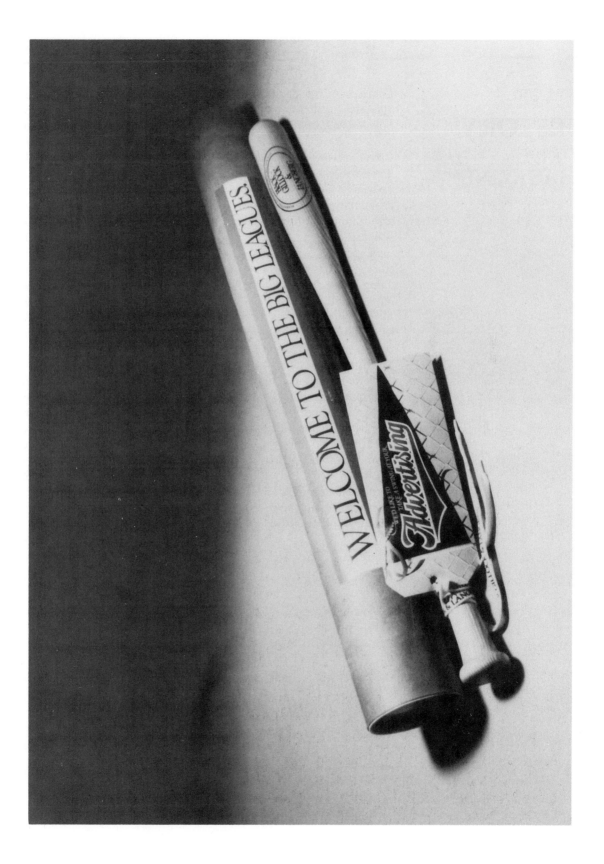

CASE
HISTORY
URGE
MAGAZINE

Courtesy of Urge *Magazine and Specialty Advertising Association International.*

Clever advertising needn't be limited to use of the usual advertising media. Sometimes, particularly when you have a rather limited target audience, you can do spectacular things with specialty advertising. The story of *Urge* magazine in Tampa, Florida, is an outstanding example.

The problem/objective was to introduce a new city magazine to advertising agencies and potential advertisers.

The magazine, a news and entertainment weekly called *Urge,* was edited for the 18-39 age group in the Tampa area. A basic theme line was developed: "Got the urge to paint the town red?" To 250 ad agencies and potential major advertisers the magazine first mailed a paint brush with a colorful shipping tag attached. Naturally, copy on the shipping tag asked, "Got the urge to paint the town red?" and explained the advantages of advertising in the new publication. This mailing was followed up with personal calls by space reps on each prospect. The space rep delivered a paint can in which was a coffee mug in paint-splatter graphics. Also in the paint can was a prototype copy of the new magazine. The paint can itself was labeled with the theme art of painting the town red.

This promotion was so ingenious that five radio stations and daily newspapers did feature stories on it. And substantial advertising was said to have been secured for the first issue of the magazine.

There's a lesson here for all advertising creative people: Think beyond the obvious.

Writing Business-to-Business Advertising

Chapter Topics

Business talking to
    business
Business advertising and
    personal selling
Types of business
    publications
Different reader attitude
News and information
Capabilities not products
Soliciting inquiries
How a copywriter prepares
Guidelines for effective
    copy
Understanding the reader's
    job function
Twenty ways to improve
    business advertising
Comparison to consumer
    advertising

Key Terms

Horizontal publication
Vertical publication
Controlled circulation
Tracking results
Trade jargon
Tailoring copy
Case history

Case Histories

United States Gypsum
    Company
United Technologies

There may have been a time when people who wrote trade ads were considered second-class citizens, but that is certainly not the case today. Consider the outstanding television advertising for IBM, Apple, Xerox, and a score of other business giants.

Of course, such ads are no longer called trade ads and they are looking and sounding more and more like general consumer ads. The new term for such selling is called business-to-business advertising. It means advertising that is *not* directed to ordinary everyday consumers of ordinary everyday products.

A Special Perspective.   The writing of such advertising follows the basic rules already laid down for you, but it calls for a somewhat special perspective. You are dealing with a situation of business talking to business. Unlike most general consumer ads, this kind of advertising is usually designed to work in conjunction with *personal selling*. Another difference is in the way your prospects view media and advertising.

Business-to-Business Media.   There are a few hundred consumer magazines, but there are thousands of magazines directed to certain kinds of business and industrial purposes. These *business publications* have many of the same characteristics as consumer magazines, but they are less likely to be sold at newsstands and their news, editorial matter, and advertising are totally oriented toward specific business interests.

The broad term business publication includes a few general business publications that appeal to all kinds of business interests. These publications cover the waterfront, reaching high-level executives in many fields: *Fortune, Business Week, Forbes,* and *Wall Street Journal,* for example. Other business publications concentrate on certain operations within many businesses, such as *Purchasing Magazine* for purchasing agents and *Sales and Marketing Management* for marketing executives; these are referred to as horizontal publications. Still other business publications cover a particular business or industry in depth, for example, *Progressive Grocer, Package Engineering, Boot and Shoe Recorder,* and *Advertising Age;* these are called vertical publications.

Next come the professional journals that go to members of the American Medical Association, American Bar Association, American Dental Association, to architects, engineers, or teachers.

Farm publications are both consumer *and* business publications, and often are geared to a single area of interest such as dairy farming.

To receive some business publications, the reader must be genuinely interested in the subject of the magazine. Outsiders cannot receive these *controlled circulation* publications even if they want to. For example, *Media Decisions* magazine is circulated free to people in the advertising business who are in charge of selecting and buying media space and time.

Different Reader Attitude.   Readers bring a different attitude to business publications than they do to general consumer magazines like

Reader's Digest, Sports Illustrated, or *People.* As a rule, the reader of a business publication is, indeed, all business. Most subscriptions to business magazines are paid for by the reader's company, and those magazines are often read on company time. The reader is thus motivated to take advertising in business papers very seriously, and is actively on the lookout for new ideas and for information about other products that can contribute to the efficient and profitable manufacture and sale of the reader's own product.

Need for Personal Sales Representative.   In the world of business-to-business selling, the *specified purchase* requires a personal salesperson or company representative. What you're selling may well be used in the manufacturing process that creates a consumer product—a machine tool, a packaging element, a measuring device. Very often, the product or service you are promoting has to be specially adapted to your customer's needs, or "specified," as the customer and your sales representative work out a solution to the customer's particular problem.

Selling Capabilities.   Often you are not selling your products per se, like boxes of corn flakes. Instead, you are selling your *capabilities* to produce exactly the element your prospect needs in manufacturing. For example, the Microswitch Company makes many, many different kinds of small switches for machinery. But when they advertise, Microswitch is not likely to be trying to sell a carload of Switch #8259; Microswitch is selling its *ability* to make a tiny switch that is exactly what the prospect needs. Once there is a match-up of need and ability, it takes a sales representative to close the sale.

Soliciting Inquiries.   This necessity for matching need with ability explains why sensible business-to-business advertising constantly solicits inquiries. Many do it with a coupon. Many do it via a toll-free 800 phone number. Almost all put a name, address, and phone number with the signature of the ad. The inquiries are coded or keyed in some manner. "Phone George at such and such a number" indicates a particular ad in a particular publication. "Phone Helen, etc." would indicate a different ad and publication.

As the inquiries come in, the business-to-business advertiser keeps records tracking the performance of the ads. The advertiser can tell which appeal brought in responses and which publication generates the best results. The sales crew completes the tracking process by noting which inquiries were converted to sales and how much dollar volume was produced per sale.

Sometimes the respondent will ask to talk to a company salesperson or representative. Sometimes the respondent seeks a booklet or pamphlet giving information about the advertiser's company. The important thing is that the advertising provides leads for the salesperson.

How a Copywriter Prepares. Occasionally business-to-business advertising is of such a technical nature that it requires a copywriter with an engineering or chemistry degree to write it. But that is rare. For the most part, business-to-business advertising is written by regular, everyday copywriters. It is very possible that your first professional copywriting assignment will be in business-to-business advertising.

Learn the Lingo. How do you prepare for the task of writing ads in a business or industrial field new to you? In addition to thinking of principal prospect, principal benefit, and principal objective, just as you would for any ad, you will want to learn the lingo of your prospect's field. By reading the editorial content of the particular publication your prospect reads you'll become aware of certain recurring key words and phrases. Make a list of them. It probably won't be a very long list, but it's vital. Once you are familiar with those words and phrases, you'll feel more comfortable about talking to somebody in that line of work. Each field of human endeavor has its own jargon—even advertising. Once you learn that, you're on your way to being a pro.

Pay attention not only to the key words and phrases, but to how the publication handles its editorial material. Studying the way it presents subjects to its audience can provide hints for your own advertising.

In addition to studying the publications in which you'll advertise, you will meet and talk with the engineers and designers who created your company's products. It is your job to elicit key facts from these scientists and translate that scientific language into simple, understandable English—preferably in a way that differentiates your client.

Tailor Copy to the Prospect. Your copy must be tailored to the job needs of the person you are talking to. Give *news.* Give *information.* And stick to the subject at hand. As David Ogilvy writes; "A buyer of flexible pipe for offshore oil rigs is more interested in pipe than anything else in the world. So play it straight."

Work hard on your headline. It's the key to success. Don't worry about long headlines or long copy; interested prospects are eager to learn everything that will help them.

You may advertise some products to different customers in different ways. Each customer has a special interest to which you must appeal. For example, in advertising bathroom and kitchen tile to the home buyer, you stress beauty and ease of care. To the home builder you stress ecomony and beauty—but beauty as a point in helping the builder to sell the house. To the do-it-yourselfer you stress ease of installation. To the architect you stress beauty and versatility allowing more design freedom.

Guidelines for Effective Copy. Here are a few more simple guidelines:

- Don't talk too big and avoid any hint of exaggeration. It is counterproductive to proclaim "The Greatest Aspidistra in the World" when talking to an audience of aspidistra experts.

■ Don't be flamboyant. Use straightforward, factual editorial techniques rather than bombastic approaches. The reader is likely to have a scientific viewpoint, and will respond to the rational.

■ Case histories of products at work on actual jobs are ideal, although they may require a lot of digging for background information. Company salespeople can alert you to good subjects. The reader likes to see photographs of an actual installation or such highly specific headlines as "This three-foot wide conveyor belt carries a ton of copper ore a quarter of a mile at a cost of eleven cents." It's real, it's true, it's factual. It's convincing. Your prospect then wants to read on to learn more facts and figures and names and places. A case history is, in effect, a third-person endorsement.

■ Personalize your copy as much as possible so that readers feel you understand the special problems of their particular job or business. Suppose you are writing an ad directed to the executive who must select the company's corporate Christmas gift. Your copy should recognize and sympathize with that individual's highly sensitive situation.

■ Your copy should be friendly and helpful, but not smartalecky. The primary ingredients of your copy should always be *news* and *information*. Use easily understood language, but without being dull. Your readers may be all business, but they are still human. Give them sprightly stuff to read—like this iron-tough headline from a steel company: "It's time to boil the fat out of steel specs."

■ Cardinal rule: Your copy should deal in specifics rather than generalities. John Caples says there is strength in the specific. Specifics *convince*.

There are thousands of business publications, and almost without exception they are specialized. Many of these magazines are published by Cahners Publishing Company, which recently offered some valuable advice in a research report:

20 WAYS TO IMPROVE ADVERTISEMENTS IN SPECIALIZED BUSINESS MAGAZINES

1. Have something to say. Say it as briefly and to the point as possible.

2. Set *one* objective for the advertisement before it's written. Decide in advance the *one thing* you want the reader to do or to remember. Then write the advertisement for the sole purpose of achieving that *single* objective.

3. After the advertising objective is set, try to achieve that objective with the *headline* alone. For many readers, the headline is the only line read.

4. Then try to achieve the advertising objective with the *illustration* alone. Some 60 percent of the advertisement's attention value is in the illustration alone.

5. Make sure that the advertisement has one main focal point visually. Do not clutter. Do not compete with yourself.

6. If the headline or illustration makes claims, use the body copy to support those claims. Use facts. *Never* exaggerate.

7. Appeal to specialized business magazine readers in terms of their *specific job interest*. What will your product do for readers in the performance of their job responsibility to their company? Will your product save time and money? Will your product eliminate downtime, rejects, customer complaints? How can your product contribute to sales or profits? Describe the *business benefits* your product can offer readers in carrying out their specific job responsibility to their company.

8. Do not expect the same message to appeal to readers with different job functions receiving different specialized business magazines. Sellers want to sell, buyers want to save, builders want to get the job done, engineers want their products to work, managers are responsible for profit. Individuals with specialized job functions have very special interests, which is why they are reading specialized business magazines.

9. Look at the editorial pages of the publication in which your advertisement will appear to see how this particular group of business readers expect to see their business information presented. Use the same type of presentation devices in your advertisement, whether they are call-outs, cross-sections, diagrams, charts, comparisons, demonstrations, drawings, photographs, statistics, or summaries.

10. Use *you* not *we*. Sell benefits to the user, not boasts of the seller. *Thee* not *me*.

11. Use space to get attention—the larger you are the more you will be noticed. And *color* always helps.

12. Avoid shouting, bragging, and boasting, all black, too gray, tricks, humor, confusion, cuteness, the plant, the boss, "me wonderful."

13. Run the advertisement. No one can see it unless you run it. Advertise as exactly and consistently as you expect to sell your product. Unless you are in a seasonal business, advertise every month if you expect to sell every month.

14. Reprint your advertisement. Mail copies to your target prospects, to your customers, to your sales force, to your internal staff. Then mail it again. You can triple your advertising effectiveness by direct mail follow-up of the same sales message.

15. Repeat your advertising in reference directories. Buyers refer to directories when they are looking for your product, your address, your telephone number, your local sales representative. Directories are your point of sale. If there is something you want buyers to know when they are making a buying decision, let it be known by repeating your advertising in reference directories.

16. Consider your advertising program an investment, and measure your return on that investment—in readership, recognition, brand awareness, and brand preference. Measure the return on your advertising investment exactly as you would measure the return on any other investment you make.

17. When you get a winning advertisement, determined by the criteria in #16, stick with it. Run it and run it and run it. Do not abandon a successful advertisement—they are too few and far between.

18. Surround your advertisement. Make sure that your entire marketing and management team sees it, knows what its purpose is, knows what kind of results it is achieving for them. Your marketing/management team should be at least twice as aware of your advertising as your prospects or customers. And that is your responsibility, not theirs.

19. Give your advertisement the "ten second test." Look at it for ten seconds, and if the prime objective of the ad does not come through to you in those ten seconds, start again. You'll be happy you did when you measure the return on your advertising investment.

20. Focus on what you want the reader to remember. . . or to do. Say it in the headline. Say it again in the illustration. Use the body copy to back it up factually, in job-interest terms. If there is even one word in your advertisement about anything else, take it out. Concentrate 100 percent on what it is you want the reader to remember or to do, and your advertisement will pay off in readership, awareness, and preference at a higher level than three out of four of all advertisements run in specialized business magazines.

Comparison to Consumer Advertising.   From the viewpoint of the advertising copywriter, business-to-business advertising becomes more like consumer advertising with each passing year. You see more selling of ideas rather than products, more institutional than product emphasis, more selling of company capabilities. More money is being spent on outstanding artwork and photography, and there is definitely greater use of dominant visuals and message simplicity. You see greater use of color, greater use of bleed space, greater use of double spreads. Why might this be so? Some speculate that big decisions are made by big executives and that big executives like big ads.

Certainly the ever-increasing use of television by business-to-business advertising may bear that out. A commercial for a computer company on the Super Bowl telecast is bound to reach a sizable cross-section of top executives in the audience—the people who make big decisions. In fact, it may lead to uses for computers that the computer manufacturers hadn't even thought of themselves.

Television or print, large ad or small, the object of business-to-business advertising remains the same: to clear the path for the personal sales representative to finalize the transaction.

CASE HISTORY
UNITED STATES GYPSUM COMPANY

Courtesy of United States Gypsum Company and its agency, Marstrat, Inc.

Here's an outstanding example of a very serious subject being treated in a very serious, professional manner—and winning high readership scores to boot.

Beginning students have a tendency to feel that people won't read long copy. They most certainly will, when that copy is pertinent to their problems. Architects and high-rise contractors read every word of this ad and then wrote in for more. Why? Because it talks their language on a deadly serious topic.

What made this particular business-to-business ad so successful? For one thing, it doesn't look or sound like an ad. It has been very carefully tailored to have the same feel or tone as the editorial content of the architectural magazines in which it appears. It is, in fact, almost a classic example of what we refer to as the editorial layout. It is clean and well-ordered. It uses a chart with great effect. The type is extremely readable, with bullets used to punch out certain key points. It contains an invitation to write for further information (a device that also helps keep tabs on readership). The copy is long, extremely detailed, and specific.

It is a no-nonsense message, presented in a highly businesslike way. We are told that United States Gypsum Company wouldn't even trust this copy assignment to the agency's skillful regular writers, but turned it over to their experienced technical editor, an engineering grad from Purdue.

He did them proud. He did the whole advertising profession proud.

HIGH-RISE FIRE PROTECTION:

Special insulations draw curtain on flame spread.

Specifying an effective fire-containment system that is proven to resist flame passage is a crucial need for high-rise curtain-wall design.

It is virtually impossible to guarantee that high-rise fires can be prevented no matter how a building is designed, since office, hotel and apartment buildings contain combustible furnishings and other contents. Facing that reality, designers concentrate their efforts on ways to effectively detect, contain and/or extinguish fires. Products and systems that perform these life-safety functions are often effective and commonly employed. However, there are key details in many systems that are particularly difficult to deal with effectively.

Important examples of details that need attention are the containment systems where two separate design systems meet, such as exterior curtain wall and the floor slab, and where a wall or floor must be penetrated. There are few effective ways to maintain fire integrity in such cases. The following checklist is intended to serve as performance criteria for products or systems being considered for fire-containment design details at curtain wall/floor slab intersections or wall and floor penetrations:
■ The fire-stopping material must maintain its dimension and integrity while preventing the passage of flame and hot gases when tested according to the standard ASTM E119 time/temperature exposure for a time period equivalent to the rating of the assembly penetrated.
■ The fire-stopping material must be noncombustible as defined by NFiPA Standard 220 when tested in accordance with ASTM E136 criteria.
■ The melt point of the material should be a minimum of 2,000°F. to withstand the temperatures that high-rise fires often achieve.
■ The curtain wall insulation must be compatible with and meet the same fire-performance criteria as the fire-

stopping material in order to maintain the fire-containment rating and integrity of the spandrel wall and floor juncture.
■ The material should be resilient enough to seal irregular or variable openings and remain in place during an actual fire.
■ The material should have a suitable attachment method to hold it in place.
■ If applied in contact with metal, the material must be non-corrosive (won't corrode steel or aluminum, as tested per Fed. Spec. HH-I-558B).
■ If used in curtain-wall applications, the material should have significant thermal insulating value ("k" value of 0.25 or less, per ASTM C518).
■ To assure durability, the material should be moisture-resistant, mildew and vermin-proof, as well as non-deteriorating.
■ The material must be economical in cost and have easy installation characteristics.

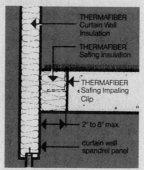

THERMAFIBER
Curtain Wall
Insulation

THERMAFIBER
Safing Insulation

THERMAFIBER
Safing Impaling
Clip

2" to 8" max.

curtain wall
spandrel panel

Typical fire-protection application in aluminum-spandrel curtain-wall system utilizes two important THERMAFIBER Fire Safety Insulations.

THERMAFIBER° Fire Safety Insulations meet or are consistent with all the criteria listed above. In fire-containment tests per ASTM E119 time/temperature exposure, a curtain-wall assembly constructed using THERMAFIBER Curtain Wall and Safing Insulations withstood the fire for over five hours, while other insulation materials in similar tests failed in less than an hour (polyurethane, 17 min.; 4-pcf glass fiber, 26 min.; 6-pcf glass fiber, 32 min.). The surface burning characteristics for these products are: flame spread 15, fuel contributed 0, smoke developed 0, per ASTM E84 (with foil facing: flame spread 10-25, fuel contributed 5, smoke developed 0).

These insulations are also highly resilient and can be "stuffed" into irregular openings. Thus THERMAFIBER Safing Insulation can be used to seal openings in walls and floors and flutes in metal decks (where they cross fire-rated assemblies), as well as the space between the floor slab and curtain-wall assembly. Both THERMAFIBER Curtain Wall and Safing Insulations have low thermal conductivity: 0.25-0.23 "k" value, per ASTM C518, depending on specified density. Assemblies with these insulations endured fire for up to 5 hrs. with aluminum-spandrel curtain wall, 3 hrs. with glass-spandrel curtain wall and 2 hrs. with granite and glass-fiber-reinforced concrete. The safing insulation endured 3-hr. tests of spandrel-slab edge applications and up to 2½-hr. "poke-through" tests.

A casebook detailing the historical and worldwide nature of curtain-wall fire-protection problems and other information about these two exceptional products may be obtained by writing to: Dept. 331-2, United States Gypsum Company, 101 South Wacker Drive, Chicago, IL 60606.

CASE HISTORY
UNITED TECHNOLOGIES

Courtesy of United Technologies.

To borrow from a famous old advertising line, probably 99 and 44/100 percent of all advertising done in America is designed to sell products and services. A very small percentage comes under the heading of corporate image advertising—advertising that can often be very challenging.

Take United Technologies, for example. A giant conglomerate, essential to America's air and space future, it is barely known by the general public, and not overly well known by its own special publics—the leaders of industry, government, and the military.

Noted for its all-type human interest messages in the *Wall Street Journal,* in recent years United Technologies has advertised consistently where it could reach the thought leaders of American government and business. The task has always been a subtle and complicated one: to make United Technologies more visible as a single, multi-industry company, a whole greater than the sum of its parts; to stake UTC's claim to technological leadership; to show that what United Technologies does is important, and that its work has meaning and merit for all Americans; to give the company a human face and worthy values to match; to gradually lead the perceptions of its tar-get audiences toward the idea of a "united" United Technologies; to convince leaders of industry, government, and the military that United Technologies Corporation is the organization best shaped to help them realize ambitious goals.

To achieve these objectives, United Technologies' most recent advertising is based on celebrating a technological achievement that all Americans can recognize and admire, thereby giving every reader a stake in UTC's success. The advertising makes very clear the role of the UTC division in the achievement, and shows how this achievement is part of a larger picture. The advertising sketches in the other divisions and their roles. When possible, the copy explains how various UTC divisions have contributed to the project being discussed, and how the technologies are herein united.

All this is done in colorful double spreads with starkly handsome layouts. The dominating photograph is real. The people in the photographs are real. The stories are fact: an early flying clipper setting a speed record across the Pacific; the strange black jet that outruns a bullet; the skylab house of America's astronauts; Igor Sikorsky with the first practical helicopter; a close-up of a space suit; the walk on the moon. Each ad celebrates what curious, ambitious, daring, driven, and determined people have

UNITED
TECHNOLOGIES

Continued

done. Are doing. Can do. This campaign lives where engineering and vision intersect.

While there has been some positive feedback, the campaign has not had much time in which to generate measurable results. But the overall aim remains constant: to make United Technologies live—front of mind—among its constituencies as the company that can harness the technology to conquer new frontiers.

212

"The work of the individual still remains the spark that moves mankind ahead."

Igor Sikorsky

In the 1920's, he built a forerunner of the modern airliner. In 1939, he built the first practical helicopter. Today, Igor Sikorsky's company is developing the first rotary-wing aircraft that will approach the sound barrier—the X-Wing.

The companies of United Technologies are working together on tomorrow's aviation technologies. Advanced materials and design by Sikorsky, controls by Hamilton Standard, power by Pratt & Whitney and inspiration from the past.

VOUGHT · SIKORSKY
VS-300

13

Writing Retail Advertising

Chapter Topics

Retail share of ad budget
Retailing is local
Four essentials of retail
  copy
Store Image
Price
Immediacy
Specifics and details
The crucial executive
Tight deadlines
Special advertising
  activities
Media of retailing
Creative staffs in retail
Help from manufacturers
Differences between retail
  and "national"
  advertising
"Retail" covers many
  businesses

Key Terms

Buyer
Trade markets
Daily deadlines
Fast feedback
Storewide promotion
Overall theme
Institutional message
Special-event copy
Clip art services
Cooperative advertising
  funds

Case Histories

Spiegel
The Plastic and Aesthetic
  Surgery Center at
  Jewish Hospital,
  Louisville

Webster's dictionary defines *retail* as "the sale of goods in small amounts to ultimate consumers."

Retail advertising seems to rate little consideration from advertising textbooks and teachers, yet it makes up the largest dollar share of America's total advertising budget. Retailing is a dynamic, pervasive, and fascinating part of the economy, offering great opportunities to many writers in many places. To succeed, however, the advertising writer must understand certain fundamental truths about retailing and about how retail advertising differs from so-called national advertising.

Retailing Is Local. Retail advertising can cover anything from a small-space special offer at a hairdressing salon to a huge double-spread for a supermarket. The media is local, the establishment is local, and the customer transaction is local.

Retailing is a local affair. The retailer, who is in effect the purchasing agent for the community, risks capital anticipating the future needs, wants, and tastes of neighbors. The retailer who guesses correctly will prosper. The retailer who fails to read the local pulse accurately goes bankrupt. To avoid this, the merchant in Peoria had better not tie that store's destiny too closely to what plays in New York.

THE FOUR ESSENTIALS OF RETAIL COPY

Many local enterprises come under the heading of retail. We will use one of them—the department store—as an example as we explore the four essential points of writing retail copy: store image, price, immediacy, specifics.

Because the department store owner or manager anticipates the customers' wants season after season, year after year, the citizens of the community develop a special feeling for the store and it becomes almost like family. The successful local merchant becomes an institution like the local government, local schools, and the local churches. This is true not only of small communities, but of the largest cities in the world. Macy's in New York, Harrod's in London, and Marshall Field's in Chicago are all tourist attractions.

This landmark reputation doesn't just happen. It is built over a period of time and nurtured through thousands of transactions. The respect, the feeling, and the affection that the local community has for a retail store becomes its greatest asset. The store's image or personality is far more precious than its location or its square feet of floor space. This is the first and most important point for you to know about writing retail copy.

Importance of Store Image

This precious *store image* is built up by every single function of the store's operation—of which advertising is naturally an obvious and ubiquitous part. But only one part. To maintain this image, the retail copywriter must never, ever write advertising that does not fit the store image. Can you picture Neiman-Marcus advertising like Woolworth—or vice versa? A department store that features high-fashion merchandise will never run ads that look like those of a discount operation. Although that's an over-simplification, it's also true that one high-fashion establishment will try to differentiate itself from a competitive high-fashion establishment. So, too, will competing discount operations. That element of your reputation that differentiates you is to be cherished and promoted.

Importance of News/Immediacy

Retail advertising, by its very nature, is legitimate *news* to the local public—of styles and fashions, of goods and services, or prices and values. People want to know these things because such news directly affects their daily lives.

Because retail advertising is news in itself, an air of immediacy should permeate the copy, for example, "just received," "new shipment," "special order," "this season's look." There are hundreds of ways to say it, but details that make the merchandise new must be given special emphasis; no doubt should be left about its availability *now*. Department store fashion merchandise is highly seasonal, and the old or current simply must give way to the new.

Importance of Price

Retail copy must give proper prominence to *price*. Sometimes price rates great emphasis, sometimes it is treated demurely, but price is always in the ad. Even in advertising for fabulous fur coats at Neiman-Marcus, the price is very much in evidence. There's a good reason for this.

Price is an essential item of information that the public demands to know and deserves to know—perhaps above all other considerations. Very often, price is what triggers the buying action. A shopper may have been eyeing a certain item for some time. Suddenly it's seen at a price that means *value;* shoppers know when the price is right. The retail advertisement that does **not** show a price on the merchandise is not playing fair with the public, and definitely not playing smart.

Importance of Specifics

In addition to featuring price, it is wise to describe merchandise in the most detailed and specific terms. Your customer isn't satisfied to know only that it comes in a "kaleidoscope of favorite colors." What does that mean to somebody whose heart is set on lemon yellow? The shopper doesn't want to know about a *range;* the shopper wants to know exactly *what* colors, *what* patterns, and *what* fabrics are available in that particular outlet *before* making a trip to the store. Is it washable? Is it a blend? The shopper who wants a lemon yellow cashmere sweater to complete an ensemble is not likely to settle for something else. By giving the customer full information your advertising contributes to the store's image for service, and contributes to its efforts to win friends.

The four keys to writing sound retail copy are:

Store Image
Price
News/Immediacy
Details

It's a small list to remember, but it's crucial.

Your Key Contact.   When you write department store copy you work with a chain of command in which the store buyer is king or queen. There is an overall merchandise manager to coordinate efforts, but the store buyers make the key decisions. They attend trade markets in New York and elsewhere, and they purchase merchandise many months ahead of time. Store buyers must know what's new, what's fashionable, what's a good value, but most of all they have to know the *customers back home.* A style that is all the rage in Los Angeles might wither on the vine in Des Moines. The buyer has to know not only geographical differences, but traditional differences.

Tight Deadlines.   The store buyer is the person who tells you what goes into the merchandise and why it is "right" for your customers. These are the points you will feature in your copy. Thus you are involved in a constant, but fascinating, learning process. And in retail you have to learn fast, think fast, and work fast because you are dealing with very, very short deadlines—*daily* deadlines that never end.

Closeness to Customer.   You have an advantage in being close to the merchandise and close to the customer. While the store buyer supplies the details and the rationale behind a certain offering of merchandise, you can see, touch, wear, operate, or eat the particular item and compare it on different sensory levels with competing merchandise. You can mingle with the customers on the floor, observe their reactions, and hear their comments about the items offered for sale. You often can also learn the customers' reactions to the store's advertising. For these reasons, occasional relief stints at the sales counter will broaden your knowledge of customer relations beyond any amount of theoretical study.

Fast Feedback.   You also have the advantage of getting fast and definite feedback from the advertising. Either the customers come in or they don't; the merchandise moves or it doesn't. You may experience some frustrations in retail, but wondering how the audience responded to the advertising is not one of them. You can't take too much credit or be saddled with too much blame for the way customers respond, however, because most retail advertising features a particular piece of merchandise at a particular price and this regulates the effectiveness of your message to a considerable degree. But there are other advertising activities that give you positive creative scope.

Special Activities.   For a storewide promotion you will be charged with creating an *overall theme* that can tie together many different items of merchandise and many store activities. The store will plan special displays and special events around your theme idea to spur local interest (such as fashion shows or a contest involving paintings by children). A large Chicago department store once keyed all activities to the theme "California Days." California designers and styles dominated the fashion departments, California furniture was front and center, and the food department extensively demonstrated California patio cooking.

The other advertising activity that will allow you to spread your creative wings is the preparation of institutional messages, ranging from those relating to store policies and services (deliveries, charge accounts, returns, announcements of new store openings) to those relating to general seasonal events (Santa's visit, Easter egg hunt), to specific community events (the high school homecoming day, the town's centennial). Macy's spectacular Thanksgiving Day Parade down Broadway in New York City now delights a national television audience. And Marshall Field's practically *is* Christmas in Chicago. Their Christmas tree is seven stories high! For years Field's ads have featured Uncle Mistletoe as they proclaim themselves "The Store of the Christmas Spirit."

Media of Retailing.   Because retailing is a local affair, local media are used. Newspapers carry most retail advertising, but retailers have gotten good results with radio and, in recent years, even with television, thanks largely to the use of videotape. And as everyone who has ever had a charge account knows, retailers make continuous and effective use of direct mail as an advertising medium. You rarely receive a bill without finding a small envelope stuffer signaling some attractive buy.

Creative Staff.   If you write copy for a large department store in a large metropolitan area, you may find yourself part of an all-embracing operation, one of several writers working with skilled layout artists. Right on the premises talented sketch artists will render finished artwork. Each artist is a specialist; one may have a flair for fashion while another may excel at showing the detail in hard goods. You'll have a complete photographic studio at hand, capable of delivering almost any kind of picture. You'll be part of a self-contained advertising "machine" that turns out highly polished messages in volume.

If you work in a more modest department store advertising set-up, you may have to rough out your own layouts and turn them over, with artwork, to the local newspaper for typesetting and final assembly. When there isn't a pressing need or there isn't a large enough budget for specially prepared artwork, there are a number of clip art services available. These huge catalogs offer professionally prepared artwork, photography, lettering, and even entire seasonal-event advertisements. With a pair of scissors you can cut out any of the catalog elements and drop them into your own layouts. You'd probably subscribe to certain clip art services yourself (men's fashions, for instance). And the local newspaper would have more general clip art catalogs if you wanted to use them. Not just newspaper but all local media stand ready to pitch in with general as well as technical assistance. They will help you select illustrations, typography, announcers, actors, music, and settings.

Help from Manufacturers.   You will also receive help from the national manufacturers whose brands your store carries. These manufacturers' advertising departments and agencies prepare advertising material for dealer use that can include everything from a single illustration of the product to an entire advertisement. Through the use of cooperative advertising funds, the national brand manufacturer may reimburse your store for a sizable percentage of your advertising expenditures.

Retail versus National Copy.   Even as you use the national advertiser's cooperative funds, you should be aware that there are marked differences between retail copy and the national copy. A Liz Claiborne ad in the *New Yorker* magazine is *national;* an ad for Liz Claiborne skirts at your store is *retail.* Here are the essential differences between the two:

1.   The retailer is concerned with store image. The manufacturer is concerned with brand image.

2.   Retail copy stimulates immediate buying action. National copy usually can produce only a long-range effect.

3.   Retail advertising puts great emphasis on price. National advertising puts little (or no) emphasis on price. (Retailers set the prices. Differences in shipping costs can influence prices.)

4.   Retail copy tends to be detailed and specific about merchandise. National copy often waxes emotional, using psychological appeals.

5.   Retail advertising receives immediate feedback from the public. National advertising rarely does—unless it is direct marketing advertising.

Although department store advertising has been used as the example throughout this discussion, "retail" does not refer only to department stores. On the contrary, "retail" covers almost any local operation dealing directly with the public. A supermarket is a retail advertiser. So is a bank, a clothing store, a restaurant, a book shop, a bakery, a dry-cleaning establishment. Some of these advertisers need the services of a full-time ad writer; some do not.

Many students will go into retail advertising immediately after graduation. It is a great, wide-open field for entry-level people, and many brilliant advertising careers have been and will be launched in retail.

CASE HISTORY
SPIEGEL

Courtesy of Spiegel and its agency, HDM Dawson Johns & Black.

Advertising is often used to create an image; occasionally it is used to *change* an image. Such was the case with Spiegel, a long-time direct marketing company out of Chicago.

All direct marketing has experienced a tremendous boom, and sales from mail-order catalogs have accelerated by many billions of dollars in just a few short years. Spiegel wanted an increased share of those sales.

Spiegel had a solid reputation with the traditional housewife and mother audience. But the role of women had been changing drastically, and more and more women were entering the workforce. Spiegel decided to appeal to this new and different target market, especially to the narrower segment of it that included active women aged 25 to 54 in households earning over $30,000 a year. Fashion-wise and shrewd judges of quality, these women had money to spend but little time to spend it on shopping. Many of them had the kind of roles in business and society that called for a fairly extensive wardrobe.

Spiegel realized it couldn't adopt a new look while selling much of the same old types of merchandise. Originally established to sell mail-order products in rural communities, the Spiegel catalog featured many basic items such as clothing, tools, tires, batteries, and home furnishings, and competed directly with Sears, Penney's, and Ward's.

With its new image as a goal, Spiegel's eliminated many of the routine department-store items from the catalog. In their place Spiegel's featured designer fashions, perfumes, cosmetics, shoes, children's clothing—brand-name merchandise.

The new advertising had to have an image as fresh and sprightly as the new catalog. It had to generate catalog requests at reasonable cost and it had to reassure those customers who might have doubts about catalog shopping as opposed to in-store shopping.

The first change was a newly designed signature that replaced Spiegel's old block print logotype. More important in reflecting Spiegel's new personality were the people shown in the advertising. They were the real thing, honest-to-goodness professional women and men, photographed in their own bailiwicks wearing clothes from the Spiegel catalog. Copy told a breezy first-person story of how the Spiegel catalog was an essential shopping tool in their lives. In every case, copy carried the reassuring note that returns were picked up free. The ads were contemporary in appearance and convincing in tone.

The new look, the new image, has paid off handsomely

219

for Spiegel. The first fall that the new campaign ran, requests for the catalog almost doubled. Sales per request have increased at a ratio far higher than cost per request. In the first four years of the campaign Spiegel's overall sales increased by over $200 million.

221

CASE HISTORY
THE PLASTIC AND AESTHETIC SURGERY CENTER at Jewish Hospital, Louisville

Courtesy of Jewish Hospital, Louisville, and its agency, Doe-Anderson.

Before-and-after demonstrations have always been effective in winning conviction. Nowhere can they be more effective than in the field of plastic surgery.

In 1985, Jewish Hospital in Louisville set out to create a comprehensive plastic surgery center, the first in the nation. Once the region's leading surgeons had been recruited, consumer research was conducted in order to focus on a target market. Research determined that the target market was women in the 18–55 age group. Approximately 40 percent of these women were somewhat interested or very interested in having some form of plastic surgery. They fell into two distinct categories. The first group had a specific physical feature that they were concerned about and thought they would like to change someday. This group was called "the Procrastinators." Women in the second group were *not* unhappy with any of their physical features, but did foresee a time in their lives when cosmetic surgery would be important to them. This group was called "the Daydreamers."

It was decided to concentrate advertising effort on the Procrastinator group. Given specific information about cosmetic surgery procedures, the Procrastinators were far more likely to respond readily than the Daydreamers.

Jewish Hospital wanted to be set apart from their competition, particularly from one hospital whose Women's Pavillion had a three-month head start advertising their cosmetic surgery services. Jewish Hospital did so by broadening services to men as well as women and communicating that the dedicated center was exclusively designed for cosmetic surgery.

Specific cosmetic surgery procedures were advertised in a bold and direct before-and-after pictorial format. Both men and women were featured in ads with such picture-headline combinations as "When you know it can't be baby fat . . . we can help you take if off" and "If you're carrying excess baggage . . . we can help you travel light."

In addition to the main before-and-after campaign, one ad promoted a quarterly seminar about cosmetic surgery. Another promoted a seminar "for men only." An umbrella institutional ad was also created, stressing the quality of the surgeons. It showed a close-up of a surgeon's hand holding an artist's brush rather than a scalpel, and the headline stated: "You need more than a surgeon for plastic surgery."

The primary medium for the campaign was print because print could carry the more detailed information

222

THE PLASTIC AND AESTHETIC SURGERY CENTER

Continued

desired by the target market. However, at the beginning of the campaign radio and television were used to create immediate awareness.

Positive results have been achieved in three key areas: over 1,000 people have attended the seminars; research indicates that the target audience perceived Jewish Hospital's Cosmetic Surgery Center to be the leading hospital for cosmetic surgery by a two-to-one margin over the nearest competitor; Jewish Hospital exceeded their first-year patient level goals.

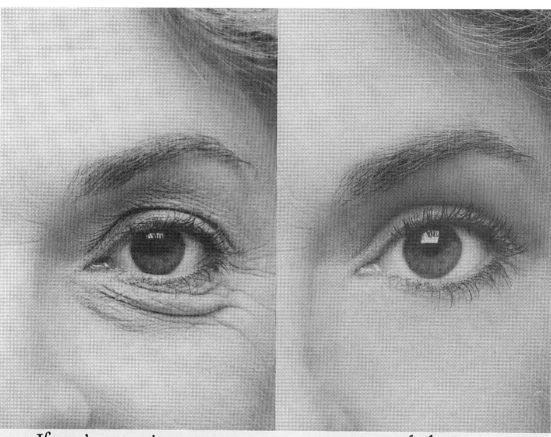

If you're carrying excess baggage, we can help you travel light.

Bags and excess skin around the eyes can make you look tired and older than you feel. Blepharoplasty, or eyelid surgery, can get rid of the bags, ease the lines, and give you a younger look. In some cases, eyelid surgery can even correct conditions that impair normal vision.

Why do it? Because you want to; because you believe that you'll look and feel better minus the baggage.

Where to go. The Center for Plastic and Aesthetic Surgery is located at Jewish Hospital, long recognized as a leader in surgery and health care services. Yet the Center is separate, devoted exclusively to plastic surgery. It's the first of its kind in the country and the only one in Louisville.

Experienced doctors and staff. On the Center's staff are some of the region's most respected and experienced plastic surgeons. They're backed by a hand-picked staff especially trained in the needs of people having plastic surgery: before, during, and after the surgery.

What to expect. You'll have privacy. Hotel-like accommodations. And the special care you need.

Cost. Because the Center was designed for aesthetic surgery, costs are lower than you'd expect. If you like, we can help you arrange financing.

Get the information you need. All cases are treated individually and results vary with each patient. To find out what you can expect, call us at 587-4000. We'd be happy to answer your questions privately and confidentially and to arrange a tour at your convenience. Videotapes are also available.

In Kentucky call toll-free 1-800-633-8923. Out-of-state call 1-800-327-3613.

The Plastic and Aesthetic Surgery Center
at Jewish Hospital

14

Writing Copy For Sales Promotion

Chapter Topics

Reasons for sales
    promotion boom
What sales promotion
    achieves
Copywriter's contribution
Forms of sales promotion
Example of sweepstakes
What sales promotions can
    and cannot do

Key Terms

"Brand image"
Profit squeeze
Temporary hypodermic
Increased trial
The coupon
Free-standing inserts
Refunds and rebates
Sweepstakes and contests
Overall theme

Case Histories

L'Oréal Studio Products
NFL Properties: "Fun,
    Food, and Football"

In recent years, marketing has seen a definite shift away from straight brand image advertising to sales promotion. In the mid-1970s expenditures ran 60 percent for advertising and 40 percent for sales promotion. In the late 1980s, the emphasis became just the reverse, some 65 percent for sales promotion and 35 percent for advertising.

Reasons for Sales Promotion Boom. It is interesting to speculate on this shift in emphasis. For one thing, there have been very few spectacular product introductions since the years immediately following World War II. That period produced a consumption revolution with such entirely new categories as television sets, high-fidelity components, and microwave ovens as well as such supermarket winners as detergents, frozen foods, and paper diapers. That boom in innovation has simmered down until today we have a marketplace of largely mature products scrambling with one another for share of market rather than increased consumption.

The other factor that has tilted the scales in favor of sales promotion over brand image advertising is economic necessity. A squeeze on profits has prompted many corporations to opt for the quick sale.

Sales Promotion Defined. By definition, sales promotion is a *temporary* incentive to buy a product or service *in addition to* the normal merits of the product or service.

Sales promotion can mean a price reduction through the use of a coupon or rebate, a free gift or premium along with the purchase of the product, or a chance to win a major gift or prize through the purchase of a product or simply by having one's attention directed to it.

True Objective of Sales Promotion. The true objective of sales promotion is to *close the sale* to the potential buyer who *already* considers the product *an acceptable alternative* in that product or service category. Sales promotion should *never* be used to compensate for poor product quality, inequitable pricing, bad distribution, or inadequate advertising support.

What Sales Promotion Achieves. Properly used, sales promotion can achieve the following objectives:

- It can increase trial of a product or service by offering an additional incentive to occasional and new users.
- It can maximize continuity of usage.
- It can make people "load up" by buying greater quantities of the product or service than they would buy normally.

Best Known Use: The Coupon. The most common form of sales promotion is the coupon offering a cents-off price reduction on the product— either at the point of sale or by return mail from the manufacturer. Coupons are generally delivered to the potential customer by way of a magazine or newspaper ad. Since the coupon ad usually appears in a highly competitive enviroment such as *food day* in a newspaper, or in the *Sunday* paper with its plethora of big, colorful, free-standing inserts, it is your job as a creative person to make the price reduction offer sound as tantalizing as possible—more tantalizing, if possible, than the offers surrounding it.

What Copywriters Can Contribute.   It is up to you to communicate the price reduction offer to the consumer quickly, interestingly, persuasively. Both the headline and body copy, however, do *not* simply sell the idea of making money. Instead, they strongly reinforce the *benefit of the product.* The best coupon ads tie in the price reduction directly with the major benefit. For example, a Kellogg's All-Bran coupon ad is headlined: "Here's 50¢ to help you get serious about fiber."

The Heart of Sales Promotion.   The heart of sales promotion theory is very simply that a price reduction on nothing means nothing to the consumer. Consumers need to be reminded of the *value of the product* so that they can perceive that the price reduction is a true bargain. A coupon ad for a food should make the food as well as the offer sound appetizing; a coupon ad for an appliance should sell the work-saving or time-saving benefits of the product as well as the money the consumer saves. That's the real key to this kind of advertising. Examples: for Lime-A-Way Bathroom & Kitchen Cleaner, "Save 50¢ and clean away hard water stains!" and for Clorox, "Save up to 75¢ and look your best with Clorox!"

Coupons by Direct Mail.   The same approach applies to a coupon delivered by direct mail, with the added premise that in the welter of direct mail we are all subject to, your copy on the outside envelope had better tease readers into believing that your offer will be both exciting and beneficial, and that it will be worth their while to open the envelope. A classic example is the American Family Publishers letter announcing in bold type, personalized with your name, that you may already have won umpteen million dollars!

As for the inside, virtually the same rules apply as for the coupon ad. Sell the product as well as the offer. Reinforce the value or benefit of the product.

Refunds and Rebates.   Another kind of price reduction is the refund or rebate offer. This kind of offer is generally found on big-ticket items like cars or computers and means that the parent company will send you a rebate check once the item has been purchased from the dealer. A couple of years ago, instead of giving money as a rebate the Ford Motor Company gave away the first two years of maintenance as an inducement to buy its cars. Currently car manufacturers are offering tremendous reductions in time-buying interest rates—far, far lower than one can obtain at a bank.

Sweepstakes and Contests.   An area of sales promotion in which you have a chance to be creative in a different way is the development of a Grand Prize structure and the means by which the consumer can win it.

We commonly see ads and commercials saying we can win a fabulous trip to Acupulco or Rome or wherever by entering a big sweepstakes. A sweepstakes is purely and simply a game of chance, and requires no skill. You win or lose through dumb luck, which is why the sweepstakes may be the most common method of offering a prize.

Since it is a game of chance, a sweepstakes cannot legally require the purchase of a product. What it *can* do is force attention to the product at the point of sale, or force attention to the coupon in an ad or insert. The result, simply by directing more people to either, is generally to increase sales for a period of time surrounding the promotion. For example, Zayre and Lee Jeans sponsored a " 'Star of the Store' Sweepstakes! Win a trip to Hollywood and a Studio Screen Test for your Child!" By giving a *name* to the sweepstakes, by working out the way in which the sweepstakes is played and by doing the advertising for it, you can lend your creativity to the sponsor in a major way.

Sweepstakes Example.   An outstanding example is the sweepstakes called "Fun, Food and Football" run every year by the National Football League. The NFL gets together twenty or so major food advertisers to participate with their own coupon ads in an insert that runs in the Sunday papers in eighty major markets. The grand prize is a trip to *both* the Super Bowl and the Pro Bowl. In addition to a coupon, each ad contains a small picture of a football helmet with team insignia on it. The helmet is the means of playing the sweepstakes.

When consumers received the insert, they phoned William "the Refrigerator" Perry of the Chicago Bears on the 900 number listed in the ad. The phone message they heard from The Fridge told them to look thoroughly at every ad to find the helmet. They they had to come into the store to play the helmet match-and-win game at the point of sale to find out if they won any of the *other* prizes. The result of all this activity was that the consumer was directed to the coupon and to the product display in the store.

These kinds of sweepstakes are intricate and fun to put together, and involve a great deal of creativity on the part of the people who work on them.

A contest is something else. It generally involves *some* skill, even in the contest that asked people to guess the number of coffee beans ground into a can of Sanka. A contest often requires judging, which is an expensive proposition. To celebrate its bicentennial of friendship with the United States, the Dutch government sponsored a contest involving the writing of a fifty-word statement on "I would like to visit the Netherlands because. . . ." Several hundred American couples from various sections of our country won a week's trip to Holland, all expenses paid, portal to portal.

The best sweepstakes and the best contests have something in common. The prize, the product, and the way of entering are mutually reinforcing. Each element is part of a broad, overall theme—like "Fun, Food and Football." Creating such a theme is a big challenge to the sales promotion writer.

Sometimes a promotion will involve the publication of a special information booklet, newsletter, or magazine. This kind of editorial writing assignment can prove challenging and interesting for an advertising writer, and it certainly breaks the pattern of ad-writing assignments.

What Sales Promotion Can and Cannot Do.   Sales promotion can almost never build a brand franchise on a permanent basis because it does not provide for continuity of idea or image.It is simply a temporary method of pushing sales. However, sales promotion is a useful, legitimate tool for the advertiser, particularly when the promotion idea and its communication ties in closely to the long-term idea communicated by brand-building advertising.

As an aspiring copywriter you should know that there is a growing list of agencies that specialize in sales promotion. They have certainly been prospering in recent years, offering starting points for many a good advertising creative person.

CASE HISTORY
L'ORÉAL STUDIO PRODUCTS

Courtesy of L'Oréal and its agency, Communications Diversified of New York.

Promotions call for creative minds, not simply to prepare the advertising but to select the grand prize and the method of winning. Here's an ingenious promotion idea from L'Oréal.

One of L'Oréal's newest and most successful brands is Studio Line, hair styling products that include sprays, gels, creme, and mousse. The line is primarily targeted for young adults (18-24) who think of themselves as fun and contemporary. The brand's packaging design and advertising reflect this positioning with the use of bold graphics and bright colors.

At one point, Studio Line had explored the idea of using a Rock Music concert tour as a promotional platform to enhance and support their positioning and sales efforts. However, the cost of staging an effective concert tour nationally was prohibitive during the brand's introductory phase.

L'Oréal did the next best thing in developing and executing a promotional program that supported the brand's fun, contemporary, trend-setting positioning. They sent the winning consumer on a fabulous rock concert tour! The objectives of the promotional program were to (a) increase sales 10 percent during the promo-

tion period; (b) generate in-store displays and feature ad activity; and (c) enhance and reinforce the brand's image and positioning.

The promotion used cents-off coupons and a music theme: "Studio Rocks." The promotion delivered a gift-with-purchase incentive and the opportunity to win "lifestyle" directed prizes. The promotion encouraged in-store efforts with a pre-pack display shipper that carried both the product and the gift-with-purchase.

Consumers were offered a hit single and a chance to win a fabulous rock tour free with the purchase of a Studio Line product. The free record was available near the display of packages and contained Peter Cetera's hit single, "Queen of the Masquerade Ball" and an audio instant-win message.

The program featuring the pre-pack Floor Stand and Eva-Tone Sound Sheets was backed by full-color magazine advertising (with coupon), by local radio advertising, and by run-of-paper newspaper advertising.

As a result of this effort, key accounts response to the program was higher than forecasted. Pre-pack shippers sold 100 percent of allocation—all of which proves that a particular segment of the market will respond if you're ingenious enough to find the right way to appeal to them.

Rock 'N' Win A Fabulous Concert Tour

Pick up your Free Peter Cetera Hit Single when you buy Studio at special store displays.
Your Single may include the Studio Rocks Instant Winner message sending you packing for a Rock Tour with the Band of your choice. Plus Hundreds of Other Rock 'N' Prizes.

NO PURCHASE NECESSARY

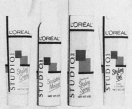

CASE HISTORY

NFL PROPERTIES: "FUN, FOOD & FOOTBALL"

Courtesy of NFL Properties and its agency, Communications Diversified of New York.

In recent years, more and more top-notch advertisers are using promotions along with or instead of long-term brand image advertising. A promotion is a short-term "hypodermic" that generates extra consumer and trade activity for a short period of time in the hope that some of the extra interest will carry over. The National Football League uses promotions for highly specialized reasons.

NFL Properties is the marketing, licensing, and publishing arm of the National Football League. Its charter is to promote and enhance the image of the NFL and generate revenues, through promotional programs, that will offset league operating expenses.

Over the years a number of major national advertisers such as Ford, Cheverolet, Miller Brewing, and Canon Camera consistently found the NFL to be an effective communications vehicle. But NFL Properties had considerable difficulty convincing advertisers that the NFL could be effective in helping sell packaged goods such as luncheon meat, frozen chicken, or cranberry juice. Even though more women watch NFL games than soap operas (women account for 39 percent of NFL TV viewership), most marketers trying to attract a female target audience resisted the notion of tying into the NFL.

The opportunity existed to develop an NFL-themed promotional program for packaged goods marketers that would (a) promote and enhance the image of the NFL via tie-ins with leading nationally advertised brands; (b) increase sales and consumption of sponsoring brands; and (c) generate high levels of awareness, interest, and enthusiasm among participating salesforces and the trade.

The key was to create a logical association between NFL games and food or food-related products. Hence the umbrella theme: "America's Favorites: NFL Fun, Food & Football." Transcending the theme were generous motivating incentives for the consumer, salesforce and trade—all packaged in a sweepstakes keyed to the Super Bowl and Pro Bowl, a complete program and event flexible enough for advertisers/sponsors to tailor for their specific needs.

The promotion shown here revolved around a twenty-four page Freestanding Sunday Coupon Insert on October 5, 1986, with a forty million household circulation in over 150 newspapers. Each of thirty-nine sponsoring advertisers purchased space in this vehicle.

A consumer could win a Super Bowl/Pro Bowl family vacation or one of thousands of other prizes by phoning Wil-

NFL PROPERTIES: "FUN, FOOD & FOOTBALL"

Continued

liam—"The Refrigerator"—Perry. To increase readership of each ad in the insert, the "Fridge" tells consumers to look for the specially marked helmets in each ad for more chances to win. To force store traffic, consumers had another chance to win by taking their insert to the store and matching any specially marked helmet to the NFL Fun, Food & Football display material.

The promotion was supported by four-color ads in *Woman's Day*, by heavy daytime network TV advertising (over fifty spots on popular game shows), and by network radio spots during prime listening hours two weeks prior to the event. There were full-page promotion ads in *Supermarket News*, a Trade Sweepstakes exclusively for buyers, and, of course, custom Point-of-Purchase materials with the winning symbols.

The results were sensational. The percent of product movement for all participating brands was +24 percent. Thirty-five of thirty-eight individual brands had product movement increases; eighteen realized increases of 25 percent or more. Nearly half a million people phoned "The Fridge"; 357,000 submitted second-chance entries; and 6,800 key buyers and store managers entered the trade sweepstakes (up 62 percent from the previous year).

"NFL Fun, Food & Football" has definitely proved itself a winner.

234

15

Other Copywriting

Chapter Topics

Variety of copywriting chores
Point-of-purchase advertising
Forms of point-of-purchase
After-sale advertising
Reinforcing the purchase decision
Yellow Pages advertising
Transit advertising
Fashion advertising

Key Terms

Package inserts
Counter cards
Merchandising pieces
P-O-P
Display space
Tie-in
Related items
Instructional tag
Directories
Directional medium
Posters and movement
Reminder advertising
Captive audience
Fashion is now
Dominant element

Case History

Spuds MacKenzie

When you become an advertising writer you also become something of a jack or jill of all trades. Over the course of your career you may be asked to write a little of everything: magazine and newspaper ads; radio and television commercials; copy for package inserts, counter cards, light-pull tags, instruction sheets, catalog pages, sales meetings, merchandising pieces, annual reports; press releases and presidential speeches. Above all, you will be asked to *name* things—promotions, sales events, new products, new models, new patterns, new colors, and so on. Naming things goes with the territory.

Other kinds of advertising writing in which you may get involved are point-of-purchase advertising, after-sale advertising, Yellow Pages advertising, transit advertising, and fashion advertising.

POINT-OF-PURCHASE ADVERTISING

In this day of widespread self-service, the manufacturer hopes that advertising has already pre-sold customers before they step into the store. But the manufacturer does have one remaining sales opportunity, at the very moment when the customers are in an active buying situation. That sales opportunity is appropriately called point-of-purchase advertising, and it offers many challenges and opportunities for the creative person.

Display space in a retail outlet—floor or shelf space—is almost priceless. There is precious little of it and it is in great demand. The retailer knows its value and is not about to use it on any display idea that does not promise increased sales or increased traffic. Retailers are flooded with display materials from manufacturers—more than they could ever use. To win them over, a point-of-purchase idea has to be very good indeed.

Fortunately, the creative person has a lot to work with because point-of-purchase material comes in many forms: window banners, decals, counter displays, mobiles, shelf talkers, over-wire banners, light pulls, easel cards, merchandising racks, and floor stands, to name a few. Displays can have light and movement; they can talk or make music; they can offer third-dimensional shapes. While most point-of-purchase pieces are composed of cardboard, they can also make use of wood, wire, plastic, glass, or metal in an incredible variety of ways. The suppliers of point-of-purchase printing ingeniously bring to reality the most fanciful idea of the most creative copywriter.

As for that fanciful idea, it must be grounded in common sense. The display must feature the product where it is easy to see and easy to pick up. (Many supermarket purchases are unplanned; an eye-catching display can move a lot of impulse items.) A display that promotes several related items is likely to get used faster than a display for a single product. Whether the display is a repeat of the overall advertising theme or offers instructional material, whether it creates atmosphere or is keyed to a promotion (contest, coupon, or premium), it must glorify the product or the brand. Although the product must be the hero of the display idea, there is little or no restriction on the idea itself.

One of the most striking and effective displays we ever saw was a standing floor display for Black Velvet whiskey. It featured a life-size woman in an evening gown, posed in back of a large box camera, ready to take your picture. Over her head a kleig-type light flashed continuously. If the life-size woman doesn't catch a customer's eye, the flashing light definitely will.

Another outstanding display featured a cardboard Eiffel Tower that soared above everything in the supermarket. Stacked around its base, which was printed in vivid tricolor hues, was a mass of French cheeses.

Recently Mr. Bartles and Mr. Jaymes of wine-cooler fame appeared life size in supermarkets, sitting on their front porch, surrounded by six-packs of their product. No customer could miss them.

From the manufacturer's point of view point-of-purchase writing assignments are important but not too frequent. The copywriter who works directly for a retail operation, however, is likely to do a lot of point-of-purchase advertising. In fact, many large retailers disdain the use of manufacturers' display materials, preferring to do it all themselves. The display can take numerous forms—from a crude sign scribbled with a marking pencil, to a mass stacking of merchandise, to an elaborate concoction of glitter and light and sound and motion.

AFTER-SALE ADVERTISING

A frequently overlooked form of advertising occurs *after* the sale is made. It is short-sighted for the merchant or salesperson to lose interest in the sales transaction as soon as it has ended because psychologists have learned through research that the purchaser is plagued with doubts for a period of time after the sale. And the larger the price tag, the greater the doubt.

The easiest and best way to reinforce the purchase decision is to attach to the item a tag (for clothing), a brochure (for appliances and other smaller mechanical objects), or a booklet (for a big-ticket items, such as automobiles) that tells how the product was made, what its superior qualities are, how to get the most enjoyment or use from it, and (if mechanical) how to operate and maintain it.

This form of advertising is particularly valuable to retail merchants, who can suffer critical depreciation on objects that have been charged and returned because the after-sale opportunity to advertise the product's virtues was overlooked.

In writing advertising for product purchase reinforcement, the nature of the item will dictate format and length. However, all such advertising must *inform* and *reassure*. If it succeeds in these purposes, the chances are high that the product will be used with pleasure, and that repeat purchases will follow.

YELLOW PAGES ADVERTISING*

When total advertising revenue is considered (including business-to-business as well as consumer advertising), the Yellow Pages are now the fourth-largest advertising medium in the country. There are approximately 7,000 directories in the United States, and in 1985 some 98 percent of consumers used the Yellow Pages an average of thirty-six times per year. As the growing population of the United States becomes more mobile each year, the average consumer must rely more often on directory advertising to locate retail sources of specific products in strange towns and cities.

Yellow Pages publishers make a distinction between the functions of the Yellow Pages and those of other media. They position television, radio, magazines, newspapers and other media as *creative* media—those that create (or stimulate) demand for a product or service. They position the Yellow Pages as a *directional* medium—a medium uniquely suited to completing the consumer search process.

Consumers who use the Yellow Pages have *already decided to make a purchase*. They are *actively seeking information*.

Yellow Pages directories are an unobtrusive, inoffensive advertising medium that can help consumers find products and services conveniently and directly. The Yellow Pages are not known for glamor, sophistication, or dazzling graphics. Nor do they lend themselves to heavy use of timely information.

As in all advertising, start a Yellow Pages advertisement with the benefit or solution to a problem, for example, "Foreign Car Specialists . . .," "Stop Roof Leaks." The American Association of Yellow Pages Publishers makes these additional recommendations:

DO

1. Think from the reader's point of view. Does the customer need more than just the telephone number? Hours of operation? Lines carried? Location?

2. Distinguish your business from the competition. Are your years in business important to customers?

3. Make it easy for the reader to find you. A map or a local landmark may help: "One block north of city hall."

---

*(Note: For almost all the Yellow Pages material, we are indebted to Professor Alan D. Fletcher of Louisiana State University and his excellent monograph *Yellow Pages Advertising*.)

4. Keep the ad clean and simple. Use white (yellow) space and avoid clutter that may inhibit readership and understanding.

5. Illustrations attract attention and can add visual excitement.

DON'T

1. Don't use the company name as the heading of the ad unless the name is descriptive.

2. Don't use more than two type faces.

3. Don't use detailed line drawings.

4. Don't use color photographs or poorly-focused pictures.

Because of the Yellow Pages size limitation and the large collection of competitive advertising in one small place, Yellow Pages display ads offer an outstanding chance for advertising writers to develop ads that will stand out from the generally routine copy and design with which they will appear.

Strive to impart an air of integrity, experience, and responsibility to your business ("established in 1938"; "official factory representative"; "local owners"). The Yellow Pages ad you write may be your only chance to convince prospective purchasers that they should visit your store.

TRANSIT ADVERTISING

Transit advertising is essentially a poster form of communication. These posters appear in airport and station terminals, on train platforms, on the backs or sides or insides of buses and street cars, on the end panels of railroad cars, and on the backs, tops, and insides of taxicabs. In short, transit poster advertising in a variety of shapes and sizes can be found on almost any moving vehicle, and in view of people on the move mechanically or on foot. Almost without exception, transit advertising is reminder advertising.

Creatively, most of this advertising is closely related to the outdoor billboard: heavy on graphics, light on words, a strong, involving, story-telling picture, and a few clever words of copy tied directly to the illustration.

Either the vehicle is moving or the people are moving, which leaves no time for subtlety. There is one exception to this general rule.

The interior transit cards on the sides of buses, street cars, subways, and commuter trains are viewed by a captive audience who may be sitting or standing directly in front of your message for a half-hour or longer. Consequently, they can see, read, and absorb fairly long copy. There may be times when you wish to take advantage of this unique situation in transit advertising.

But for the most part you'll want a dominant picture and very few words.

FASHION ADVERTISING

Fashion advertising is a world unto itself—a world of style, a world of flair. Illustrations are smashing; layouts are innovative; copy is lyrical, mystical, and, occasionally, almost incomprehensible.

It is a world peopled by persons in the know communicating to other persons who want to be in the know. Fashion is new. Fashion is now. Fashion is today. You have to know what's up to the moment or you can't write it at all.

We can prepare you for the world of fashion with only one solid bit of advice. Make the picture of the garment the dominant element in your ad. Make your item look irresistible, and let it absolutely monopolize the space. The unfashionable quotation "What you see is what you get" is never more true than in fashion advertising. Keep copy to a minimum. Make it factual, but give it sparkle.

CASE
HISTORY
SPUDS
MacKENZIE

Courtesy of Anheuser-Busch, Inc., and its agency, DDB Needham Worldwide.

Your text tells you to "strive for the unexpected" in advertising. Rarely has there been anything so unexpected in advertising history as the emergence and instant popularity of Spuds MacKenzie. A star overnight!

Spuds MacKenzie started quietly enough in 1985 as a poster aimed at Bud Light's secondary target audience of the "contemporary adult." The audience consists of men, from minimum age to age thirty-four. The young, fun crowd. The original poster design had Spuds in a party hat, wearing a college fraternity sweater (Delta Omega Gamma—D-O-G), in front of a glass filled with Bud Light. It featured the line "Spuds MacKenzie—the Original Party Animal." People flipped over this precocious pooch.

Spuds MacKenzie was first introduced in television commercials in California and Texas, again targeted to the "contemporary adult" market. His popularity boomed, and in late 1986 Spuds MacKenzie went national on prime-time television. In most cases, Spuds is in a party situation, the center of attention, surrounded by adoring young party-goers, or performing as a world-class athlete. Spuds says nothing, but it's obvious he is having a good time, as are all those around him. And that's just the point! Hip, fun-loving people like to share the good times with Spuds and Bud Light. This light-hearted approach has struck a responsive chord with America's beer drinkers in a big way.

Bud Light's mainline "bar call" campaign supplemented by the Spuds MacKenzie campaign, have produced phenomenal results. Bud Light has become the second best selling light beer and fifth best-selling beer nationally. In 1987 Bud Light experienced the highest advertising awareness levels ever for the brand. Bud Light also passed Miller Lite in ad awareness among contemporary adults; in fact, as judged by Video Storyboards, in 1987 Bud Light passed Miller Lite to become the best-liked beer advertising among consumers surveyed.

All of which proves two things: It pays to have people call you by name. Spuds MacKenzie is a beer's best friend.

Spuds MacKenzie, Bud Light's Original Party Animal, knows there's no better way to party than with an ice cold Bud Light. The light beer with the first name in taste. So get up. Get down. Get funky. And party right with Bud Light. **Everything else is just a light.**

SPUDS AND YOUR LOCAL ANHEUSER-BUSCH WHOLESALER THANK YOU FOR MAKING BUD LIGHT NEBRASKA'S #1 LIGHT BEER.

16

The Nutshell Principle:
Key to Success

Chapter Topics

The nutshell principle
Billboard viewing
Demands on creative
   person
Marriage of picture and
   words
Strip away unessentials
Product as signature
Helpful hints
Expanding on poster idea
Good poster ideas adapt

Key Terms

Big and brief
Story-telling situations
Recognizable symbol
Non-subtle
"Teasers"
"Capsule medium"

Case History

Fischer Packing Company

The *nutshell principle* or *poster principle,* which can advance you from being a good copywriter to being a great copywriter, embraces the ability to tell the story in a nutshell. It consists of a selling idea expressed in a strong, dominant visual with a few clever words of copy married to the visual. Although the nutshell or poster principle obviously applies to the medium of outdoor advertising, the billboard, *it can be the key to outstanding advertising in all media.*

Peculiarities of Billboard Viewing.   An outdoor billboard must be read from a moving vehicle traveling at an average speed of 35 m.p.h. The outdoor billboard may be a few hundred feet away from a viewer who has perhaps five seconds to comprehend your message.

Demands on Creative Person.   Because of the billboard's fleeting impact, the visual dominates. Your idea must be big and brief, able to be understood at a quick glance. You will need illustrations and symbols that are instantly meaningful and that involve the viewer emotionally. The best illustrations convey a story-telling situation in which the viewer fills in missing gaps of information. One poster based on the copy line "Dean's Milk Grows Giants" showed just a pair of scuffed-up sneakers from which the feet and ankles projected up through the top of the billboard. It had novelty, simplicity, and humor. Most of all, it had universality. People viewing that poster put themselves into the same situation. They understood instantly.

A poster for a utility company showed a single clothespin to represent washday. Even in this age of automatic washers and driers, the clothespin communicated meaning in a flash. It was an instantly recognizable symbol.

The ideal poster is a perfect marriage of picture and words, with each supporting and explaining the other. The copy line should stem from the illustration; the illustration should expand on the copy line. Example: For the San Diego Zoo the head and neck of a giraffe extended diagonally across the poster with the words: "The world's greatest zoo is in your neck of the woods." Example: For the Fischer Packing Company five hot dogs stuck up from the bottom of the billboard to resemble four fingers and a thumb, with the copy line: "Wieners you can count on." Example: A jar of Mobil #1 synthetic motor oil was shown sitting on top of a snow bank with the words: "Cold remedy."

Eliminate Unessentials.   In creating a poster use as few elements as possible. As a rule, copy should not exceed five to eight words. In the visual, see what you can take out rather than what you can put in. If, for example, your idea has to do with cooking on a camping trip, you do not have to show a whole forest with a lake and mountains in the distance. *Focus in tightly on the key element.* Show your cooking fire up front, large, with the hint of a tent flap and tree behind it. That's enough to get the story across.

Product as Signature. One element of a poster is the product itself, prominently displayed in glorious full color. Thus displayed, perhaps toward a corner of the space, the product or package becomes the signature of the message, eliminating the necessity of including the product name in the copy line. For example, if you show a close-up of a smiling kid with a face full of chocolate and there is a handsome Hershey Bar off to one side, you don't have to say "Hershey Bars are yummy in the tummy." You just say "Yummy in the tummy." That's a corny example but it shows you how to save a couple of those precious few words.

Helpful Hints for Copywriters. Tips for creating successful outdoor poster advertising include:

1. Keep your ideas *simple* and *strong*. They must have impact and be understood instantly. Volkswagen showed a motorcycle cop ticketing a chagrined Beetle driver with the copy line: "They Said It Couldn't Be Done."

2. For longest recall, play to the emotions, to which humor can be closely related. Another Volkswagen poster shows the owner inspecting a flat tire, with the copy line: "Nobody's Perfect." British Airways showed a Concorde supersonic plane in flight, with the copy line: "For those who've already arrived."

3. Avoid indirection or subtlety. People don't have time to consider what your message means. One outdoor poster showed the burner on a gas stove with jets of flame leaping up, and the copy line: "No Waiting." Another billboard showed a big Yellow Pages phone directory with the copy line: "Best Seller."
    The exception to avoiding indirection is teaser advertising, where successive parts of the message appear on successive posters. These serve to build expectant interest in a message that will not become clear until the final poster. The most famous example of this type of advertising was done years ago by Burma Shave. Each successive poster contained a line of a limerick, and only on the final poster did they identify their product.

4. Strive for originality to produce the greatest memorability. One of the most famous posters ever run showed a baby buggy with the copy line: "Only convertible that outsells Ford."

5. If possible, tie your poster to the central advertising or selling theme of your campaign. To a great extent, poster advertising is used as a supporting medium, reinforcing the main selling effort on television, in magazines, or in newspapers.

Posters must contain the story in a nutshell. They look like fun, but they are not all that easy to write. However, if you can develop skill at coming up with sound poster ideas you should automatically be a superior copywriter in all other media, because *a good nutshell idea can almost always be expanded upon.*

Expanding on Poster Idea. One of the great poster ads of all time showed a group of nuns entering a VW van, with a copy line that line was sheer genius: "Mass Transit." It portrayed a benefit in a graphic way. It was clean, simple, memorable. It communicated at a glance.

This poster idea might have been easily adapted to other media. It could have been a solid magazine ad as is. Or it could have provided a dramatic illustration at the top of a magazine or newspaper ad with a moderate amount of body copy following.

A television commercial might open with a long shot of the church steeple, then zoom in close as the chimes struck. The camera cuts to a ground-level archway. Out the door come the nuns, perhaps one by one to dramatize the number of them. The Mother Superior might call out each sister's name as it was her turn to load in the bus.

Would that same idea work for radio? We hear church bells. An announcer tells us where the church is. We hear the nuns shuffling out of the church, intoning some kind of chant. We hear the Mother Superior calling out names as they are to load in the van. Perhaps one sister is late arriving. Will there be room for her? You know it—plenty of room! And so on.

Good Poster Ideas Adapt. A good, solid poster idea—a nutshell idea—often adapts beautifully to other media. In his book, *The Compleat Copywriter,* Hanley Norins of Young & Rubicam refers to outdoor posters as "the capsule medium."[1] If you can compress a strong selling message into a crisp and colorful capsule, you will almost surely be a successful communicator.

John O'Toole, Chair of the Board of the Foote, Cone & Belding agency said that "an effective poster is two things: it is unexpected and it is relevant. *Unexpected* and *relevant.* Those two characteristics of an effective poster, it will be noted by those who have heard me talk about advertising before, are the very same attributes I have always said are the essentials of an advertising idea for any medium.

"*That is why I always advise that creative work begin with a poster, no matter what medium the advertising is to eventually appear in.* If it can be expressed as an unexpected and relevant poster, it probably can be turned into a magazine or newspaper ad. And, yes, into a television or radio commercial."

Harken to those words!

---

1. Hanley Norins, *The Compleat Copywriter* (New York: McGraw-Hill Book Co., 1966), p. 243.

CASE HISTORY
FISCHER PACKING COMPANY

Courtesy of Fischer Packing Company and its agency, Doe-Anderson.

Few marketing challenges are tougher than that of a regional meat packer going up against the big national competitors every day of the week. Fischer Packing Company, serving Kentucky and surrounding states, has successfully battled the biggies based primarily on two factors: (a) quality products and (b) a bold and consistent use of the outdoor medium.

For three generations, Fischer's Mellwood Bacon has been Kentucky's most popular, best-selling, and best-tasting bacon. Fischer and its advertising agency, Doe-Anderson of Louisville, wanted to capitalize on that reputation for quality. In 1965 they decided to position Fischer as "The bacon-makin' people" ®, a folksy, friendly message that held great meaning for their customers. Through planned phases of advertising, that image was transferred across the entire range of Fischer's fine meat products—hams, hot dogs, luncheon meats.

A unique part of the Fischer communication program has been strong and regular use of outdoor advertising. Fischer has not missed a single month on the boards since the campaign was launched in 1965. Outdoor not only offers large, colorful, and appetizing product pictures, but it acts as a reminder just before the point of purchase. Seen consistently, outdoor posters take on the aspect of an old friend to customers and retailers. Because the messages were changed monthly, their happily punny headlines regularly became conversation pieces with the public.

The very first Fischer outdoor board stated simply: "Jack Sprat eats Fischer's Mellwood Bacon." Others have been just as audacious and amusing. A mustardy hot dog on a bun is headlined: "Mustard's last stand." A hot dog on a wiener roast stick says: "Put us out on a limb." Most irreverent of all showed Fischer's luncheon meats in a hero sandwich with a copy line inviting you to: "Feed your multitude with loaves and Fischer's."

Fischer's outdoor boards are perceived not just as ads but as personal messages from a friend. This warm feeling has contributed over time to the effectiveness of every Fischer television commercial, radio spot, or newspaper ad.

The success of the unusual relationship Fischer has established with its customers is supported at the check-out counter and verified through Nielsen Market Share Data and other research. Fischer products are a strong Number One in their marketing area.

247

17

Advertising Copy Research

Chapter Topics

Copy testing
Various research
    techniques
Checklists
Suggestions for testing
Forms of pretesting
Consumer panels
Coupon or inquiry tests
Split-run tests
Market tests
Theater testing
Forms of posttesting
Starch Readership Surveys
Gallup-Robinson
Burke Day-After Recall
Motivation Research

Key Terms

Pretesting
Posttesting
Consumer jury
Paired-comparison
Split run
Recognition test
Recall test

Case History

Home Box Office

Many kinds of research—product research, market research, consumer research—have a direct bearing upon advertising. In chapter 2 we stressed the vital importance of "up front" research and detailed how some of that research was done.

Once we have reached a point where the advertising is finally prepared, we need to evaluate our idea through the use of research. Research that examines the effectiveness of the advertising itself is formally termed "advertising research" but is more familiarly called "copy testing."

Agencies and clients constantly seek ways to determine whether advertising dollars are reaching the right people at the right time with the right message. To assist them, a number of research techniques have been devised over the years. Bearing diverse names, most have claimed to be the ultimate panacea for an industry that deals largely with uncertainties.

THE FIRST ADVERTISING CHECKLIST

Recognizing this basic problem of uncertainties and perceiving the commercial value of a solution, two brothers named Townsend devised a plan in the late 1930s for checking advertising copy against a list of twenty-seven points that they believed represented the basic persuasive elements every ad should contain. Among the twenty-seven check points advocated by the Townsend Method were:

- Identification
- Attention
- Interest
- Proof
- Sincerity
- Five points relating to basic motives: safety, love, comfort, self-actualization, self-indulgence
- Request for action[1]

Although highly controversial ever since its introduction, the Townsend Method was widely used by smaller agencies and by advertisers of all sizes, and it continues to have defenders who use it in some modified form. Detractors of the system have claimed that the use of checklists would inhibit creativity and would tend to make all advertising identical. They have also said that any checklist depends entirely on the personal judgment of the user, and that no two people would ever rate the same advertisement the same way.

---

1. *Advertising Age,* October 11, 1943.

ANOTHER ADVERTISING CHECKLIST

Despite these objections, the beginning copywriter can be aided by making sure that certain elements are included in every ad. A simpler list, stated in more modern terms, might include eight things that every ad should do:

1. Attract attention
2. Create interest
3. Provide information
4. Develop empathy
5. Build credibility
6. Assure memorability
7. Stimulate desire
8. Compel action.

Although most copywriters feel that checklists inhibit creativity, a brief guide can be helpful. For without attention, interest, desire, and action no advertisement can succeed, no matter what the product. And with information, empathy, credibility, and memorability added, the chances for success are raised.

PRETESTING

After advertising copy has been written, management must decide whether to test the advertising before or after it runs, or both. Some agencies and advertisers favor pretesting as a form of insurance that their advertising can be as productive as possible. However, since most pretesting takes place under conditions that can only simulate the real market, there are certain guidelines that should be followed in using pretests and certain basic questions that need to be answered. Among the latter are:

1. What elements of the advertising should be measured?
2. What measurement device should be used?
3. How should the measurement be done?
4. Who should do the measurement?
5. Where should the measurement take place?
6. When should the measurement be made?
7. What safeguards can be taken to assure maximum validity of the testing?

SUGGESTIONS FOR TESTING

If an advertisement is to be measured, the precise elements of measurement should be identified: awareness of the ad (was it seen?); interest in the ad; response to the ad (was it liked?); credibility of the ad (was it believed?); memorability of the ad (was it recalled?); usefulness of the ad (did it inform? was it understood?); motivation of the ad (did it stimulate desire?); and sales results of the ad (did it compel action?).

In selecting pretest devices, thought must be given to the stability of the test, and five things must be considered, in this order:

1. How reliable is the test? Will you get the same results with repeated measures?

2. Does it have high validity? Are you really measuring what you think you're measuring?

3. Can we afford it?

4. Can it be done within our time schedule?

5. Who will do it?

FORMS OF PRETESTING

The following forms of pretesting are in general use by advertisers and their agencies:

1. The consumer panel, or jury

2. The coupon

3. The split-run

4. The test market

5. The simulated market

6. The theater test.

The Consumer Panel

The consumer panel can be composed of members of your family, members of a group to which you belong, or simply people selected at random from your acquaintances, of whom you ask questions to learn their reactions as consumers.

In a more formal state, a panel of consumers or potential consumers is brought together to rate advertisements or elements of advertising. To offer an acceptable degree of validity, panel members must meet these three basic requirements:

1. They must be *typical* of the market that uses the product or service advertised;

2. They must be *interested* in the product (most women would have no interest in men's shaving cream);

3. They must be *potential users* (if you are testing advertising for a set of the world's great books, panel members must be literate and educated).

The panel will be shown two or more ads, and asked to rate them according to which ad most appeals to them or interests them in the product. A variation frequently used for the consumer panel is to ask them to select the one ad of a pair that they like best. This ad is then joined with a second ad, and the selection process is repeated. In such a *paired-comparison,* the best ad of the group tested is ultimately selected through the process of elimination. This technique is often used for gaining insight into probable consumer responses to advertising themes. It is also used to learn which of several creative approaches—headlines, copy blocks, logotypes, etc.—evoke the most favorable consumer response.

Advantages of the consumer panel can be listed as follows:

1. They work. Correlation has frequently been high between consumer panel ratings and sales of products advertised.

2. Cost is low. When a panel has been convened, a number of ads or elements of ads can be rated at one session.

3. They require little time.

4. If the panel has been carefully chosen from representative members of the market, it will reflect the viewpoint of the consumer. To be sure that this is so, care must be taken to select panelists whose age, education, vocation, income, and residence is similar to that of your core (or target) market.

All copy tests have their drawbacks. Those of the consumer panel method are eight-fold:

1. Panel composition does not always match the market closely enough.

2. The size of the panel may be inadequate to yield statistically significant findings. Two hundred has been suggested as a minimum number from which to derive valid judgments.

3. The attempt to measure separate elements is not always a true reflection of actual consumer response, as people looking at print copy respond to an overall effect, rather than to an ad in fragments.

4. Interest in an ad may not necessarily reflect a purchase decision response.

5. Too frequent use of panel members dulls their response stimuli, and can adversely affect the validity of their judgments.

6. Purchase pattern of product may be unrelated to consumer needs of the panel members. For example, panel members may record

opinions about kitchen appliances, but those with comparatively new ones in their homes will be out of the market for years to come.

7. Opinions of panelists cannot always be accepted at face value, as they may not be willing to admit in a group situation that they are "turned on" by a sexy ad, or "turned off" by classical music, or vice versa!

8. The cumulative effect of advertising campaigns is not reflected in panel responses to single ads, or to various elements of the advertising.

Coupon Testing

Coupon or inquiry testing is easy to do, and incurs no extra cost. You simply design an ad to include a coupon, or make an offer somewhere in the copy that invites an inquiry or purchase. If your company is a processor or packer of foods, for example, you might offer a free cookbook that features recipes using your product.

The response to the coupon or the offer can be easily tabulated and analyzed to yield an immediate measurement of the number of people who have seen and read your test ad, or who have been motivated to make a purchase.

If you wish to validate your judgment that one version of the ad you have written is the most compelling of several, inquiry testing can be done simultaneously with two or more versions of copy appearing in different publications. A variation of this can be to run the same ad at different dates in the same publication.

Split-Run Testing

The split-run test is the running of two or more variations of the same ad in the same position in the same issue of one publication. For example, you may have written three headlines that seem to have predictable sales motivating power. Your gut feeling is that one is better than the other two, but your copy supervisor and the advertising manager of the client company (or your boss and the president of the company store) each likes one of the others. A split-run of an ad with a coupon or an offer hidden in the copy of each will tell you whether one headline is, in fact, more compelling than the others, whether all are equally successful in bringing about the readership of the ad, or whether none has significant appeal.

Split-runs can be used to test any creative element of your ads or to determine whether the cost of one extra color or full color is justified by the returns. However, no research technique has yet been devised with no drawbacks for the advertisers, and split-run testing has been criticized as giving an unrealistic evaluation of potential sales in the marketplace. It also has been said that split-run tests provide little insight about the reader, and no information about those who do not respond at all.

Without denying these obvious limitations, it is clear that a split-run offers three advantages:

1. It gives a reasonable reflection of what will happen when the ad runs, that is, it will be seen under natural and realistic reading conditions, with no built-in variables stemming from the comparative skills of interviewers.

2. It will provide a definitive insight concerning responses relative to place of residence if used in publications with national or multiple regional distribution. This makes it possible to zero in on various market segments with appeals predetermined to work.

3. As split-runs are done with ads that actually run (as opposed to those that are only mocked up), the cost of the advertising is not purely a research expense, but has as much chance to produce business as any advertising effort.

Sales Market Testing

Sales market testing is used most often in connection with new products. By running a trial campaign in only one market, it is possible to learn in advance what sales results are likely to be. In using this form of test, advertisers must promote in cities or areas having no known bias toward the product, pro or con, and that are representative of the market about which information is sought. Like split-run testing, market tests also can be used to premeasure the pulling power of various copy approaches or media. They can be particularly effective when used for consumer products with a frequent purchase pattern (convenience goods) that is quickly responsive to advertising appeals.

Simulated Market Testing

The simulated market test is based on the premise that people respond differently in a store than they do in the abstract, and that their buying actions can be predicted accurately only when placed in an actual purchase situation. To make this form of testing possible, respondents are selected who are representative of the product market for convenience goods sold by the advertiser. They then are bused to a store where the product to be tested is sold. There each member of the test group is given an equal sum of money. (For highest validity, the amount received should be several times the cost of the product.) Instructions are given to the group to buy any brand of the product that is being tested by the undisclosed advertiser—regardless of their current need for the product.

After purchases have been made, the panel of shoppers is returned to the research headquarters where their product selections are tabulated. They fill out a questionnaire designed to uncover the reasons for their purchase decisions.

The advantage of this kind of test is that it relatively accurately measures purchase action at the point of sale where the stimuli for decisions are not artificial. The disadvantage is the cost of selecting a panel of test shoppers, bringing them to and from research headquarters, and providing them with the money to make their purchases. To be of value as a copy testing device, this test can be conducted before and after a regional or metropolitan campaign with different test groups. This will reveal the degree of impact the advertising has on actual sales.

Theater Testing

In the theater test, respondents predetermined to be representative of the product market are assembled in a theater to view a first-run movie or pilot TV program. First, however, respondents are given a questionnaire on which to note numerical choices of brands in the advertiser's product field as well as in other product fields. Once completed, the questionnaires are collected and the group is shown the movie in which commercials are interspersed to simulate home viewing. At the end, questionnaires are again distributed, and brand choices recorded a second time. In theory, any difference between the first and second questionnaire will represent the impact of the commercial. Some theater tests register respondent reactions, second-by-second, to each segment of the test commercial.

The advantage of this test is the comparatively low cost. The disadvantages are these:

1. The testing situation is an artificial one in which respondents are forced to make judgments that may not accurately reflect their true feelings.

2. The ratings of television advertising by viewers may have little relationship to actual purchase decisions.

3. The group situation of the audience can affect the validity of the response.

FORMS OF POSTTESTING

Starch Readership

Posttesting of advertising copy is done by many companies that invest large sums in advertising. Among the best known, oldest, and most widely used posttesting service is the Starch Readership Study, first offered by Dr. Daniel Starch in 1932. The premise of the Starch Advertising Research Service is that effectiveness of print advertising can be determined by measuring recognition of the advertising among its target audience and correlating that measurement with the intensity to which the target audience was exposed to the advertising. The Starch Advertising Readership Service is available to any advertiser who runs a schedule of ads one-half page or larger in the magazines studied by this organization.

In the Starch service, interviewers gather information from a sample of readers in twenty to thirty geographic areas that parallel the circulation of the magazines studied. All respondents must be at least eighteen years of age and must match the predetermined demography of the readers of the magazine being researched. Each sample must contain between one hundred and two hundred interviews with qualifying members of each sex.

Starch interviews take place after the magazine under study has been on sale long enough for readers to have seen it. With monthly magazines, interviewing begins two weeks after the initial sale date and lasts for three weeks. With weekly and biweekly magazines, interviewing begins three days after the initial sale date and lasts for seven days.

In the interview, respondents are first asked if they have the magazine being studied, and have read any part of it. If the response is affirmative, respondents are then questioned about each advertisement being studied in the magazine, page by page. With this technique, Starch is able to provide subscribers with three measurements:

1. The percent of respondents who have seen and *noted* any part of the ad under study;

2. The percent of respondents who have read any part of the ad and *associated* it with the product or service of the advertiser;

3. The percent of respondents who have *read most* (half or more) of the ad copy.

By careful analysis of the Starch figures, an advertiser can measure the impact of an ad, and can tell whether it is attracting attention, creating interest, and sustaining readership. In addition, Starch data can be useful in these comparisons:

1. One ad in a campaign against another;

2. One campaign against another;

3. The advertiser's ad against those of other advertisers in a specific product group whose ads are being measured by Starch.

In addition to the readership measurement technique used by Starch, the *recall method* is used to determine the effectiveness of print ads. There are two forms of the recall system: *aided* and *unaided* (sometimes called "pure"). In the unaided form, respondents are shown the magazine under study and asked what ads they remember seeing in it. In the aided form, respondents are given helpful clues, such as being shown advertisements in the magazine in which company names and logotypes have been obscured. They then are asked to tell what brand is being advertised in the ad.

Gallup & Robinson Readership

One of the leaders in the field of recall measurement is Gallup & Robinson Advertising Research, Inc. Founded by Drs. George Gallup (of the Gallup Poll) and Claude Robinson (who founded Opinion Research Corporation), this organization uses a combination of aided and unaided recall to measure the impact of the magazine advertising of blue chip clients. In the Gallup service, a staff of trained interviewers in various parts of the country call at the homes of people who represent the readership of the magazine in which the advertising appears. The Gallup technique follows this chronological order:

1. Respondents are qualified (or disqualified) by being asked to name at least one editorial feature of the issue of the magazine under study.

2. If qualified, the respondents are given cards on which appear the names of advertisers in that issue, as well as nonadvertisers. Respondents are then asked to recall any ads of these advertisers in the magazine. If they say they remember any, they must prove it by describing the ad adequately.

3. Next, respondents are asked what sales message the ad contained, and whether they were impressed with it.

4. If the respondents are still qualified by the answers given, the interviewer verifies the recall by opening the magazine to the ads the respondents recalled. The respondents are then asked if they have ever seen these ads in other magazines.

5. Respondents who pass through the first four questions successfully are then asked about age, education, occupation, income group, etc. This provides background controls for all respondents used.

In the Gallup method, the most important insight available to corporate clients is the playback of the advertiser's message in the comments of respondents. From this knowledge, it can be learned how to rework the copy for maximum impact on the reader. Because the "recall" rather than "recognition" method of testing is used by Gallup & Robinson, their scores usually run lower than Starch scores. However, both firms render a valuable service to advertisers and their agencies.

Television Testing

Since the cost of television advertising entails a greater investment on the part of the advertiser than do the other media, it is considered critical to obtain as much insight as possible into the effectiveness of commercials on the viewing audience.

The ideal research of television, as well as radio, would provide pretesting measurement of commercials. Since television began, there have been a number of attempts to provide pretesting insights, none of them outstandingly successful.

Prominent among the posttesting techniques of broadcast advertising is the measure of recall and perception. In this service, the methods are similar to those used for print advertisements.

Conducted by house-to-house interview or by telephone on the day following the commercial broadcast, the interviewer first qualifies the viewer as having seen or heard the broadcast. If this test is met, questions then are asked about the product and brand advertised, the advertising theme, the impact of the message, and anything else in which the advertiser has an interest.

Burke Day-After Recall

An example of posttesting is Burke Marketing Research, Inc.'s Standard Day-After-Recall for the testing of television commercials on the air. The objective of the Burke technique is to measure the immediate and essential characteristic of a television commercial, that is, its ability to communicate an advertising message and to be remembered. The Burke method involves telephone interviews on the day following the test telecast. These interviews are conducted in three or four cities selected from more than thirty cities located in six defined geographic areas of the country. The Burke sample takes 200 viewers of the test program who were actually in the room with the TV set, and who were not asleep or changing channels at the time of exposure to the test commercial. It can include homeowners, working men or women, or teenagers, depending on the market of interest to the advertiser. To those who use its service, the Burke organization furnishes a report that provides a quantitative measure of communications effectiveness (how many saw and heard the commercial), a summary of all that was remembered about the commercial (the recall of key advertising messages), and a verbatim transcript of all ideas recalled from the commercial (playback). An advantage of the Burke service is the relatively modest cost. A possible disadvantage is the level of validity of the information gathered by telephone.

In the advertising industry's never-ending search for insight that would help create advertisements that would have the most favorable effect on sales, many devices have been offered by researchers and explored by advertisers. Among them was the "Pupilometer" test, which claimed that deep-seated responses to advertising messages could be determined by measuring with a camera the size of the pupils in the eyes of readers as they looked at the advertising. If the pupil expanded, the reader was said to be aroused by the ad. If it contracted, the ad did not hold the reader's interest.

It would seem, from the nature of this research technique, that advertisers are willing, even eager, to spend money on any device for which reasonable claims for validity can be offered. If this is true, the heavy investment in advertising made by American business more than justifies a serious and continuing effort to develop better techniques for measuring the effectiveness of commercial messages broadcast by both electronic media.

MOTIVATION RESEARCH

In the measurement of deep response, no summary of advertising research bearing on copy testing would be complete without the mention of motivation research. This technique, spearheaded by famed psychologist Dr. Ernest Dichter, burst on the advertising world like a comet in the 1930s, shone like a star through the 1940s and '50s, and began to wane in the 1960s.

Still used by some advertisers but no longer favored by most, motivation research is concerned with buying behavior. It attempts to explain why people act as they do and to define ways in which they can be induced to change attitudes and modify actions. Based on the premise that people cannot always understand their behavior and responses without professional assistance, motivation research techniques include depth interviewing by psychologists and the administration of projective psychological tests. These are designed to induce subjects to project their true feelings, through interpretation of pictures, completion of sentences, or in other ways related to psychological devices.

Efforts to gain insights through advertising research are not always successful. However, there is enough evidence in the files of agencies and advertisers to suggest that, although a marriage of research and creativity sometimes may seem to be the union of an odd couple, it can often lead to a longer and more successful relationship between agency and client, and between client and customer.

CASE HISTORY
HOME BOX OFFICE

Courtesy of Home Box Office and its agency, Kobs & Draft Advertising, Inc.

Here's the story of a four-way copy test by direct mail that is a good example of how the creative strategy can be tested and measured.

In an increasingly competitive—and always shifting—cable TV marketplace, Home Box Office is always looking for the most effective direct mail strategies. Over years of testing, HBO had found the most effective executions to be hard-sell, offer-driven packages with brown "Kraft paper" outer envelopes, similar to the paper used in grocery store shopping bags. However, HBO also wanted to produce direct mail advertising that was flashier and projected more of an image of exciting entertainment.

The goal of this particular Spring 1987 four-way test was to create colorful, high-impact packages that still performed cost-effectively in the marketplace. At the same time, a new hard-sell package titled "Kraft II" was also developed to determine if the control could be beaten on its own terms.

The control panel was an offer-driven brown Kraft "NCR" package, so named because the reply device used an NCR-style carbon form.

The first test package was another offer-driven package, "Kraft II," which featured a hard sell of the eighty-seven-cent installation offer on the outer envelope. Inside, every element of the package (letter, brochure, reply card) was built around the eighty-seven-cent offer.

The second test package was a 6" × 9" "Innovation" package presenting HBO as the premier supplier of original and innovative home entertainment. Whereas in the past the positioning of HBO's product had always been "blockbuster Hollywood movies . . . and more," this package positioned HBO as offering "innovative original programming . . . plus the great movies you've come to expect from us." HBO wanted to find out if original programming could provide as strong a hook to the consumer as Hollywood movies did. The assumption was that in this time of VCRs, with consumers being able to rent movies before they come to HBO, the attraction of blockbuster movies might have lost its luster.

The third test package was the 9" × 12" "Image" package. The purpose of this package was to position HBO as "hot and exciting." As in previous efforts, blockbuster movies were given more importance than HBO's original productions. The use of dramatic full-page product shots and relatively short copy combined to position HBO as high-impact, exciting entertainment.

In both the "Innovation" and "Image" packages the

261

eighty-seven-cent offer was strongly emphasized, but it was not necessarily the predominant message of every piece in the package, as it was in the control cell and in the "Kraft II" test package.

The big 9" × 12" "Image" package pulled the highest gross response, but the significantly higher cost for producing the package made it less cost-effective on a cost-per-subscriber basis.

The winner on a cost-per-subscriber basis was "Kraft II," a package that, like the control, was hard-sell and offer-driven, thus verifying the creative strategy that HBO had been following for two years.

The fact that the 6" × 9" "Innovation" package did not pull well, even in gross response, indicates that people still sign up for HBO because of blockbuster Hollywood movies (even though research shows that once they have HBO, they tend to *stay on* as subscribers because of the original, innovative programming on HBO).

RESULTS:

	% Responses	Cost per Subscriber Index
"NCR" Control	1.81%	100
Kraft II	1.93%	91
Innovation	1.30%	164
Image	2.25%	221

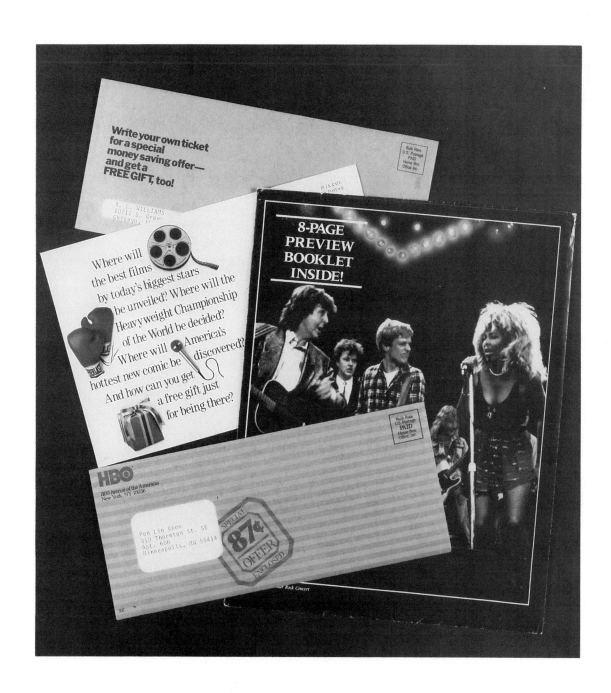

18

Advertising to Foreign Markets

Chapter Topics

Expanding markets
Past mistakes
Bilingual personnel
Purchase of foreign
    agencies
America's own "foreign"
    market
Size of Hispanic market

Key Terms

Get the name right
Bicultural
Hispanic market
"Nationals"

For many years, major U.S. corporations have enjoyed a large and expanding overseas market, with some foreign division or subsidiaries becoming key profit centers. Despite this happy circumstance, some business firms have, in the past, made important mistakes in the naming of products distributed in foreign markets. An example that comes to mind from a number of years ago is a sanitary napkin deodorant called Quest, which was marketed in Latin America by International Cellu-cotton Products Company, then the marketing arm of Kimberly-Clark Corporation for Kotex, Kleenex, and Delsey. Despite successful initial distribution in all key markets, the product failed with the Latin consumer because of its name, which is pronounced much like "que est," or "what is it?" As Quest was a new product in Latin America, potential customers said to themselves, "If they don't know what it is, why should I buy it?"

Advertising agencies have also been faulted in the past for running advertising in foreign markets that was prepared in the United States and that evoked adverse response from nationals of the country in which the ads appeared. As recently as fifteen years ago, one of the authors asked a class of thirty-eight advertising students at the University of Puerto Rico to bring to class examples of print advertising that they considered highly effective or ineffective. As an example of bad advertising three students pointed to a full-page newspaper ad for the New York Life Insurance Company, which showed a diverse group of professional men in the clothing they wore to work. The ad intended to signify that New York Life Insurance was for men in all professions and to upgrade the image of the life insurance salesman to a professional level. However, as the students pointed out, the models shown in the photo, which occupied two-thirds of the page, were ludicrous depictions in the Puerto Rican market, as all of the men shown wore heavy-soled, northern type shoes, two of them wore dark felt hats (never seen on men in Puerto Rico), and four of them looked like members of other ethnic groups. When the ad was called to the attention of the manager of the local office of one of the three largest U.S. agencies, he defended it on the ground that it had been designed in the New York office.

Today, such product naming and advertising design mistakes occur with much less frequency, as most manufacturers and their agencies do market testing in depth before committing a product to a foreign market. In the unlikely event that the advertising happens to be prepared in a U.S. creative department, the work is done by bilingual and bicultural personnel before it is submitted for critique to the branch office in the country where it is scheduled to appear. Beyond this, today many of the agencies that have expanded to foreign shores have done so by purchasing an existing foreign agency and integrating it into the corporate family. As a result, the advertising needs of foreign markets continue to be well met by natives who are thoroughly familiar with every nuance of language and culture of the country. Because of this intelligent approach to the dissemination of advertising messages in foreign lands, American-owned advertising agencies have become important leaders in foreign advertising communities and their clients have been served with significant success.

Although advertising in foreign markets once meant markets in foreign countries, the American Spanish-speaking market has burgeoned to an estimated $120 billion in 1987, with the top five U.S. Hispanic markets being Los Angeles with 3.6 million Hispanics, New York with 2.5 million, Miami with 936,200, San Antonio with 889,300, and San Francisco with 786,900. With the growing affluence of the 18 million Hispanics in the United States, American companies are budgeting hundreds of millions of advertising dollars each year to reach this segment of the buying public. In 1987, these budgets increased nearly 20 percent over the preceding year, with such major U.S. corporations as Procter & Gamble, Kraft Foods, McDonald's, Philip Morris, Johnson & Johnson, Miller Brewing, and others in the vanguard.

To reach this ever-growing Spanish-speaking market, advertisers are using the 600 full-time Spanish-language TV and radio stations as well as the hundreds of newspapers printed in Spanish, thousands of outdoor posters, and hundreds of thousands of transit posters. As a result of this increased activity in the Hispanic market, many of the major U.S. advertising agencies have added specialized Hispanic divisions. Other agencies are farming out their Spanish-language advertising to specialty shops, which handle market research, advertising concepts, creative execution, media selection, and placement.

Although we have emphasized the Hispanic market in the United States, active markets exist for North American manufacturers and service companies in Europe, Latin America, Asia, and Africa; and a number of the leading advertising agencies have branch offices or affiliations with local agencies in the principal cities on other continents. Even though these offices in foreign countries usually are staffed with national employees, the possibility always exists for overseas service for those advertising people who aspire to work and live abroad. Thus, the student who seeks a career in advertising or marketing will be advantaged by accepting every opportunity to learn a second language and to travel in the country of choice, for a time can be foreseen when those with language skills and supporting cultural insights will enjoy a distinct advantage in the market place over their peers.

對國際性投資事務丁無往不利

(No one translates international investments like The Travelers.)

Introducing The Travelers International Index Fund.

The Travelers understands the language of international investing like no one else.

Our International Index Fund brings to plan sponsors, for the first time, a way to truly capture the opportunities of international investing. That's because The Travelers International Index Fund tracks the *FT-Actuaries Europe—Pacific Basin Index,*™ the new standard measure of performance for international equity markets.

A recognized leader in international investing, The Travelers has a record of successful index tracking, professional investment management and competitive fees. Key reasons why we manage over $22 billion in retirement assets.

To learn more, contact Tom Willison, Vice President, at 203-277-2150. Or, write to him at The Travelers, Asset Management & Pension Services, One Tower Square, Hartford, CT 06183.

The**Travelers**

The Travelers Insurance Company and its Affiliates, Hartford, CT 06183.

19

Advertising Writers: Where They Work and What They Do

Chapter Topics

Five obvious businesses for copywriters
Writing for an agency
Writing for a retailer
Writing for the media
Writing as a free-lancer
Writing for direct marketing
Writing for a manufacturer
Other option: public relations
Public relations assignments
Public relations as a career

Key Terms

Clients
Full-service agencies
Creative directors
Day-to-day deadlines
Writer-producer
On-the-spot alterations
Catalog copy
Instructional literature
Publicity
Annual reports
Internal publication or house organ

Precisely what a copywriter does depends on where the copywriter works. Specific duties are keyed to the particular job situation.

WHERE DO ADVERTISING WRITERS WORK?

There is demand for skilled and ingenious advertising writers in five types of business organizations:

1. Advertising agencies
2. Retail stores
3. Direct marketing companies
4. Manufacturing firms
5. Media.

In the nonproduct, nonprofit sector of human activity, advertising writers may be employed regularly by such diverse organizations as universities, churches, foundations, government agencies, charitable institutions, political parties, labor unions, and trade associations. Many copywriters also have found rewarding careers with corporate public relations departments, the public relations groups within advertising agencies, or public relations firms.

Writing for Advertising Agencies

An advertising agency is a private business peopled by highly skilled advertising specialists. The agency hires out its services—primarily on a commission basis—to many industrial firms with goods or services to be sold. While agencies work anonymously and tend to be small in comparison to the clients they serve, a number of agencies have earned broad recognition. Among the most famous are J. Walter Thompson Company, N.W. Ayer ABH International, DDB Needham Worldwide, Batten, Barton, Durstine & Osborn, Inc., Young & Rubicam, Foote, Cone & Belding, and Leo Burnett Company. These advertising giants are full-service agencies, offering clients all the essential advertising functions of art, copy, account management, media buying, research, and production.

Some of the United States' leading corporations, such as General Motors and General Foods, employ the services of several different advertising agencies to promote their various products and brands. A number of major companies such as Quaker Oats have established in-house advertising agencies as part of their own marketing structure.

Duties of an Advertising Agency Writer

Most agency copywriters prepare consumer copy addressed to the buying public at large for various media such as magazines, newspapers, television, radio, or outdoor posters. Some writers specialize in industrial or technical writing. Some specialize in direct marketing copy, while others write only direct mail pieces. The average agency copywriter, in addition to writing advertisements for all media, may be called on to write everything from a product instruction tag, to the script for a sales meeting, to a speech for the president of a client company. Thus, agency copywriting offers a highly varied menu. The work of advertising agency copywriters is supervised and approved by creative directors in large agencies and by the agency principal in small agencies. Despite careful review of all advertising writing, personnel of the client company always sit in judgement on agency copy, checking to see that it meets these criteria:

1. It contains all the facts necessary to inform prospects about the company's product, service, or philosophy.

2. The facts are accurate and legally defensible against government scrutiny.

3. The facts are presented in a way that the client believes to be persuasive and in a manner distinctive from the advertising of competitors.

4. The writing of the particular advertisement is appropriately related to the overall theme of the advertising effort.

5. The copy (and theme) is well suited to the image of the client that now exists, or that the client wishes to present to the public.

Writing for a Retail Advertiser

Advertising and advertising writers are vital to all the country's retail operations. This is true not only of such outstanding merchants as R.H. Macy in New York, but of the much smaller corner store. All use advertising writers to some degree, and some retailers employ dozens of writers. There is more retail advertising done in the United States than any other kind of advertising. Every day of the week, the copywriter who works directly for and in the retail organization performs what has been called the primary function of advertising in our society: spreading the news in the marketplace. The copy prepared by the retail writer sells merchandise via local newspaper, radio and television stations, and direct mail. In addition, the copywriter must occasionally be able to develop a promotional campaign built around a store-wide theme and to write publicity releases for it. The day-to-day deadlines of retail advertising tax the creative ingenuity and the stamina of even the ablest writer. Retail copywriting is not only an exacting and exciting art in itself, but the discipline it enforces is excellent preparation for writers who later work for agencies.

Writing Retail Copy for the Media

Most students of advertising writing are likely to end up writing retail copy—not working for the retailer directly, but working for the media that the retailer hires. The local newspaper, radio station, and television station serve many retailers in their localities who know little or nothing about writing advertising and who are not large enough to hire an agency. Working for a newspaper, you will be part salesperson for the paper, part creative director for the retailer. You call regularly on the retailer to get information about what is to be featured in the advertising. As you become better acquainted with the retail business situation, you can originate fresh ideas and directions—and sell them to the retailer. You can give leadership to the retail advertising and become a "take charge" creative person making a genuine contribution.

If you work for a local radio or television station, you will perform much the same function for many retailers. You will call on the retailer for merchandise information, then come up with an engaging idea, write the commercial script, and get it okayed. As you learn more about production you will be given more responsibility in the studio. Advertising writers at television stations are very likely to be writer-producers, responsible for originating the commercial idea *and* seeing that it gets on the air.

Writing Retail Copy as a Free-lancer

You can also service local retail accounts on a free-lance basis. Then, indeed, you must wear many hats. You solicit the business in the first place, win it, then continue to keep the client pleased with your work. You dig out the background information, analyze the situation, apply creative strategy, and come up with an advertising idea. You present and sell the idea and select the media that will carry it. Then you have to see that the advertising is produced properly and delivered to the media promptly. There is lots of work and worry for the free-lancer, but it amounts to a solid contribution in support of the retail clients.

Writing Retail Copy for a Small Agency

If you work for a small agency handling several retail accounts, you'll soon learn that a copywriter is not *just* a copywriter. A copywriter is a member of a creative team, all pulling together, each crossing strict job boundary lines to contribute to the success of the whole venture. The copywriter may look up media figures, cut mats for layouts, interview customers, call on dealers. Like every member of a small agency, the copywriter wears many hats and must have several strong qualities. First among them, of course, is a vivid imagination and a good command of words. There is constant demand for fresh ideas, and the writer must be able to generate them quickly for hundreds of different situations. Then the copywriter has to execute those ideas in interesting, clear, and persuasive language. In addition to these communications skills, the copywriter must work well with other people—not only getting along with them, but getting the best out of them. Finally, the writer in a small agency must have the ability to adapt to fast-changing circumstances. In emergencies, the copywriter must be able to make quick decisions and on-the-spot alterations.

Writing for a Direct Marketing Company

Direct marketing selling has long been an American institution, producing such mercantile giants as Sears, Montgomery Ward, Aldens, and Spiegels, all famous for their mail-order catalogs. Today a new generation of shoppers orders from catalogs by phone and in person as well as by mail. These large direct-response firms—the so-called mail-order houses—hire scores of copywriters, most of whom are kept busy preparing catalogs and fliers, issued periodically throughout the year. These writers quickly learn the value of each word, for they see their copywriting efforts measured overnight by the orders placed for merchandise advertised.

Writing for a Manufacturer

Most manufacturing corporations of any size maintain their own advertising departments and employ copywriters. In some companies, the advertising department may consist of only a few people; in others, it can be a staff of dozens. Even though the company may use an advertising agency to prepare its national advertising, there is still plenty of writing work to be done. The company advertising department may prepare copy for special dealer newspaper advertisements, catalog pages, merchandising brochures, instructional literature, display pieces, and sales training booklets. The department may even edit the company publication and contribute designs and copy for the company's annual report.

Some companies that manufacture highly engineered machinery and equipment believe their advertising can be best done by those with professional training in the technology involved. Accordingly, the job of writing industrial advertising is sometimes assigned to people trained in various engineering disciplines.

This brief survey provides a picture of where most advertising writers work and what sort of things they do on their jobs. But a good advertising writer doesn't always have to work in advertising. There is at least one other obvious option.

THE PUBLIC RELATIONS FIELD

It is an easy and natural transition for an advertising writer to shift into public relations work. And vice versa, of course. There has long been a considerable amount of crossover between people in advertising careers and people in public relations careers. Because of this, we are including in this advertising text the following background material on training for public relations, and the preparation of various public relations items.

TRAINING FOR PUBLIC RELATIONS WRITING

Until recently, public relations personnel were drawn from the newspaper profession, principally because of the familiarity of newspaper professionals with the writing style and form preferred by news editors. These newswriters had also learned the responses and habits of editors, and had personal acquaintance with many of their number. Since most public relations material is submitted to editors in the form of news releases—from which they select those few items that appeal to them and that they believe will interest their readers—the logic of this reasoning is inescapable.

With the advent of broadcast media, the custom of choosing public relations writers from the fourth estate began to change. Since news editors were no longer predominantly newspaper personnel, it was not necessary for a public relations writer to have the entrée of a newspaper past. At the same time, academic majors and degree programs in advertising and public relations developed at leading schools of journalism and communication.

The result has been new generations of public relations writers, men and women highly trained in the various arts of influencing the public and intent on pursuing specialized careers in the broad area of public communication.

For women particularly, this situation has marked an important employment breakthrough. The ratio today of women to men who are engaged in public relations work is drawing close to one-to-one. In fact, in most corporate public relations offices the number of women is now greater than the number of men. Many women are being given responsibility for the management of public relations departments.

PUBLIC RELATIONS WRITING ASSIGNMENTS

If you should become a writer of public relations material, you will probably be given a wide variety of assignments. Among them might be the following:

1. News releases
2. Publicity stories
3. Articles
4. Books
5. Annual reports
6. Speeches
7. Position papers
8. Print advertisements
9. Letters to stockholders and customers
10. Brochures
11. Internal publications
12. Miscellaneous tasks.

The News Release

Of these possible assignments, the one on which you will spend much of your time is the news release. At one time, all newspapers had staffs of reporters whose job it was to get out and dig up the news. Although reporters for newspapers as well as television stations still bring in most of the feature stories used, the majority of news printed and broadcast today comes over the various wire services and in the mails in the form of news releases.

These news releases are routed to editors whose job it is to determine what is newsworthy enough to be disseminated in print. Highly objective in most cases, these editors have a basic interest in only one thing: does the item have broad interest for their readers or viewers? Since there is only so much air time in each day and a relative limit on the number of newspaper pages to be printed daily (or weekly), editors must make choices among news items. For understandable reasons, they select for reading only those items that are most succinct and that appear to contain all necessary facts.

For this reason, every writer of news releases must adhere to certain rules of the trade if the copy is to be considered seriously for use in print or broadcast. If it does appear, the writer has succeeded in the job; if it does not, the writer has failed. And although there may be other reasons why the release was not selected, the suspicion is always present that the fault lay in the writing.

To assure the highest possible level of success with releases, a writer should be sure that each one contains these specific points:[1]

1. *Who* was involved?
2. *What* happened?
3. *Where* did it take place?
4. *When* did it occur?
5. *Why* did it happen?
6. *How* did it occur?

The example given by Cutlip and Center is this: (Who?) John Jones (What?) died (Where?) in his home at 10 Main Street (When?) at six o'clock Wednesday evening (Why?) of a heart attack. (How?) He had complained of difficulty in breathing, and was dead when the physician arrived.

In addition to the above points, every news release should conform to these rules:

1. The headline should be in capital letters.
2. The first paragraph should begin at the vertical center of the page.
3. Paragraphs should be indented five spaces.
4. Each page of the release should be numbered, and the release should be double spaced, with wide margins. This will enable editors to make corrections easily or to note additions or comments should a decision be made to use the release as the basis for a story.
5. Pica (large) type should be used.
6. The release should be dated.
7. The release should be as short as possible to do justice to the facts.
8. Sentences should be as short as possible and multi-syllabled words should be avoided unless necessary for adequate description.
9. At the bottom of the release there should be typed the name, address, and phone number of the person to be contacted for further information about the story.
10. The release should be mailed as soon as possible after the news item it recounts has occurred.
11. Where appropriate, the release should be sent to the editor concerned with the category of news into which the release falls. For

---

1. Cutlip, Scott M. and Center, Allen H. *Effective Public Relations* (Englewood Cliffs, N. J. , Prentice-Hall, Inc., 1971), pp. 419-20.

example, a release covering a sports item should be sent to the sports editor.

12.   Wherever possible, the release should be sent to an editor by name.

The Writing of Publicity

Publicity is a specialized area of public relations, in which the basic aim is to make some person or product well known to the general public.

The most notable examples of successful (if not always accurate) publicity are found in the annals of show business, where publicity agents dream up stories about their clients. The stories are designed to improve the client's public image in a way that will generate maximum press and broadcast coverage and stimulate increased attendance at the gate.

Since so much of public relations involves the goal of publicity for people or products, here are three basic rules for writing publicity stories to give them some chance of being used:

1.   Stick to the truth. Sheer puffery will no longer be printed.

2.   Give all necessary facts, and state them as early as possible.

3.   Write your story in such a way that it can be cut (as it probably will) at any point without doing serious injustice to the key points you are trying to get across.

Public Relations Articles

Most public relations writers will have a chance, at one time or another, to write articles. When this opportunity comes, these few rules will help assure the use of your article:

1.   Be sure it is devoted to a timely topic. If your company, or client, is celebrating its 100th birthday, a story about what was happening in the country when the company was founded could be considered timely.

2.   Be certain the article has a quality of popular interest, or is of probable interest to the specialized readership of the publication(s) to which it will be sent.

3.   Be sure it is well written, with tight sentences and a logical transitional flow from paragraph to paragraph.

4.   Where possible, try to match the article to the general style of the publication in which you would most like to see it printed.

Books as Public Relations Tools

When you have acquired enough seasoning as a writer, and your track record indicates that you can accomplish lengthy writing projects on schedule, your chances of being assigned the writing of a book about your company are fairly high. If this opportunity comes, take it, by all means—for if you do a good job with the book, your chances of getting free-lance book assignments are high, since the number of book projects available exceeds the number of writers capable of doing research, turning it into readable form, and meeting fixed publication dates.

Annual Reports

Annual report writing was once done only by corporate fiscal officers, and was as dry as library dust. But with the expansion of stock ownership among the general public, other uses for annual reports began to be recognized. When this occurred, public relations writers (along with advertising agencies) were given most annual report assignments. They sought to use annual reports not only to impart dry facts and figures but to influence stockbrokers, bankers, lawyers, and others whose investment counsel is frequently sought. The results have greatly expanded the usefulness and distribution of these reports, and no publicly held company can afford not to put its best foot forward in an annual compendium of facts relating to its corporate progress and future plans.

Speeches

Speeches and position paper assignments come more frequently to writers in public relations offices of large corporations or to staff members of public relations firms whose client list includes companies of considerable size.

If successfully performed, these assignments often offer an inside track to jobs on the staff of corporation presidents. Ultimately, these skills might lead a writer into the political arena, preparing speeches and papers for a candidate or elected official.

The best adult preparation for work of this sort is to read widely and observe life in all of its aspects. The better the education you have had, and the more seriously and successfully you undertook your term paper assignments, the higher the chance that you will find speeches and position papers to your liking.

Letters

Any letters you are assigned to write to stockholders and customers will reflect the character of the company. As in the case of corporate advertising writing, the precise purpose or goal of the letter should be clearly understood before the assignment is begun. Otherwise, there will be no way in which the results of your efforts can be measured successfully.

Brochures

Today most brochures are prepared by advertising people who work for the company or its agency. However, occasional needs arise for a booklet designed to develop or change an attitude toward a company or industry. When this occurs, the writer will need the same amount of insight required for print advertising assignments. The writer must know in detail how the public to which the brochure is addressed now sees the corporation (or industry), and precisely what public images or modification of images are required.

Internal Publications

Internal publications or house organs are published by large and small companies, and include newspapers, periodic newsletters, and magazines. Like annual reports, such publications can be used successfully to influence brokers and bankers, and they often are employed for this purpose.

However, by far the most advantageous use of an internal publication is as a form of communication between corporate management and its employees, and between the company and the community. Used as a human relations tool to favorably influence employee attitudes, the internal publication should be designed and written with these rules in mind:

1. The writing should be objective, not slanted toward management, and all sides of a question should be fully covered.

2. Items of genuine interest and news value should be explored editorially. This will increase the value of the publication by broadening the involvement of employee readers, and will go far toward creating an image of objectivity and scope.

3. Corporate employees should be encouraged to contribute news and fiction to internal publications. Such contributions can be edited carefully (like any other piece of copy), and are often of surprisingly good quality. When they appear in print, employee pieces have a high readership potential and create goodwill among employees and their families, friends, and acquaintances.

4. The special interests of employees and their families should be recognized and dealt with editorially. Some examples: pitfalls to look for in purchasing a home, ways to save money for college education, investment suggestions for retirement incomes.

5. Design and write your material as though it were to be submitted to a commercial publication. Your readers cannot help but compare the company's internal publication with the magazines or newspapers they read. The credibility of your editorial material will rest

largely with its presentation, that is, its appearance as well as its content.

A PUBLIC RELATIONS CAREER

Writing for public relations purposes is a skill that can be developed by anyone with curiosity and an interest in words, ideas, and people. But public relations is also a field requiring commitment to honesty and integrity. Great public relations practitioners such as Ivy Lee have displayed a high level of integrity and have educated their clients to believe that truth is the only safe commodity in which to deal. From a craft that began as a manipulative art has developed a profession that attains a higher level of respect with each act of honest practice. Without public relations, our business enterprise would be less well served. With every ethical use of the skill, the interest of public relations clients is advanced beyond the level of information dissemination to the level of credibility.

The use of their talents and integrity by public relations writers can be an advantage that will not yield to any amount of chicanery or distortion—for as amply demonstrated in the Watergate cover-up, the truth, in time, will out. When it comes, better that it originated with your client or employer. Any explanation that is given under those circumstances for an adverse aspect of your client's business will be believed, and you will have succeeded in your goal of influencing public opinion in a way that is favorable to your cause as well as to your profession.

20

Hints on Seeking an Ad-Writing Job and Other Jobs

Chapter Topics

Preparing the sample book
Special target audience
The portfolio
Writing the résumé
Writing the cover letter
The interview
Hints on seeking *any* job
Doing research
Zeroing in on the target
Persistence is the key
Use of contacts
Vocational questionnaire

Key Terms

Sample book
Campaign emphasis
Tag line
Portfolio
Résumé
Self-analysis
Cover letter
"Cold turkey" letter
Directory of Advertising
   Agencies
Directory of National
   Advertisers
Cultivate the executive
   secretary
"Old boy" network

Advertising writers are rarely hired on the basis of looks, personality, or charm. Instead, they are hired strictly on the basis of creative talent, on a demonstrated ability to generate selling ideas. The following information tells you how to get ready to market yourself to a creative director.

THE SAMPLE BOOK

A sample book, in which you demonstrate your creative ability by putting together an exhibit of your thinking and writing, is crucial to any copywriter's job search. Your sample book is *you*.

As a student you have little or no professional track record, so you have to create your own samples from scratch. Here are three ways you may go about doing that:

1. You may invent a new product to advertise. The product should appear to have some useful purpose. (Don't do a campaign for something like three-dollar bills.)

2. You may invent a new feature or a new use for an already established product. Look through the kitchen and bathroom cabinets of your home.

3. You may take a product with an established advertising campaign and give that product a totally new advertising campaign. Avoid changing one of the acknowledged great campaigns.

Emphasis on Campaigns

Notice the emphasis on the word campaign. Advertising practitioners seek *ideas that can be extended*. They like advertising approaches that can be extended over time and through every facet of a marketing program. For example, the "Pepsi Generation" advertising theme has itself already been extended through two generations of soft-drink consumers.

How to Display Campaigns

Here's how to handle a campaign idea in your sample book:

1. For each new campaign in your sample book, create at least three ads. It is not necessary to do more than three, although you may if you want to.

2. For the initial ad in the campaign, type complete copy and prepare a rough layout for that copy.

3. For the second and third ads in each campaign show only the rough layouts.

4. Each rough layout should contain a reasonably understandable illustration, a headline, and a tag line. The headline and tag line should be lettered as best you can. The tag line or recurring theme line is usually at or near the bottom of the layout. The three headlines and illustrations in your c mpaign will all be different but the tag line remains the same through all three ads. The tag line is what helps tie the three ads into a campaign.

5. The first ad in each campaign is placed in the portfolio so that the complete typewritten copy is on the left-hand page and the rough layout faces it on the right-hand page.

6. The rough layouts for the second and third ads in the campaign follow on the next two pages.

   With your samples thus organized, the experienced creative interviewer can take in your headline, illustrations, and tag line at a glance—and tell if you have a truly creative idea.

A Special Target Audience

The target audience for your sample book is not your professor, your classmates, or even a logical consumer prospect. On the contrary, your target audience is a highly talented, highly skilled, highly experienced appraiser of creative work, someone who is sophisticated, discriminating, demanding, someone who "has seen it all." All your samples have to do is make such a person blink with surprise and delight.

How Many Samples?

Your sample book does not have to contain a score of examples, but everything in it should be done to the best of your ability and should make the reader see that product in a new light. Six to eight campaigns should be sufficient. Remember—headline, illustration, tag line. Include only work of which you are intensely proud. Among your sample campaigns, include three or four that lead off with a television script (and possibly a simple storyboard) followed by two rough layouts of magazine ads. Toss in an occasional radio script to show that you can handle that medium as well. Add a couple of billboard ideas; they are super demonstrators of creative talent.

   Never include a school assignment paper on which there are instructor's comments or a grade (even an A+) because: (a) a school assignment underscores the fact that you are an amateur, and (b) showing an instructor's comments to a professional is bad psychology. If you wish to use one of your outstanding school assignments, retype it completely.

   Put the best thing you've ever done at the beginning of the book, as first impressions count heavily. You might consider including one off-the-wall idea. It jolts the interviewer and shows that you may have far-ranging potential.

THE PORTFOLIO

Place your samples in a portfolio, which is generally slightly larger than a briefcase. The center of the portfolio is a looseleaf book of heavy black paper pages, each of which is totally enclosed in a clear plastic oversheet. You slip each sample between the black paper page and its clear plastic cover, and it will stay put without pasting or taping. Because the book is looseleaf, you can put as many or as few pages into the finished sample book as you wish. Or you can shift pages around in any order you choose. You might want to rearrange the sequence of exhibits depending on the interests of the particular company you are interviewing with.

The looseleaf book of samples is bound to a soft leather or plastic carrying case, zippered on three sides, with a small carrying handle at the top. Each outside cover of the carrying case has an inside flap or pocket into which you can put extra résumés or any other exhibits of your skills that you might want to have handy during the interview.

What If You Can't Draw?

Many aspiring copywriters worry about the quality of their drawings and lettering, and wonder if they should hire professional help. This is not necessary. You are being evaluated on your creative thinking, not on your skill as an artist. Most creative directors are comfortable with stick-figure art as long as the idea is clear. On a TV storyboard, you might consider hiring somebody to do the series of sketches for you. In any event, if the artwork is not yours, say so at once.

Never stop working on your sample book to improve it, and continue to experiment with new samples. Why? Because you will be a better copywriter with each successive effort.

THE RÉSUMÉ

While you are getting samples of your work ready, you should be putting together your résumé. A résumé is a fact sheet about yourself. The wording is crisp and telegraphic, using sentence fragments rather than complete sentences, and you state facts only, not opinions or feelings.

Identify yourself at the top—name, address, phone. (Do not include a small photograph of yourself. This practice is frowned upon nowadays.) After you have identified yourself, state your job objective. If you are too explicit and narrow, you may be ruling out some job possibilities.

For example, use a broad term like "advertising writer" rather than "agency writer."

Next list your pertinent work experience, if any, followed by your educational records, all in reverse chronological order (most recent experience listed first). If the jobs you've held have all been incidental to schooling, list your educational background directly after your job objective. Follow this with honors and activities, both civic and academic. Summer jobs and part-time jobs appear next if they are not included earlier. Highlight any points that will make you look desirable to an employer.

At the end of the résumé, you may include references or you may say something like "References furnished upon request."

Length of Résumé

It is best if you can hold your résumé to a single typewritten sheet of paper. Rightly or wrongly, practitioners resent a multi-page résumé from a novice. They can't help feeling that a young beginner hasn't lived long enough to rate more than a single-sheet résumé.

Have a number of résumés on hand because you will be handing them out at a great rate. Take extra résumés with you to interviews. You can't anticipate how many different individuals you might be handed over to in the course of one office visit.

Creativity in Résumés

Since advertising is essentially a creative business, some students get rather creative with their résumés. Often the résumé will become a folder on colored paper, perhaps even with little cartoons or sketches. This sort of innovative treatment is fine within reason, though it is not necessary by any means. You cannot go wrong with a single typewritten sheet of white paper. But if you feel the need to jazz up your résumé, be sure to do it with taste. Keep it orderly, neat, and of a size and shape that fits easily into a regular file folder.

The Cover Letter

Of great importance for the aspiring ad writer is the cover letter that carries the résumé and asks for a personal interview. The object of the cover letter is to obtain an opportunity to show your sample book. Some people refer to this cover letter as a "cold turkey" letter because it is sent to somebody you don't know and who doesn't know you.

What a Cover Letter Can Do for You.   A good cover letter offers a golden opportunity to do three things:

1.   To give vital, detailed information about yourself in a highly personal manner.

2. To differentiate yourself from all other applicants.

3. To display a certain flair in communicating.

Rewriting Pays. Your cover letter may be the most difficult piece of copy you will ever write in your life. We have seen students rewrite a cover letter half-a-dozen or more times to get it just right. The extra effort pays off. If your letter is routine or drab, you will not stir up much response. If it is too flashy, braggadocio, or gimmicky, you may make a bad impression. For example, don't compare yourself to Superman, solver of all problems; Superman has been done to death!

A Matter of Self-Analysis. A good cover letter calls for self-analysis. You have to do a sort of creative strategy review on yourself. Even if you appear to be the most ordinary person in the world, there must be something you've done, seen, or felt that makes you a distinctive personality. Build on that. Write that first sentence or first paragraph a hundred times if you must because that first sentence is what will pull the employer in and lead him or her to say, "I'd like to meet this person."

Cover Letter Examples. Nobody can tell you how to write this kind of letter because each applicant's life story is that person's own. One of the most productive "cold turkey" letters in Chicago copywriting circles began: "Have you ever worked on a garbage boat? Well, I have." It went on from there and ended with this postscript: "Even if you can't hire me, see me anyway. The story about the garbage boat is pretty interesting."

One young woman began her cover letter by saying, "Did you ever leap 200 feet off the side of a cliff, suspended only by a rope and the seat of your pants. I did. Once. It's called rappelling, and the way I felt just before my feet left the ground that day has since been equaled only by the way I feel right now, as I prepare to leap from the security of college into the strange new world of advertising."

One young man began his cover letter this way: "Have you ever painted flagpoles, buried a body or dodged bullets as a range officer at a public shooting facility? I have. I have performed some similarly bizarre tasks in several of my other jobs. However, I have never written advertising copy for a firm like yours." He tells more about himself and begins his final paragraph with this sentence: "If you would enjoy meeting one of the few men who has been in a grave and is still willing (and able) to talk about it, my portfolio and I would appreciate the opportunity to present ourselves to you." In that same letter, the applicant enclosed a free sample of his work—an idea for an outdoor billboard.

Press for Interview. Whatever the angle of approach in your cover letter, it must be interesting. Try to keep it short—no more than one page. And always close the letter by asking for an interview date to show your work.

Sad to say, no matter how brilliant your letter, some people will not respond and you will have to follow up with phone calls. When you can't get the creative director on the phone, enlist the aid of her or his secretary. No matter how much it hurts your pride, be persistent. Keep calling, keep asking, until you get that interview.

The Interview

Once you get an interview, show up looking and acting businesslike—then play it by ear. Over and over we hear creative directors who evaluate young talent say there is no substitute for *enthusiasm*. Radiate love of copywriting. Let them know you'd rather write copy than eat.

Some interviewers like to have you explain why you did things a certain way as you show your samples. Some interviewers don't want you to talk at all while they are reviewing your campaigns. Some will bait you to see how you respond. Some will compliment you on a particular ad of yours; others will say the same ad is dreadful and should be removed from your book. Learn to live with these varying responses and don't be too quick to tear your book apart on one person's say-so.

All creative directors are busy, busy people, harassed from all sides all day. They have little time to spare for interviewing, and some of them are so busy that they will ask you to leave your sample book. This is all right if the agency is reputable, but be very cautious about leaving your original copy anywhere. Ask instead if you can leave a set of Xerox copies of your material.

Where to Look

To whom should you apply? You'll probably have to put together your own list of best prospects although some categories of business have directories to guide you. Two of the most prominent in advertising circles are the Directory of National Advertisers and the Directory of Advertising Agencies. The agency directory lists agency accounts and the names and titles of its key personnel. For a large agency, pick out the loftiest-sounding title that has the word "creative" in it. Like "Executive Vice-President in Charge of All Creative Services." For a small agency, if there is not a high-sounding "creative" title, write to the president who will route your letter to the proper person. As a rule, agency personnel directors have little to do with screening creative talent. If you are contacting a large corporation (not an agency), however, you *can* write to the personnel director, or to the executive vice-president in charge of marketing or to the advertising director.

There are two excellent and relatively inexpensive recent volumes on the advertising creative job hunt: *How to Put Your Book Together and Get a Job in Advertising* by Maxine Paetro, currently Vice-President and Creative Manager for DFS Dorland Saatchi & Saatchi agency in

New York, and *How to Get Your First Copywriting Job* by Dick Wasserman, Vice-President and Creative Director for the Foote, Cone & Belding agency in New York.

Handling Rejections

Chances are that in spite of all your fine efforts you are going to get some turn-downs—perhaps a number of them. *Do not take turn-downs personally.* If an agency says it has no openings at present, it doesn't mean they hate you and your work. It simply means what it says—they have no openings at present. After a decent interval, try them again.

After an interview, always send a thank you note or card. If a creative director seems to like your work but has no spot for you, ask if he or she can suggest somebody else for you to approach; keep the lines open. If you have had a satisfactory interview but no job offer, remind that outfit from time to time of your continued interest in them. No agency can get mad at you for wanting to work for them.

Because advertising writing jobs are highly desirable, you can't expect to find one the first time out. That's rare. Do not be discouraged. If you want with all your heart to be a writer, keep on writing until you make somebody notice you. The effort is well worth it.

HINTS ON SEEKING *ANY* JOB

While this book is designed for a course in advertising writing, we realize that most students in such a course are not primarily interested in copywriting as a *career*. But they are interested in finding a good entry-level job—a job that can lead to a career. Consequently this chapter includes advice on seeking *any* job.

As usual, the procedure begins with the preparation of a résumé.

The Résumé

In seeking any position, you need to construct a summary statement of your background. Called a résumé, this statement should be brief enough to encourage your interviewer to read it before the job interview begins and long enough to include the highlights of your life. It also will be advantageous if your résumé can be done in a somewhat creative way that sets it apart from the many others that will rest on the desk or in the files of your interviewer. Keep in mind that no matter how creatively you may present your background statement, it is the content of the résumé, not the form that will gain you the advantage you need.

There are a number of schools of thought about the best form for résumés to take; your college placement office or librarian can refer you to helpful reference works.

Your résumé needs to be accompanied by an individualized letter addressed to the person who has authority to make decisions about job interviews. This could be a personnel executive, a creative director, or the supervisor of the department in which you aspire to work, such as the executive vice-president in charge of account services. It could also be the president of an advertising agency or other corporation, depending on the approach you decide to use.

Job Hunting Questionnaire

The questionnaire at the end of this chapter is designed to help you identify and clarify your vocational choice and your target and in validating the probability that your interests and needs can be met in the vocation. Before answering the questions, read them carefully. If you find any that you cannot answer, do the research they require, then answer all the questions.

For this initial research, you can use your college or local library, where you will find current editions of business directories, such as the two previously mentioned. The first, the Directory of Advertising Agencies, lists all agencies of any consequence, their officers, and their principal clients, while the second, the Directory of National Advertisers, lets you know which corporations are likely to have advertising departments. After you have completed the questionnaire, study your answers. They will reveal a much clearer picture of what you want in a job and where you are most likely to find one that will be rewarding and fulfilling.

Doing Research

Upon completion of your library research, augment your insight by talking with the most senior officer available to you at the bank used by you or your family. Ask for as much non-confidential information as possible about the companies under consideration by you as potential places of employment. If this research effort reveals insufficient information of value, visit the office of a large stockbrokerage firm and talk with its research librarian. Try to obtain copies of annual reports or stock prospects relating to the industry or firms you are considering. And begin to read advertising trade and business magazines to orient yourself to problems and opportunities in the industry.

Zero in on Your Target

After you have completed your research and filled out the questionnaire, follow these next steps:

1. Narrow your job search to one particular agency or corporation.
2. Decide in what way and in what probable job you can make a significant personal contribution to the agency or other corporation.

3. Try to determine what sort of personal growth patterns might be justified for you by your training and aptitudes.

4. Draft a letter to the person you identify in your target agency or other corporation as having the authority to hire you. The name and title of this person can be learned by a telephone call or personal visit to the *secretary* of the chief executive officer. Never ask to speak to the boss. Secretaries know how the power structure works and if you impress them favorably, they can guide you through possible pitfalls in the corporate structure. A secretary may even decide to make a telephone call on your behalf to the person with whom your case will rest.

5. Always write the secretary of the C.E.O. a personal letter of thanks. Offer to keep him or her informed of your progress in attaining your goal of employment in the company, and do so. In this way, you will have made an important ally, if not a friend. It is the executive secretaries in the world of commerce who have the ears of their bosses and who can subtly influence personnel decisions.

The Cover Letter

Draft a letter to the person identified by the executive secretary as the one who can make hiring decisions in the work area you have targeted. In this letter, tell why you want to make a career in that particular agency or company, clearly indicating your familiarity with its corporate history and its position in the industry, and identify the work area in which you expect to make a significant contribution. For example, if you have lived or traveled in Japan, delineate your familiarity with the customs or language or cultural link to one of the countries in which they have clients. Zero in on this as a possible plus factor in giving consideration to your application.

State that you will telephone the addressee in two weeks to learn when it might be convenient to meet you or to arrange for you to meet with an executive to whom your letter has been referred.

Persistence Is the Key

If your first try does not produce the interview you seek, try again and again until you succeed. The value of persistence can be seen in the experience of a determined young man with an honors degree from Harvard Law School who chose Harrisburg, Pennsylvania, as the place he wanted to live. Identifying the leading law firm in that city, he determined to become associated only with it, and he sought an interview with the senior partner, who refused to see him on the ground that no vacancies for associates existed currently or in the foreseeable future. Undaunted, this young man began to visit the law firm every day, to spend mornings and afternoons in the commodious waiting room, reading law journals and books. When questioned by partners, he responded that as his goal was to work only for that firm, he would wait in the room provided for that purpose for a vacancy to arise, in the meantime thoroughly familiarizing himself with the laws of Pennsylvania. After months of this routine, the senior partner stopped in front of the young man one morning and said, "Good grief, man, are you still here?" "Yes, sir," he replied, "and unless you object, I'll be here until a vacancy opens up, as this is the only law firm I want to join." "Well," said the senior partner, "I guess your persistence has worn us down. Come into my office and we'll talk about it." When he died, in his early sixties, that young man had been head of the firm for over twenty years. Courteous and reasonable goal-oriented determination *can* create job openings where none exist.

The Interview

The following suggestions will help you make the most of your interview:

1. Dress conservatively and as expensively as your purse (or credit) will allow, for as Benjamin Franklin wrote in *Poor Richard's Almanac,* it is by such things that most people know you, especially on initial meeting and in a vocation where contact with people is a critical factor.

2. If you are a man, be sure your hair is cut in a fashion acceptable to senior business executives and that your fingernails are cleaned and trimmed. If you are a woman, avoid dramatic, faddish hairstyles, use make-up sparingly, if at all, and avoid colored nail polish and false eyelashes.

3. Be sure that your teeth are clean and your breath is fresh.

4. Answer all questions politely, respectfully, truthfully, and completely.

5. Avoid asking your own questions unless you are so requested, and do not interrupt.

6. Do not gush, tell jokes, or make any comment extraneous to the business at hand, which, among other things, is an appraisal of your social poise, your manners, and your ability to communicate forcefully and succinctly.

7. Sit still throughout the meeting: keep your hands relaxed, do not pick at anything, tap with your fingers, or swing a crossed leg or foot.

8. If you are a smoker, do not smoke during the interview, even if you are offered a cigarette. A great and growing majority of corporate executives see smoking as a sign of bad judgment, and the offer could be a subtle test of judgment and self-control.

9. Speak in a firm, steady, moderate voice, and avoid such unnecessary words as "like," "you know," "and uh," and "I mean."

10. Stress the contributions you believe you can make to the firm, and give your reasons.

11. Reveal your knowledge of the firm's history, its products, services, customers, or clients and anything else gleaned from your research that relates to the industry's challenges and opportunities.

12. Do not bring up the subject of compensation. If it arises, indicate that what you seek is an opportunity to prove your value on the job, and add that you will rely completely on the firm's equitable salary policies and salary scales.

13. Do not bring up the subject of earned vacations, sick leave, or retirement policies. If the subject is raised by the interviewer, make an appropriate comment, but do not dwell on it.

14. If asked what your career goals in the firm might be, indicate that you have given serious thought to the subject and state your immediate, intermediate, and long-term goals in the firm's employ.

15. Do not press for an immediate answer about the possibility of your selection.

16. Let it be known that the firm to which you have applied for a job is your first choice of employers. Give thoughtful and valid reasons for this based on your research and your analysis of your qualities as a match for the firm's needs.

17. Indicate that you can be available for any further interview.

18. Above all, be polite, honest, modest, and low-key. Avoid extravagant or questionable statements, and display an admirable level of humility, all while suggesting an air of quiet self-confidence.

19. If you lack self-confidence, and fear that you may come off poorly in an interview, write a hypothetical script of the questions that might be asked by the interviewer—especially those that could give you the most trouble—and your answers. Rehearse the script with a partner until you feel more comfortable about the interview.

Use of Contacts

Three more suggestions could be of value:

1. If you have any family, social, or school contact that might be useful in providing meaningful introductions to senior executives of the firm of your choice, take advantage of them. In every free country, the business world spins on its axis by the power generated by "old boy" networks; introductions made by people of influence who know you can open doors through which you may not be able to pass on your own efforts.

2. Follow up on all leads related to your vocational goal.

3. If you receive a turn-down from the firm you have selected as your target, ask the executive who gives you the bad news for suggestions on uncovering the kind of job you seek. Often such people will know of openings in competitive companies, and may feel an obligation or desire to give you what help they can in your search, especially if you have made a highly favorable impression.

If you have done your research with serious purpose and diligence, and if you are able and willing to follow the suggestions made above, your chances of making an excellent impression are outstanding. And if a job vacancy exists for which you are qualified, the odds in favor of your being chosen for it are on the order of 50 to 1. Beyond this, if no present job exists in which your skills can be used, the chances are high that one will be created for you—for not one job applicant in a thousand will have had sufficient insight and drive to follow the steps you have taken to prepare yourself for selection as an employee of the firm to which you have applied.

If instead of a career in advertising, you have chosen another vocation or profession, the same methodical approach to research will serve you well, and your local library or professional association can furnish you with directories that give full information about the qualifications required to become a member of the employment group you wish to join. Armed with these insights, you should be able to make valid decisions regarding your career target in the geographical area or city in which you hope to live and work.

THE VOCATIONAL QUESTIONNAIRE

1. Given a choice, in what part of the country (or world) would you most like to live?_____ .

2. Why?_____ .

3. Are the reasons for your choice short- or long-term ones, i.e., will they still be valid five, ten, or twenty years from now?_____ .

4. What city or town in the area of your choice has the most appeal for you?_____
_____ .

5. Have you ever visited this city or town?_____ . If not, why does it appeal to you?
_____ .

6. Do you have any family or friends there who could help you with business or social contacts?_____ .

7. If not, are there any present or potential school contacts who could be of help to you?_____ .

8. In what industry would you most like to work?_____ .

9. Why?_____ .

10. Do you have any special training, experience, talents, or interests that could be of value to a firm in this industry?_____ . If so, what are they?_____
_____ .

11. If not, why have you chosen that industry?_____
_____ .

12. Is there a firm in this industry in the city or town of your choice?_____ . If so, have you carefully researched that firm?_____ .

13. If you have done this research, did any aspect of what you learned have special appeal for you?_____ . If so, what has special appeal for you and why does it attract you?
_____ .

14. Can you see any way this appeal matches a special contribution you might make to that firm?_____ . If so, what is this contribution?_____ .

15. If no special contribution by you to that firm is possible at present, is there any training or other preparation that might make your services of value?_____ . If so, what is this training or preparation?_____
_____ .

16. From your research, are you sure that the firm or industry of your choice can meet your vocational interests and your personal needs?_____ . If not, why not?_____
_____ .

17. Is there a viable second choice of firm or industry that might be a better match to your needs and interests?_____ .

18. If there is a second choice, have you researched it as an alternative target for your services?_____ .

19. How stable is the firm or industry you have chosen?_____
_____ .

20. Using your best insight from research, does the firm and industry of your choice have a high probability for growth? (Explain)_____
_____ .

21. Has your research identified the principal bank with which the firm of your choice does business?_____ . If so, have you visited an officer of this bank to learn what you can of the firm?_____ .

22. Does this information confirm your choice, or cause you to consider an alternate choice?_____ .

23. Using the banking sources available to you, your family or friends, have you studied a Dun & Bradstreet report on the firm you have selected as a target?_____ .

24. If so, did it confirm your judgment in finding a good match between the firm and your special needs and interests?_____ .

25. Have you sought the counsel of anyone whose judgment and objectivity you respect in helping you to evaluate your own assets in relation to the profile of the firm you have chosen?_____ .

26. Did this conversation validate your own judgment of a match between your assets and the firm?_____ .

27. Is there evidence of good management in the firm you have targeted?_____ .

28. Does there appear to be a solid second echelon of management that can replace current managers?_____ .

29. Have you talked with a knowledgeable stockbroker about the firm of your choice?
_____.

30. Did this conversation serve to validate your choice?_____ .

31. Does the firm you have chosen have a training program for those in the work area of your choice?_____ .

32. Has your research produced evidence of a history of promotions from within the firm?_____ .

33. Has your research uncovered any evidence of nepotism?_____ .

34. Is the stock of the firm held by a small or large group of shareholders?_____ .

35. If the stock is held by a small group, are they involved in the management of the firm?_____ .

36. If the shares are publicly held, what has been the market history of the stock?_____ .

37. If the shares are publicly held and if you can afford it, have you purchased at least one share of stock in the firm you have chosen as your target?_____ .

38. Have you thoroughly researched the history of the firm?_____ .

39. If the firm is a public corporation, have you studied the last three annual reports?
_____.

40. If so, did they confirm your choice?_____ .

41. Have you used the products or services of the firm or its clients?_____ . If so, can you identify with them?_____ .

42. In your opinion, do these products or services live up to the claims made for them? _____ .

43. Are you familiar with the advertising of the firm and/or its clients?_____ .

44. Have you visited any of the firm's places of business?_____ .

45. If so, what did you learn that is pertinent to your selection of the firm as your target for employment?_____

_____ .

46. Have you talked with any of the firm's personnel?_____ .

47. If so, what did you learn about the firm?_____

_____ .

48. Have you talked with any of the firm's clients or customers? If so, what did you learn about the firm?_____

_____ .

49. Have you identified the principal competitors of the firm?_____ . If so, have you talked with any of them?_____ .

50. On the basis of your intensive research, are you still satisfied that you have chosen the most viable target for your services?_____ .

Writing for New Business

Chapter Topics

Meaning of term "new business"
The lifeblood of agencies
Acquiring new business
Organizing for new business
Questions regarding new business prospect
Research for new business
The new business presentation
Agency "house" campaigns
Books as new business tools
How to keep new business
Where do new business writers come from?

Key Terms

Conflicts
Compatible management
Agency billings
Speculative presentation
"House" advertising

Case History

J. H. Benedict & Associates

Writing for new business (that is, soliciting potential clients for an agency) is a somewhat esoteric form of writing, little understood by many practitioners and most teachers of advertising. In addition, the very acknowledgment that new advertising accounts must be sought is distasteful to many who prefer to give emphasis to the creative aspects of advertising agency life rather than to their necessary selling efforts. For these reasons, little mention of agency methods of business acquisition can be found in advertising textbooks or agency training manuals.

Believing that this fact of agency operation should be revealed to the student of advertising writing, the authors give in this appendix a brief review of agencies' new business activities and their seemingly tenuous relationship to writing. Although none of the preliminary contact work and little of the background research involve the advertising writer personally, most new business is acquired only after a **written** presentation. In most agencies, such presentations are prepared by men and women who are or have been writers.

HOW MOST AGENCIES ACQUIRE NEW BUSINESS

In the advertising business, the annual sales volume is referred to as "billings," and agencies are classified in the trade by the total dollar volume spent through them by their clients. In a well-managed agency that does excellent creative work and gives outstanding service to its clients, the amount of money spent by clients on advertising usually increases in some proportion to the increase in sales produced by the advertising. This, in turn, elevates agency billings. Thus, it can be said that much agency growth results from offering a service that attains the marketing goals of its clients.

At the same time, satisfied clients often recommend that other companies give business to their agency. Good service not only adds to the dollar volume from current clients, but adds new advertising accounts to the total agency billings.

Despite this idealized view of agency growth, agencies and their clients **do** have disagreements. Agencies lose accounts for a variety of reasons. This is normal attrition, and leaves all agencies with concerns about the acquisition of new accounts. They devote the time and energy necessary to hold or attain the level of billings desired for the agency.

Agency Organization for New Business

Logically called "business development," the sales efforts of an advertising agency are usually placed under the direction of a senior partner or officer of the firm. This person uses professional experience and high-level contacts to uncover inside or outside information that might lead to a new advertiser. A sophisticated and profit-oriented agency owner or manager will establish and adhere to certain guidelines in the selection or approval of new business prospects.

Writers in advertising agencies can benefit from an understanding of the economics of agency management and the critical relationship between the growth of an agency and continuing career advancement for themselves. The student of advertising writing should have some idea of the criteria used by agency principals in qualifying new business opportunities as desirable. Although these criteria can vary from firm to firm, usually they include such questions as these:

1. Is there any conflict between present and prospective clients?
2. Would serving the prospective client preclude an early solicitation of a much more desirable account?
3. Does the prospective client have a good product or service, with growth potential?
4. Does the prospective client have good management?
5. Is this management compatible with the agency management?
6. Is the prospective client in good financial condition?
7. Are the advertising and marketing goals of the prospective client clearly defined and realistic?
8. Has the agency had specific experience in the prospective client's industry?
9. How many advertising agencies have served the prospective client over what period of time, and what does the record show of these relationships?
10. Why does the prospective client want to talk with new agencies?
11. Is the agency structured and staffed to meet the advertising needs of the prospective client?
12. Can the agency anticipate making a reasonable profit on the prospective account? Is so, how soon.?

If answers to such questions show no problem areas, active solicitation of a desirable advertising account is considered to be in order.

Research for New Business

Once a decision has been made to solicit an advertising account, the role of management becomes temporarily subordinated to that of the agency's research and marketing staffs. These staffs are now put to work preparing the definitive insight into the prospect's company, industry, product(s), competition, and markets that is necessary for the making of creative decisions.

At this point, if the agency is large, a creative director (or team) will be given the job of developing a selling strategy (Rosser Reeve's

"Unique selling proposition"). A writer (or writing team) will be assigned the actual writing project, which may include the creation of an advertising theme as well as the preparation of any advertising ideas that will be shown to the prospect.

If the agency is a member of the American Association of Advertising Agencies, it will be prohibited from making a purely speculative presentation of a proposed advertising campaign to the prospective client. Creative work will be limited to the marketing research that is usually necessary to orient the agency to the prospective client's business and marketing problems.

If the agency is not a member of the AAAA, or if the prospect has offered to pay for creative ideas, the presentation will usually include a complete advertising plan and comprehensive ideas for its execution. In this case, the writer approaches the job much like any other writing assignment. After absorbing all research facts available, the writer relates them to the marketing goals of the prospective client and translates this information into an advertising campaign.

The New Business Presentation

When a prospective client invites an advertising agency to make a formal solicitation for its account, the chances are high that the agency will decide to put together a new business presentation. A date will be set— usually not more than three months away, and frequently sooner—for the meeting between agency and prospect.

This meeting will usually be attended by the agency president (if the account is large enough, or if the agency is small), the vice-president in charge of the office from which the account will be served, and the men and women who will supervise the account, write the copy, and (sometimes) direct the art. Depending on the nature of the account and the size of the agency, a marketing person and someone responsible for the agency's research effort will also be present. And if the account is one for which a heavy television schedule is being recommended, the head of the television department of the agency will be on hand.

This group of agency people will be assigned various roles in the new business presentation. The script by which it will proceed will be very carefully written and rehearsed. If you should be tapped to write a presentation for an advertising agency, the following rules may prove useful.

Some Rules for Writing New Business Presentations

1. The first thing to avoid is a history of the agency. No matter how grand and glorious the record of your agency has been, or how long and successfully it has existed, the client does not care. If your firm happens to have a glamorous or highly creative reputation,

this will already have attracted the prospect, who does not need to be reminded of the things already well-known, but will, in fact, be adversely impressed by the agency's lack of modesty in thumping its chest when it should be concentrating on things of value to the prospect.

2.   Even at the risk of your job, refuse to incorporate into your script any prolonged reference to the work the agency has created for any of its clients. Agency owners and managers often see this as an irresistible opportunity to overwhelm the prospect with the agency's expertise. Prospective clients, on the other hand, find it boring, repetitious (if they don't know about this work, and hadn't been impressed with it, they would not have extended the invitation), and completely off the point—their concern is not "what have you done for other companies?" but "what can you do for me?"

3.   Begin your script with as much marketing and research insight as the agency has been able to pull together. Use it in a way that immediately qualifies your agency as knowledgeable in the prospect's industry. Move from this into the full expression of the agency's intimate comprehension of the client's specific business. When this point has been made with care, you should develop to the fullest your agency's understanding of the advertising and marketing tactics of the prospect's competition.

4.   At this place in your presentation, you have either qualified or disqualified your agency. You are now ready to deal with the creative aspect of the presentation, which must be directly related to and based on the agency's marketing insight into the prospect's business. If this is well handled, your agency can score with less than an award-winning caliber of creative work. If it is not clear that the creative effort is based on your knowledge of the prospect's marketing needs, this part of the presentation will fall as flat as a work of art that is seen but not understood.

5.   In developing the presentation of the advertising that the agency has prepared for the prospect, start quietly and gradually build to a crescendo. For example, if your agency is recommending 30 percent print, 20 percent radio, and 50 percent TV, save the television for last, where it will linger longest.

6.   If packaging, logotypes, product names, or other design opportunities are part of your script, they should now be woven in as a form of frosting on the cake.

7.   At this point, the prospect has probably reached at least a tentative decision. However, to stay on the side of the angels, your script should now pull together in summary fashion all elements of the presentation, ending on a high but sincere note of anticipatory pleasure and mutual success in the important business partnership that the agency is seeking.

Agency Advertising Campaigns

In addition to the pursuit of new business opportunities by senior executives, some agencies take their own advice and run advertising campaigns extolling the virtues of their own agencies. Such campaigns are usually written by a senior copywriter who has intimate knowledge of the agency and its history. Writers assigned to the agency's own house account often have achieved top management positions based on their skill in turning research insights into selling strategies that work.

Among the many agency campaigns seen by the authors, the newsletter of Grey Advertising, Inc., is a notable example. Called "Grey Matter" and printed on gray paper, the newsletter is sent to clients, friends, and prospects and is said to be an effective new business tool.

Other notable agency advertising efforts observed by the authors have included those of Ogilvy & Mather, Marsteller, Ketchum, MacLeod & Grove, N.W. Ayer ABH International, and Campbell-Mithun.

Broadcast media have traditionally been significantly absent from house advertising programs of advertising agencies, probably because of the high cost of television and the highly obtrusive as well as intrusive nature of both broadcast media—along with their waste audience for a highly selective market. Also, the fleeting nature of broadcast advertising is a substantially limiting factor. Instead, house programs have to date been concentrated in the print media of magazines, newspapers, and direct mail.

Other Writing for New Business

Prominent among other forms of writing designed to attract new advertising clients are books written by agency principals, especially when published by recognized publishing firms and distributed through regular channels to the hardcover or paperback book markets.

Believing that a demonstrable correlation exists between the ability to produce a publishable book and effective advertising copy, N.W. Ayer & Son (for many years the preeminent agency in the United States) encouraged its copywriters to write on any subject. Once published, the books were on permanent display as tangible evidence to clients and prospects that the copywriters at Ayer were skillful enough to produce writing that could be sold commercially.

Of even greater value to Ayer was a comprehensive history of that agency written in the 1930s by a professor at the Harvard Business School. Revised and republished by the Harvard University Press after World War II, this book was used as a new business tool by the agency. It was very successful in convincing blue chip advertisers that Ayer was a highly competent and successful agency.

In the years since, a number of well-known advertising people have written books that have met with significant success. One of the first of these, *Reality in Advertising,* was written by Rosser Reeves in 1961. As board chair of the Ted Bates agency, Reeves advanced his theories about advertising, including the need for every advertiser to develop a "unique selling proposition" as a shortcut to success for his products.

Soon after Reeve's book appeared, David Ogilvy broke into print with his autobiography, *Confessions of an Advertising Man.* A highly self-confident and talented Britisher of Scottish birth, Ogilvy's career evolved from chef in a Parisian hotel, through advertising research with Dr. George Gallup in Princeton, to the founding of an agency in New York. In his book, Ogilvy explains how he used the small Hathaway shirt account to parlay his company into one of the top ten American advertising firms, and reveals in personal detail how he reached the pinnacle of success in a highly competitive business in an alien land.

In 1966, Hanley Norins, vice-president and creative director for the Young & Rubicam agency in New York, wrote *The Compleat Copywriter.* A delightful analysis of the work style of an advertising writer, this book has been used by teachers of advertising writing as a supplementary text although it is not written in textbook form.

Another autobiography appeared in 1970 under the provocative title of *From Those Wonderful Folks Who Gave You Pearl Harbor.* Authored by an ebullient and highly talented Italian-American named Jerry Della Femina, this book derives its title from an agency creative meeting in which the author proposed this phrase as an advertising theme for a Japanese manufacturer who was entering the American market via a New York agency. Fired for his untimely display of levity, Della Femina moved in and out of five Manhattan agencies in six years. Finally deciding that he should be his own man, he opened a creative agency that has flourished. His book describes the many hilarious behind-the-scenes antics involved in the production of the successful advertising with which Della Femina has been associated.

Written by men of widely different cultural backgrounds and highly dissimilar approaches to the creation of advertising, these books had one common denominator: each was a potent tool for use in the new business efforts of the author's agency.

HOW TO KEEP NEW BUSINESS

So far, we have recounted ways in which new business is acquired by advertising agencies and have given some criteria for the selection of potential clients. And although these criteria can have very significant bearing on the retention of new advertising accounts by virtue of their selective nature, the following important factors can extend the industry average for retention from seven years to the life of the client corporation and/or the advertising agency.

1. Senior agency executives should not take a key role in the new business presentation unless they will be involved in the administration of the account. The reason for this is that senior agency personnel, by virtue of the drive and talent that led them to form the agency or to evolve to the top in its management structure, usually have dynamic and compelling personalities, which can be critical factors in acquiring new advertising accounts. However, new clients then expect the level of talent available to them to be equal to that which was displayed in the presentation. When it isn't, when they never see or hear again from the president, the executive or senior vice-president, the creative director, or other senior officers who may have been involved in the presentation, they begin to feel cheated, and the disenchantment process has begun. Conversely, when one or more of the people who took an active role in the presentation assumes supervision or active day-to-day involvement with the account, clients feel involved in a continuing partnership that they themselves brought into being by the exercise of their judgment in choosing the agency. As a result, their attitude toward their account team is inclined to be cooperative and approving. And as long as the relationship between sales and advertising continues to be favorable, and as long as the person who most influenced the decision to hire the agency remains in a key management role in the marketing area of the client corporation, the chances for longevity of the account are high.

2. Whatever promises are made in the presentation by the agency personnel must be scrupulously fulfilled. When this is not the case, the first cracks in the client/agency relationship are bound to appear.

3. Careful thought should be given to any major personnel changes in the team assigned to the account. Unless the client requests a change in the structure of an account team (which sometimes happens for a variety of reasons, usually for a conflict in personalities), it should remain intact. The reason for this is that, even when the account supervisor comes from the same industry as the client, a minimum of twelve months is required for account personnel to acquire enough familiarity with the account to render their best level of service. In cases where an account supervisor or key account team member receives a promotion or a transfer that means being replaced on the team, the client should be given ample notice of a change in account team structure, and the replacement team member should be introduced to the client by the departing executive. Further, this executive should work with the replacement for at least thirty days, or until the client has had multiple exposures to the replacement and has indicated comfort with the new relationship.

4. At the slightest sign of friction between the client and a member of the account team, a senior agency executive should endeavor to

learn the cause of the friction. Where required by good business judgment, this executive should meet with the client in candid discussion of the relationship problem. If internal investigations or discussions with the client reveal an existing or potential conflict of philosophies or personalities, the agency person should be replaced at once with a new team member who is or can be expected to be persona grata to the client.

5. In all dealings with the client that relate to agency accounting practices or to billings for services or production costs, it is imperative that the agency be scrupulously honest, as any attempt to pad billings by hiking production charges or time costs for services is guaranteed to bring about an eventual rupture in the client/agency relationship—for no one likes to feel cheated. In any discussion between the parties arising from a disagreement about billing, the agency is on very thin ice, and unless an early and friendly resolution of the conflict is forthcoming, it will only be a question of time until notice of contract cancellation is received from the client. To minimize the chances of this sort of dissension, agency accounting management personnel should meet with the financial executive in the client company who is responsible for approving agency bills for payment to explain in detail the system for deriving and billing charges. Once these procedures are clearly understood and agreed to by the client, the possibility of conflict over billing will be greatly reduced, and the odds in favor of indefinite retention of the account by the agency will have increased immeasurably.

CASE HISTORY
J.H. BENEDICT & ASSOCIATES

Courtesy of J. H. Benedict & Associates.

Beginning with the house ads of N.W. Ayer nearly one hundred years ago, the largest agencies have long known the value of advertising their services as a means of attracting new business. However, self-advertising by small agencies is less often encountered, as they seem to have less faith in the success of house advertising than in advertising for their clients.

An outstanding example of a superb house advertising campaign by a small agency appears here as an inspiration to those owners of local agencies who still believe that a small staff and a limited client market constitute a valid reason to rely exclusively on word-of-mouth recommendations and never-ending "birddogging" for uncovering new business opportunities.

The small agency whose house advertising is shown here, J.H. Benedict & Associates, began its business life in Daytona Beach, Florida, in 1974 and used self-advertising on a staggered schedule in local publications. Perceiving a growing opportunity for professional advertising counsel on Florida's Space Coast, Benedict opened a branch office in Cocoa Beach in January 1987. To launch his agency in the business community, he ran the full-page ad shown here in the Sunday business section of *Florida Today*, a younger companion publication to *USA Today*. The same one-page ad also ran in the *Brevard (County) Business News*, a weekly tabloid-size journal for local business people. These initial one-time, full-page announcement ads were followed up with weekly insertions of the same ad format in 1 column × 5 inches, using varying copy messages, one of which is also shown here.

As a result of this modest but well-conceived mini-campaign in print, the Benedict branch agency received an average of three responses to each ad, enabling Benedict to expand in Cocoa Beach from a staff of three to nine professionals in the first four months of the continuous campaign—to prove once again that advertising doesn't cost, it pays.

Tips for the New Ad Writer Who Works Alone

Chapter Topics

Art direction and
    production for the
    amateur
Working with local
    suppliers
Typefaces and
    measurements

Key Terms

Standard Rate and Data
Point system
Serif and sans serif
Roman and italic
Spacing/leading
Reverse type

A FEW THINGS THE WRITER SHOULD KNOW ABOUT ART DIRECTION AND PRODUCTION

Layout, illustration, and typography are generally the responsibility of the art director. To a considerable extent, so is mechanical production (getting the ad ready to print). But what happens when the writer has to handle the whole work alone? This might happen occasionally in a small company or in a free-lance situation.

If you're not an artist, you're not. If there is no advertising art director at hand, track down the closest graphic designer you can find—even if you have to run a classified ad to locate one. Then try to work out some arrangement for the two of you to consult together. The effort will be worth it. Lacking that, you will have to fall back on one of the oldest clichés in art circles: "I don't know anything about art, but I know what I like."

Sharpen and develop your own taste in what is visually pleasing. Clip ads, illustrations, photographs, and type settings that you admire. When dealing with the suppliers of these items, be positive. Politely insist on getting the effect you want. You are the creator of the idea, and the final result should definitely reflect your own imaginative touch.

Refer to the seven basic layout formats shown in this book. One of the seven will probably suit your purposes for any given situation, and the various ways of using illustration can be applied to help you solve almost any problem. At the very least, use these two checklists to help you get started.

If you are a novice at creating layouts, you will benefit by following two basic principles of visual communication: keep it simple; let one element in the ad dominate the space.

The more cluttered and complicated you make your layout, the more difficult it is for the reader to grasp. See what you can take out, rather than what you can put in. You will be doing your readers a favor.

The dominant element is the part of the ad that will catch the reader's eye first. It is the most important part of the ad, and should set the tone for the rest of the ad. All things in an ad cannot claim equal importance, or you will end up with a mishmash that does not stop people and bring them in to your message.

Working with Local Suppliers

No matter how remote and untrained you may feel at times, you will still be dealing with people who can help you. Local media people, printers, and typographers have the skills and equipment to see you over the rough spots. Perhaps you are struggling with a newspaper ad for a small free-lance client, and you have a definite idea in mind. Show your rough layout to the ad manager of the local paper in which the ad is to appear. You might have with you an ad you admire and say, "I want it to look like that." The newspaper ad manager can instruct you in the mechanics of putting the ad together. The paper will have some variety of type from which you can choose, art catalogs from which you can clip an illustration or display heading to insert in your ad, and a variety of borders that can set your ad apart. Certainly, you and the newspaper ad rep working together should be able to do a reasonable job. Caution: put every instruction in writing and keep a copy.

Large display ads in newspapers may not need borders since their size alone sets them off. Magazine ads (half pages and larger) almost never use borders; it's a waste of space.

You'll receive similar helpful treatment from the broadcast media that will carry your advertising. The local radio stations can offer you all kinds of syndicated music and sound effects to add life to even your simplest message. They can suggest announcers and actors to you, and of course they will record. The local television studio will make a producer and studio and crew available to videotape your message. You can lean on them until you learn a few of the ropes yourself.

Magazines are specific about what you are to furnish them for printing. See the specifications in Standard Rate and Data. Most likely the magazine will ask for camera-ready material from which it will make its own printing plates. If the magazine asks for color separation negatives, you have to give your camera-ready material (artwork, typography, and a tight mechanical layout) to a printer who will make the negatives and ship them to the publication.

If you work with a local printer on a brochure or folder or mailing piece, you'll be given plenty of assistance. The printer has probably turned out many different jobs over the years, and can show you samples to guide you. The printer can also offer you a selection of typography that is likely to be more varied than the newspaper's.

If you work with a typographer, you'll find a wide selection of typefaces and styles. Typographers should have reasonably good taste; listen to their advice.

Type Faces and Measurements

In selecting type for an ad, you'll discover that there are many, many faces or families of type—each with distinguishing characteristics. All typefaces come in graduated sizes that are measured in points (72 points equal one inch in height). All typefaces come in at least two styles, roman and italic. Roman letters have a straight stem, and account for probably 95 percent of the type you see in publications and books. Italic letters have a slanted or sloped stem and are used chiefly for emphasis. You will rarely see copy of any length set in italic because it is too difficult to read.

Many typefaces have short appendages or strokes at the ends and edges of letters called *serifs*. They actually help the eye to read. Other typefaces have sharp, crisp edges and are called *sans serif*. An example is Franklin Gothic, the typeface in which so many newspaper headlines are set. Sans serif typefaces look great in display with lots of space around them, but can be difficult to read when set in a long piece of text.

All typefaces have capital letters and small letters (called upper and lower cases). Remember to leave space (leading) between lines. Stick primarily to the traditional combination of capital and small letters because that is what people are used to. Copy set entirely in capital letters is very difficult to read.

As a rule, set your type in a straight horizontal line. Don't angle it or stack it.

Most type prints black on white. The opposite is called *reverse*. The use of white on black can sometimes give a dramatic effect in display headlines, but avoid setting an entire block of copy in reverse.

Accompanying these bits of advice is a sample type specimen sheet. Any publication, printer, or typographer has these for you to choose from. Select a typeface you think appropriate and then select a size that seems suitable for your purposes. Check your rough layout and measure how wide the type area is. (In typography, area is measured in *picas*. There are 12 points in a pica and 6 picas in an inch.) Now apply that same measure against the line of type you selected on the type specimen sheet. If your layout calls for a column three inches (18 picas) wide, count the number of characters in the type line that will fit in that measure. Now count off that number of characters against your own typewritten copy, remembering to count spaces between words and sentences. This tells you how much of your copy will fit in one line. Continue the process through the balance of your typewritten copy until you know how many lines deep your copy will run. If your layout will accommodate that many lines, good. If not, you'd better start cutting that copy.

These little hints about typography are simple but they may help get you started. You'll learn a great deal more in an on-the-job situation.

Garamond Book

ABCDEFGHIJKLMNOPQRSTUVWXYZ
abcdefghijklmnopqrstuvwxyz

1234567890
.,;:?!"""()-—*/$%&

30 Point

Effective selectivity itself is not easy to achieve; it is an ONE CANNOT SIMPLY C

6 Point

Effective selectivity itself is not easy to achieve; it is an ongoing process. One cannot simply collect a year's supply of submissions, perhaps five hundred or a thousand manuscripts will be sufficient to ONE CANNOT SIMPLY COLLECT A YEAR'S SUPPL

7 Point

Effective selectivity itself is not easy to achieve; it is an ongoing process. One cannot simply collect a year's supply of submissions, perhaps five hundred or a thousand manuscripts ONE CANNOT SIMPLY COLLECT A YEAR'S S

8 Point

Effective selectivity itself is not easy to achieve; it is an ongoing process. One cannot simply collect a year's supply of submissions, perhaps five hundred or a ONE CANNOT SIMPLY COLLECT A YEAR

9 Point

Effective selectivity itself is not easy to achieve; it is an ongoing process. One cannot simply collect a year's supply of submissions, perhaps five hundr ONE CANNOT SIMPLY COLLECT A Y

10 Point

Effective selectivity itself is not easy to achieve; it is an ongoing process. One cannot simply collect a year's supply of submissions, perhaps five ONE CANNOT SIMPLY COLLECT A

11 Point

Effective selectivity itself is not easy to achieve; it is an ongoing process. One cannot simply collect a year's supply of submissions, perh ONE CANNOT SIMPLY COLLECT

12 Point

Effective selectivity itself is not easy to achieve; it is an ongoing process. One cannot simply collect a year's supply of submissions, ONE CANNOT SIMPLY COLLEC

14 Point

Effective selectivity itself is not easy to achieve; it is an ongoing process. One cannot simply collect a year's supply of sub ONE CANNOT SIMPLY COLLE

24 Point

Effective selectivity itself is not easy to achieve; it is an ongoing ONE CANNOT SIMPLY COLLE

20 Point

Effective selectivity itself is not easy to achieve; it is an ongoing process. One cannot simply collect a year's supply of submissions, perhaps five hundred ONE CANNOT SIMPLY COLLECT A

18 Point

Effective selectivity itself is not easy to achieve; it is an ongoing process. One cannot simply collect a year's supply of submissions, perhaps five hundred ONE CANNOT SIMPLY COLLECT A Y

16 Point

Effective selectivity itself is not easy to achieve; it is an ongoing process. One cannot simply collect a year's supply of subm issions, perhaps five hundred or a thousa ONE CANNOT SIMPLY COLLECT A YEA

Point Size	6	7	8	9	10	11	12	14	16	18	20	24	30
Characters Per Pica	4.23	3.62	3.17	2.82	2.54	2.31	2.11	1.81	1.59	1.41	1.27	1.06	.85

Ethics and Social Responsibility

One characteristic, beyond all others, will determine the velocity and level of success or failure that will mark your career. And without doubt, that characteristic can be defined as ethical conduct.

Because the word ethics has come to represent behavior, its meaning needs to be expanded to include *moral* considerations that, although they obviously affect behavior, are more appropriately representative of decisions upon which behavior is based or, if you wish, choices made between right and wrong *thinking* as well as acting. In brief, ethical conduct stems from one's moral judgment.

In today's world, where business, political, and spiritual leaders in profusion are found wanting in honesty and moral restraint, it is not always easy to find role models of success that are based on probity and integrity, and the imperative message that out society seems to send to its young is that the end can fully justify the means.

In the face of the seemingly inevitable rewards for dishonesty in a culture that places its highest value on the acquisition of capital rather than on personal achievement, it is not always easy to be guided by conscience in moral considerations, for strongly desired goals often get in the way of moral restraint. But be assured that whatever it costs in deferred career advancement will be repaid manyfold if you can earn the reputation for fair dealing. In the final analysis, virtue *is* rewarded, not only in the friendship and trust of those with whom you work, but in the ultimate attainment of your goals.

Beyond the exhortation to let your personal conduct reflect your highest ideals, it is suggested that all practitioners in the field of mass communication have an obligation to recognize their social responsibility to the vast audience that is exposed to the form and nature of its messages as well as to the messages themselves. Nowhere is this more critical than in the area of television broadcasting, for as many younger people have grown up watching television in preference to reading, the advertising messages projected through the TV set have had a stronger and more extensive impact on younger viewers. And because television is an active rather than a passive medium, the intensity of emotional response can be greater than that resulting from exposure to inanimate visuals. When these aspects of television advertising are added to the power of repetitive visual messages and the comparatively greater freedom in the use of sexual symbols in television, it can be seen that the social impact of advertising messages is greater today than it has ever been.

Just as those who possess power have an obligation to accept responsibility for its use, the profession of advertising must acknowledge the obligation to consider the social impact of its messages and the imagery it employs to deliver them. Should advertising agents and those who pay for the messages they deliver to the public fail to recognize the need for disciplined restraint in developing and projecting concepts that can adversely affect the morals of the young in particular and society in general, it will sow the seeds for an inevitable harvest of public censorship in the form of increased government regulation.

All who aspire to careers in the creative side of advertising should consider the possibility of the adverse impact on society when preparing messages designed to bring about changes in consumer behavior. Much of the role modeling that once took place in the family unit results today from the influence of advertising on lifestyles and social behavior.

Although students of advertising need to understand the social impact of the messages they design, they need also to recognize the difficulty in exercising restrictive creative judgment that does not reflect the attitude of advertising management, for all advertising concepts and messages are approved on management levels above that of the copywriter. A dichotomy in the acceptance of social responsibility can and does result, to plague the advertising writer whose perceptions and restraints are not shared by those who issue copy directives.

Beyond this fact of a copywriter's life lies the problem of ethics when writers are required to deal with claims or depictions perceived to be dishonest or misleading; it can be difficult for the advertising writer to reconcile the needs of the assigned task with personal moral restraints. In such cases, it is the view of the writers of this text that although occasional ethical compromises must be made in the interest of employment continuity, a writer who disagrees with the ethical values of advertising management should begin to look for a copywriting job in which ethical considerations are known to exist. Only in this way can you make your own statement of disapproval of advertising practices that you perceive to be strongly unethical or misleading.

In the end, personal restraint in response to the temptation to cross the line between truth and falsehood, right and wrong, for the sake of short-term gain is bound to be rewarded by the respect and trust that causes men and women to elevate those of their number with integrity to positions of authority—for although false leaders can and do emerge, their days are necessarily limited by self-serving motivation and behavior.

W. KEITH HAFER

GORDON E. WHITE

Accordion Fold: Folds in paper that open like an accordion.

Action response devices: Commonly used in direct marketing advertising to make it easy for respondent to take final step. Pop-up coupons are most notable form.

Advertising Council: Not-for-profit organization, supported by all facets of advertising industry, that produces essential public-service ad campaigns created by volunteer agencies and carried free by the media.

Agate line: A measurement of newspaper column depth. There are fourteen agate lines to one inch of depth.

Agency billings: The total amount of advertising dollars placed in the media by an agency for its clients. Not to be confused with agency income or agency profit.

Animatic: A television storyboard filmed in such a way that it resembles a regular commercial. Often used for test purposes. Illusion of motion is achieved through such camera usages as pans, zooms, and dissolves.

Animation: Use of series of still drawings in movies to give illusion of motion; Disney cartoons.

Announcer: In American radio and TV commercials the announcer is essentially a salesperson and is accepted as such by the public.

Art Director: Person primarily concerned with putting all elements of a message into a layout or format that communicates strongly.

Audio: That portion of TV commercial script that has to do with sound, voice, music.

Basic Selling Concept: Total advertising concentration on the product's unique selling proposition (a strong claim of benefit that cannot be, or is not, offered by a competitor).

Basic Selling Idea: See Basic Selling Concept.

Beauty Shot: TV term for carefully staged close-up of product; also called *glamour shot*.

Bleed: A printing term indicating that the printed matter extends right to the edge of the page; no margin.

"Blind" headline: A curiosity headline that does not reveal the principal benefit instantly; a headline intended to intrigue the customer into reading further. "The Case of the Barking Cat."

Body copy: The main text of a print ad, following headline and subhead.

Boom: Up, down, or over camera shot achieved by mounting camera on a crane.

Brainstorming: The term used by Alex Osborn to describe a certain form of group ideation that, among other things, rules out negative thinking.

Camera-ready art: Pictures and type assembled in precise layout form to be photographed as next-to-last step in print reproduction process.

Captive audience: An audience that cannot escape your ad; a rider in a crowded bus, for instance.

Case history: A business-to-business ad based on an actual product installation, reported in impartial detail; in essence, a third-party endorsement.

Clip art: Catalog of professionally prepared artwork subscribed to by local media from which local retailer can select or clip an item to paste right in an ad.

Closure: Universal human tendency to report a complete figure or sentence for an incomplete one.

Coated stock: Paper with a smooth finish.

"Cold turkey" letter: A cover letter to a prospective employer whom you don't know and who doesn't know you.

Communications objective: An advertising objective relating to the communication itself, such as awareness, comprehension, familiarity; as opposed to a sales objective.

Comprehensive: A print ad layout with type, photos, or tightly drawn illustrations, all precisely assembled to look like finished, printed ad.

Consumer jury: Any number of consumers from whom an advertiser seeks opinions on products and advertising.

Consumer panel: Scientifically selected number of consumer families permanently available for expressing opinions on an advertiser's marketing and advertising plans.

Coop: Short for cooperative advertising, an arrangement whereby national advertisers contribute funds toward the advertising of their products by a local merchant.

Copywriter's Rough: The roughest kind of sketch by the copywriter showing how writer's idea might appear in print; first step in layout process.

Cover letter: A job-seeking letter that accompanies your résumé.

Creative Strategy: Basic formula for intelligent advertising; analyzes situation and decides in advance *what* you want your advertising to say.

Creative Tactics: Method by which you implement the creative strategy; *how* you're going to say it.

Crop: To eliminate parts of a photograph or piece of artwork in the printing process.

Cut: In television, an instantaneous change of picture.

"DAGMAR": A 1961 treatise by Russell Colley entitled "Defining Advertising Goals for Measured Advertising Results." It advocated adoption of communications goals rather than marketing or sales goals as a fairer test of advertising effectiveness.

Demographics: Most basic research characteristics of an audience: age, sex, education, income, family make-up, etc.

Demonstrable product difference: A product advantage that can not only be claimed but be *shown* in a convincing manner.

Differentiation: What every advertiser hopes to achieve in the minds of consumers; that benefit, feature, or image that makes a product stand out from competitors.

Direct marketing: A form of selling/advertising that eliminates the middleman, goes direct from producer to customer.

Discrimination: The avoidance of making the same response to a similar but somewhat different stimulus.

Dissolve: In television, the fading out of one picture as a new picture fades in.

Dolly: Television term whereby the entire camera moves forward or back.

Doughnut: A gap in the body of a recorded radio commercial into which live copy can be inserted at the local station.

Down: A broadcast production term referring to reduction of volume.

Dummy: Rough, early layout of a proposed folder or brochure.

Effects: Various visual designs in television generated electronically on videotape; a wipe, for example.

Empathy: The ability to put yourself in the other person's shoes; this is the quality most essential in a good advertising writer.

Establishing shot: Generally a long shot that features the setting for a commercial; it "sets the stage" for the action to follow.

Fact sheet: A list of key product points in descending order of importance; given to announcer who uses list in ad-libbing commercial plugs for product or service.

Fade: Bring picture or sound in or out slowly.

Feedback: The measurable response to advertising, by sales, by coupon returns, by requests for offers, by inquiries; all direct marketing advertising produces feedback.

Film clip: A scene or series of scenes using already-existing film footage.

Finished layout: A print layout made to correct publication size and detailed enough to obtain client's okay to produce.

Fleeting message: Unlike a print ad that stands still, a TV or radio commercial "moves" very fast; difficult for viewer/listener to comprehend a complicated message that flies by in thirty seconds, even fifteen.

Focus Group Interviews: Research interview sessions with small groups of logical prospects for a product. The interviewer encourages free flow of opinion that is recorded on audiotape for use later by copywriter; not quantitative research but gives copywriter keen insight into views and words of customers.

Free-lance: A creative person who works alone, doing advertising on a per-job basis, not a permanent employee of an agency or advertiser organization.

Free-standing insert: Multi-page ads produced elsewhere and tucked into the folds of a local Sunday paper.

Freeze frame: Picture motion suddenly stopped to highlight one element.

"Gathering Raw Materials": Term used by copy veteran James Webb Young in reference to the copywriter's initial search through all kinds of background information.

Generalization: A response elicited by a different but similar stimulus than that which we are familiar.

Gravure: One of the three basic printing methods; involves inking from a sunken surface.

Gutter: Inner margin of a magazine paper next to the binding.

Halftone: Print production term referring to reproduction of continuous tone artwork such as a photo; the artwork is photographed through a glass screen of perpendicular lines that convert the printing image into dots.

Hard sell: The use of direct, obvious, and heavy-handed means to present an advertising message.

Headline: The principal statement of benefit or promise in an ad; considered by many copywriters as most important element in a print ad.

Hidden offer: In test ad, a special offer or inducement "buried" near end of the main text; not obvious like a coupon.

Horizontal publication: A business-to-business publication that covers a certain job function across many industries.

"How to" headline: A headline that promises to reveal information in a very direct and open way: "How to prepare summer salads."

Impulse items: Relatively inexpensive and unimportant items that catch your eye while you are shopping for something more important or more mundane.

In: Broadcast term meaning to introduce or begin an audio effect: bring in music here, for instance.

Insert: A separately printed piece placed in a regular magazine or newspaper; Sunday papers carry many free-standing inserts.

Institutional copy: Retail advertising based not on merchandise but on the store's philosophy or on the store's services, such as the handling of charge accounts.

Interlock: System of synchronizing and projecting separate film reel and sound track for final approval of a TV commercial.

Island ad: Smaller than page-size magazine ad printed in center of page with editorial material surrounding it.

Italic: Type with a sloped or slanted stem; used chiefly for emphasis.

Jingle: Generally refers to a selling message put to music.

Justified type: A type setting in which every line is carefully spaced out so that there are even edges on both sides of the setting.

Keyline: A layout indicating exactly where illustrations, type, and other elements go in an ad; for guidance of photo-engraver.

Key Number: Used in coupon ads and "hidden offer" ads to see which appeal and which publication pulls in the most responses.

Key visual: The scene in a TV commercial that embodies the basic concept of the message. Example: the white hot metal being shaped into a sword for a Marine Corps officer.

Kill: Broadcast term meaning don't use, strike it out, or remove.

Lab: Where movie film is developed and processed.

Layout: Visual arrangement of all the elements in a total proposed print advertising message.

Letterpress: One of the three basic printing processes; involves inking from a raised surface.

Line art: Any artwork composed of solid blacks and whites; reproduction does not involve a half-tone screen.

Live action: TV commercial involving real people and objects, as opposed to animation.

Location: Setting for commercial that is *not* in a studio.

Logotype: The name of a product or company signing an ad; usually involves a special design.

Marketing Objective: An objective relating to sales, usually expressed as share of market.

Marketing Variables: Conditions that affect sales: product, price, packaging, general economic conditions, weather, retailer cooperation, competitive activity, etc.

Match cut: TV term involving cutting from camera shot of one object to a similarly shaped object in a different location.

Match dissolve: A slower process of the above.

Mechanical: See Keyline.

Movieola: Compact film-and-sound editing machine that enables film editor to check footage of the commercial action frame by frame.

Nutshell story: The key to superior communication; the ability to distill a selling idea down to its bare essence, stripping away all unessentials; a poster idea.

Objectivity: The ability to see more than one side to a question.

Off register: When color printing plates are not perfectly aligned.

Offset: One of the three basic forms of printing; uses inking from a flat surface.

Opticals: Visual effects such as fades, dissolves, wipes, supers, etc.

Out: Broadcast sound term meaning end it, get rid of it, take it out.

Out of sync: When picture and sound are not perfectly aligned.

Overlay: Transparent cover over artwork showing color breakdown and other instructions for printer.

Overrun: Printing an excess number of copies.

Paired-comparison: A print copy pretest wherein a respondent is shown only two prospective ads at a time and asked to pick one.

Pan: Horizontal movement of camera head, left or right, from a fixed pivot.

Personal Profile: Idealization of an ad-maker's single most likely consumer; this fictional character is given a name, a family, a history, a set of attitudes—all based on marketing research facts; great help to copywriter in preparing person-to-person communication.

Photoboard: A printed piece resembling a TV storyboard; using still photos from the commercial, generally used to merchandise the advertising to the trade.

Photomatic: Same as an animatic, except that still photos are used instead of drawings.

Pica: Typographical measurement; 1/6th of an inch.

Pictures in the Mind's Eye: The effect the writer of radio commercials produces; the imagination of the listener fills in the blanks, does almost all the work.

Pinpoint targeting: The primary advantage of using direct mail; you can design a mailing to reach precisely the people you want to reach.

Pitch: Slang term for any kind of sales presentation, but particularly when an agency is soliciting a new account.

Pitchman: Slang term for salesperson, particularly a radio or TV announcer.

Point: Typographic measure of size; there are 72 points to an inch of depth, 12 points to a pica.

P-O-P: Term used referring to displays in retail outlets. P-O-P is short for Point-of-Purchase.

Portfolio: The carrying case containing the creative person's sample book used in the job hunt.

Positioning: Establishing your product in a certain niche in the public's mind: a sports car, a family car, a performance car.

Posttest: A test of ad copy *after* the advertising has appeared in the media.

Pre-emptive claim: Making a claim that competitors cannot use or have not used, thus putting you in the position of "owning" a product advantage.

Pre-production meeting: The key to efficient TV production; a meeting attended by key production house people, by agency people, and by client people to review a commercial idea thoroughly *before* it is shot. All questions of casting, wardrobe, settings, props, locations, etc., are discussed and settled.

Pretest: A test of proposed ad copy *before* any of it appears in the media.

Producer: Person totally responsible for coordinating all details of TV or radio production, from casting talent to providing lunches on location.

Production house: Company outside the agency hired to shoot a TV commercial; the production house generally supplies the director, camera people, lighting experts, etc.

Production spot: Radio term referring to a commercial that is produced in a studio, and duplicates of which are sent to all stations on the media list.

Progressives: Term in color printing referring to a set of four-color plates or films in which colors are shown separately and then in combination, first yellow, then red, then yellow and red together, then blue, then yellow, red, and blue together, then black, then all four together.

Props: All physical materials used in a commercial.

Psychographics: A consumer research designation for examining people by way of their attitudes, lifestyles, etc.

Public service: Advertising done for a nonprofit organization.

Reason-why copy: Body copy that *proves* in a specific way the promise made in the headline of the ad.

Recall test: A print copy test in which respondents must recall material in a magazine before they qualify as readers—much more stringent than a recognition test; Gallup-Robinson is a recall test.

Recognition test: A print copy test in which respondents are shown ad in publication and asked if they had seen it previously; Starch Readership Survey is a recognition test.

Recurring theme: A consistent tagline of copy in display, running through all the advertising in a campaign; These are the words people remember and use to identify advertising.

Reinforcement advertising: Those forms of advertising that support your main selling campaign; If TV is your primary medium, billboards in key markets might carry reinforcement advertising.

Remote: An announcement aired live from a location outside the studio.

Rep: The person who represents a medium or a supplier and sells their organization's services to an agency.

Repro proof: Proof of a typesetting so clean and perfect that it can be photographed as part of the ad's artwork.

Résumé: The cold, crisp, factual story of your life on a single typewritten page.

Reverse type: Type set in white against black background.

Ripple dissolve: A TV transition that appears as though water has rippled across the film, washing away one scene and revealing another. A ripple dissolve (or shimmer dissolve) may begin and end a commercial "flashback." Frequently used in "before and after" or "cause and effect" demonstrations; almost always used to introduce a dream sequence.

Roman: Type with a straight-up-and-down stem; the overwhelming majority of type we see is Roman.

R.O.P.: Run of Paper; your ad may appear anywhere in the newspaper, not in a special position.

Rough layout: Somewhat sketchy representation of what a print ad will ultimately look like; made to actual size, but with elements only roughly indicated.

Sales analysis: Actual sales figures can be very revealing: does the product sell more in one outlet than another? in one region than another? at one price than at another? in one season than another?

Sample Book: A collection of an ad-writer's work, often speculative, used in the job search.

Sans Serif Type: Modern type faces without tiny appendages at the ends of each letter; these crisp, sharp letters work best in display rather than in solid blocks of reading matter.

Scientific advertising: Direct marketing advertising is referred to as "scientific" because it is rigorously tested in the marketplace; results are a matter of factual knowledge not guesswork.

Segue: Pronounced seg-way, it refers chiefly to musical transitions in radio, sliding from one tune to another, generally to indicate a change in time, mood, or place; good story-telling device.

Selectivity: In marketing, the narrowing of target audiences by way of media choice and copy appeal.

Self-interest headline: By far the most effective kind of headline because it is keyed directly to the customer's self-interest, not the advertiser's: "New Way to Save Money on Home Heating."

Serif type: Traditional type faces that have little strokes or appendages at the ends of each letter; these tiny stokes, or serifs, help the human eye to read.

Shimmer dissolve: See Ripple Dissolve.

Slate: At start of each scene or take, a small chalkboard with a hinged slapstick is photographed because it has handwritten information identifying the scene; slates are often done verbally in videotape production.

Slice of life: In television commercials, a dramatic situation intended to represent "reality."

Special event copy: Retail advertising geared to some special occasion such as Christmas, Easter, the local high school or college homecoming, etc.

Speculative presentation: Elaborate preparation of an advertising idea presented by an agency to a prospective client on the gamble of winning that prospect's account.

Split run: A print posttest, usually of major appeals, in which every other magazine or newspaper that comes off the press carries Ad A or Ad B. Every element is constant except the two test ads—same publication, same day, same page, same position, same surrounding editorial or ad material; consumer viewing and response conditions are totally natural.

Split screen: Special effect dividing TV screen to show a double image, or to show two separate pictures at the same time.

Spread: An advertisement of two pages running across a magazine.

Stand up: Use of person in TV commercial speaking and gesturing directly to viewer.

Still: A picture without movement, used in a television commercial.

Stock art: Existing pictures/photos available to be purchased for use in advertising.

Stop motion: Movie film taken by exposing one frame at a time; inanimate objects are usually moved by hand a fraction of an inch for each exposure and when the film is played back at normal speed the inanimate object moves.

Store image: How store is perceived in minds of the public.

Storewide promotion: A selling event that embraces many departments of a store and many different kinds of merchandise.

Storyboard: Synopsis of commercial idea, told in a series of sketch drawings with typed instructions and dialogue below each scene. Storyboards are used to (1) present ideas, (2) obtain a client okay to produce, and (3) obtain bids from independent production houses.

Straight copy: A radio commercial consisting of typewritten words only; usually read by whichever local station announcer might be on duty at time commercial was scheduled.

Strategy statement: The essentials of a creative strategy expressed in a statement of three or four sentences or perhaps a crisp paragraph.

Subhead: A display line in a print ad that follows the headline and expands on it.

Subjective camera: The audience becomes an actor, that is, the camera photographs all the action solely from the audience point of view.

Super: Superimposition of a name, benefit, slogan, product package, etc., over the principal scene on the screen; vital means of visual emphasis and reinforcement.

Swipe file: Visual material gathered from various sources over time to be used in a comprehensive layout or storyboard.

Swish pan: A pan movement of the camera head done so fast that the viewer sees only horizontal streaks on the screen; also called a zip pan.

Syndicated music: First-rate music recordings, subscribed to by local stations and made available to local advertisers.

Take: A completed scene in TV commercial.

Talent: Actors; broadcast performers.

Teleprompter: Device that rolls script in view of talent who have difficulty learning lines.

Testimonial: Endorsement of a product in its advertising by an identified user, whether a celebrity or ordinary customer.

Thumbnail sketch: Art director's small, loose sketch of possible ad; follows copywriter's rough; definitely the experimental stage of layout development.

Tie-in promotion: A selling effort that involves several different products keyed to a common theme, such as "Let's Have a Patio Party."

Tilt: Vertical movement of camera head, up or down, from fixed pivot.

Trade ad: Business-to-business ad directed chiefly to wholesalers and retailers of the advertiser's product.

Trade character: Distinctive person or thing used throughout every phase of a product promotion; identifying element to which all other efforts are hitched.

Trucking shot: Camera moves alongside object being photographed; standard shot in automotive commercials, where camera is mounted in a truck.

Typography: Everything concerned with the setting of type in a print message.

Under: broadcast term meaning to hold particular sound, dialogue, music in the background while something more crucial is being featured up front.

Up: Broadcast term meaning to increase the volume.

Vertical publication: A business-to-business publication that covers a single industry in depth.

Video: That portion of a TV commercial script that describes picture and action.

Videotape: VT; electronic production of commercials in which picture, sound, and effects can be recorded simultaneously and played back instantly.

Voice over: Written as VO in script; meaning an off-camera narrator.

Widow: Typographic term referring to one or two words left hanging at the end of a paragraph.

Wipe: A television transition whereby one scene is wiped off the screen to reveal a different scene underneath.

Zip pan: See Swish Pan.

Zoom: To move in or out on a television scene by manipulating the lens only; lens is named a Zoomar lens.

BIBLIOGRAPHY

Baker, Stephen. *Systematic Approach to Advertising Creativity.* New York: McGraw-Hill Book Company, 1979.

Baldwin, Huntley. *How Television Commercials Are Made.* Evanston, Ill.: Northwestern University, 1970.

Bedell, Clyde. *How to Write Advertising That Sells.* New York: McGraw-Hill Book Co., 1952.

Book, Albert C., and Cary, Norman D. *The Radio and Television Commercial.* Chicago: Crain Books, 1978.

Book, Albert C., and Schick, Dennis C. *Fundamentals of Copy and Layout.* Chicago: Crain Books, 1984.

Britt, Steuart Henderson. *Consumer Behavior and the Behavioral Sciences.* New York: John Wiley & Sons, Inc., 1967.

Burnett, Leo. *Communications of an Advertising Man.* Chicago: Leo Burnett Co., Inc., 1961.

Burton, Philip Ward. *Advertising Copywriting.* Columbus, Ohio: Grid Publishing, Inc., 1978.

Caples, John. *Making Ads Pay.* New York: Dover Publications, Inc., 1966.

———. *Tested Advertising Methods.* Englewood Cliffs, N.J.: Prentice-Hall, Inc., 1974.

———. *How to Make Your Advertising Make Money.* Englewood Cliffs, N.J.: Prentice-Hall, Inc., 1983.

Colley, Russell H. *Defining Advertising Goals for Measured Advertising Results.* New York: Association of National Advertisers, 1961.

Cutlip, Scott M., and Center, Allen H. *Effective Public Relations.* 4th ed. Englewood Cliffs, N.J.: Prentice-Hall, Inc., 1971.

Della Femina, Jerry. *From Those Wonderful Folks Who Gave You Pearl Harbor.* New York: Pocket Books, Inc., 1971.

De Voe, Merrill. *Effective Advertising Copy.* New York: Macmillan Publishing Co., Inc., 1956.

Dunn, S. Watson. *Advertising Copy and Communication.* New York: McGraw-Hill Book Co., 1956.

Dunn, S. Watson, and Barban, Arnold M. *Advertising: Its Role in Modern Marketing.* Hinsdale, Ill.: Dryden Press, 1978.

Engel, James F., Kollatt, David T., and Blackwell, Roger D. *Consumer Behavior.* 2d ed. New York: Holt, Rinehart & Winston, Inc., 1972.

Ernst, Sandra. *The Creative Package.* Columbus, Ohio: Grid Publishing, Inc., 1979.

Flesch, Rudolph. *The Art of Clear Thinking.* New York: Harper & Row Publishers, Inc., 1951.

Fox, Stephen. *The Mirror Makers.* New York: Random House, 1984.

Glim, Aesop. *Copy—The Core of Advertising.* 2d rev. ed. New York: Dover Publications, Inc., 1963.

Haskins, Jack B. *How to Evaluate Mass Communications.* New York: Advertising Research Foundation, Inc., 1968.

Higgins, Dennis. *The Art of Writing Advertising.* Chicago: Crain Publications, Inc., 1965.

Hotchkiss, George Burton. *Advertising Copy.* 3d ed. New York: Harper & Brothers, 1949.

Jewler, A. Jerome. *Creative Strategy in Advertising.* Belmont, Calif.: Wadsworth Publishing Co., Inc., 1985.

Kassarjian, Harold H., and Robertson, Thomas S. *Perspectives in Consumer Behavior.* Glenview, Ill.: Scott, Foresman & Co., 1968.

Kobs, Jim. *Profitable Direct Marketing.* Chicago: Crain Books, 1979.

Lucas, Darrell B., and Britt, Steuart Henderson. *Measuring Advertising Effectiveness.* New York: McGraw-Hill Book Co., 1963.

Malickson, David L., and Nason, John W. *Advertising—How to Write the Kind That Works.* New York: Charles Scribner's Sons, 1977.

Marsteller, William A. *The Wonderful World of Words.* Chicago: Marsteller, Inc., 1972.

Martineau, Pierre. *Motivation in Advertising.* New York: McGraw-Hill Book Co., 1957.

Mix, Don. *Stalking Big Ideas in the Advertising Jungle.* Garnerville, N.Y.: Allen/Bennington, 1986.

Moriarity, Sandra E. *Creative Advertising: Theory and Practice.* Englewood Cliffs, N.J.: Prentice-Hall, Inc., 1986.

Nelson, Roy Paul. *The Design of Advertising.* Dubuque, Iowa. William C. Brown Co., Publishers, 1973.

Nolte, Lawrence W. *Fundamentals of Public Relations.* Elmsford, N.Y.: Pergamon Press, Inc., 1974.

Norins, Hanley. *The Compleat Copywriter.* New York: McGraw-Hill Book Co., 1966.

Ogilvy, David. *Confessions of an Advertising Man.* New York: Atheneum Publishers, 1964.

Ogilvy, David. *Ogilvy on Advertising.* New York: Vintage Books, 1985.

Osborn, Alex. *Applied Imagination.* New York: Charles Scribner's Sons, 1963.

O'Toole, John. *The Trouble with Advertising.* New York: Chelsea House, 1981.

Paetro, Maxine. *How to Put Your Book Together and Get a Job in Advertising.* New York: Hawthorn Books, Inc., 1980.

Reeves, Rosser. *Reality in Advertising.* New York: Alfred A. Knopf, Inc., 1961.

Robertson, Thomas S. *Consumer Behavior.* Glenview, Ill.: Scott, Foresman & Co., 1970.

Rogers, Edward J. *Getting Hired.* Englewood Cliffs, N.J.: Prentice-Hall, Inc., 1982.

Roman, Kenneth, and Maas, Jane. *How to Advertise.* New York: St. Martin's Press, 1976.

Sandage, Charles H., Fryburger, Vernon, and Rotzoll, Kim. *Advertising Theory and Practice.* Homewood, Ill.: Richard D. Irwin, Inc., 1981.

Schultz, Don E. *Essentials of Advertising Strategy.* Chicago: Crain Books, 1981.

Schwab, Victor C. *How to Write a Good Advertisement.* New York: Harper & Row Publishers, Inc., 1962.

Seiden, Hank. *Advertising Pure and Simple.* New York; Amacom, 1976.

Simon, Raymond. *Public Relations: Concepts and Practice.* Columbus, Ohio: Grid Publishing, Inc., 1976.

Steiner, Gary. *The Creative Organization.* Chicago: The University of Chicago Press, 1965.

Stephenson, Howard. *Handbook of Public Relations.* 2d ed. New York: McGraw-Hill Book Co., 1971.

Stone, Bob. *Successful Direct Marketing Methods.* Chicago: Crain Books, 1979.

Taplin, Walter. *Advertising: A New Approach.* Boston: Little, Brown & Co., 1963.

Walters, C. Glenn, and Paul, Gordon W. *Consumer Behavior: An Integrated Framework.* Homewood, Ill.: Richard D. Irwin, Inc., 1970.

Wasserman, Dick. *How to Get Your First Copywriting Job.* New York: Center for Advancement of Advertising, 1985.

Whittier, Charles L. *Creative Advertising.* New York: Henry Holt and Co., 1955.

Young, James Webb. *A Technique for Producing Ideas.* Chicago: Crain Publications, Inc., 1960.

Zeigler, Sherilyn K., and Johnson, J. Douglas. *Creative Strategy and Tactics in Advertising.* Columbus, Ohio: Grid Publishing, Inc., 1981.

INDEX

A

Achievers, 20. See VALS
Acquiring new business, 298–303
Adams, Mason, 147
Adolph Coors Company, xiv
Advertising
  as selling, 2
  competitors, 65
  criteria of good, 2
  placement, 65
  primary function, 271
  writing, 2
Advertising Age, xvi, 2
Advertising checklist, 251
Advertising copy research, 249–260
Advertising Council, xv, 31
Advertising Hall of Fame, xii, xiv
Advertising must fit company image, 214
Advertising pre-prints, 194
Advertising research called "copy testing", 250
Advertising research, "up front research", 20
Advertising to foreign markets, 266–67
Advertising writer, 3
  appreciation of language, 3
  aptitude, 3
  duties of, 3
  personal characteristics, 4–9
  qualities, 3
After-sale advertising, 237
Agency copywriting offers wide menu, 271
Alexander Hamilton Extension Institute, 184

American Academy of Advertising, xvi
American Association of Advertising Agencies, 300
American Association of Yellow Pages Publishers, 238
American Bar Association, 202
American Dental Association, 202
American Express, 35, 120
American Medical Association, 202
American Telephone and Telegraph, 120
Anheuser-Busch, 178, 214
Animatics, 167
Annual Reports in public relations, 278
Arm and Hammer, 65
Armstrong, Andy, 120
Arrow shirts, 64
Association of National Advertisers, 44
Attitude change
  forced use, 29
  reinforcement, 30
  repetitions, 29
  repetitions with variations, 29
Attitude formation, 28
Attitude measurement, 28
Audio, 164

B

Bacon, James, 108
Bang-tail envelopes, 189
Bartles and Jaymes, 158, 237
Bartlett's Familiar Quotations, 81
Barton, Bruce, 184, 189
"Basic Advertising", xvi

Basic appeals test in marketing, 190
Basic art direction and production, 310–12
Basic principles of visual communication, 310
Basic Team and One, 84
Bates, Ted Agency, 303
Batton, Barton, Durstine and Osgood, xii, xiv, xvi, 67, 86, 270
Bean, L. L., 189
Belongers, 20. see VALS
Benedict, J. H. and Associates, xiv
Benny, Jack, 147
Biased source of information, 62
Bibliography, 327–29
Bi-culturals and bi-linguals in foreign advertising, 266
"Big Ben", 64
Billings, 298
Black, Gillock and Langberg, case history, xiv, 196
Black Velvet, 237
Bob and Ray, 147
Body Copy
  believeability, 115
  brevity, 114
  customer examination, 114
  eliminate non-essentials, 114
  facts, 115
  form, 113
  generalities don't communicate, 115
  guarantees, 115
  highly respected names, 116
  length, 113
  memorable, 114
  outstanding success story, 116
  performance tests, 117

record-setting sales, 117
third-person endorsements, 117
Books as public relations tools, 278–9
Boom-up, boom-down, 162
Boot and Shoe Recorder, 202
Bon Appétit Books, 188
Bosley, Tom, 147
Brainstorming, 80
Brand image less important, 226
Britt, Professor Stewart H., 27
Brochures in direct mail, 192. See direct mail
Brochures in public relations, 279
Bud Light, 158, 241, case study, 178
Budweiser, 65
Built-in prospects, 189
Bullets in ad copy, 187
Burger King, 139
Burke Day-after recall
how interviews conducted, 259–60
what report contains, 259
Burnett, Leo, xv, 31, 78, 120
Business ads provide leads for salesmen, 203
Business magazines read on company time, 203
Business magazines, subscriptions, 203
Business publications, 202
Business-to-business advertising, 202
Business writing sells capabilities, 203
Business writing solicits inquiries, 203
Business Week, 202

C

Cadillac, 61, 65
Camera-ready advertising, 132
Cahners Publishing Company, 205
"California Days" promotion, 217
Campbell-Ewald Company, xv
Campbell-Mithun, 302
Campbell soup, 45, 147
Capacity for criticism, 6

Caples, John, xii, xiv, 184, 190, 193
Cardinal sin in advertising, 62
Carnegie, Dale, 184
Carnival Cruise Lines, xiv, 125–6
Case history, 62
Catalog pages, 236
Chalfant Crafts, Inc., xv
Change in stimuli, 23
Chicago Tribune, 22
Chivas Regal, 24, 65
Churchill, Winston, 86
Clarity Cloverleaf Rueff, xv, 106
Classic four page creative formula, 80
Clio awards, 37
Clip art services for retail ads, 217
Closure in ads, 25
Coca-Cola, 147
Colley, Russell, 44
Color in ads, 24
Commercials, radio, 146
Commissions for copywriters, 270
Communications Diversified of New York, xv, 230–3
"Compleat Copywriter", 157, 246, 303
Computers in direct marketing, 184. see direct marketing
Consumer behavior, 22
"Confessions of an Advertising Man", 193, 303
Consumer business publications, 202
Consumer panel, method, drawbacks, 253–4
Consumer panel, testing copy, 252
Contacts in job-hunting, 292–3
Contest, defined, 228
Controlled circulation publications, 202
Cooperative advertising funds, 218
"Coping With Life", xv
Copy-art team, 84
Copywriter
and direct mail, 226–9
appeal to customer interest, 204
as salesperson, 188
close to customers, 216

five tips for, 245
learn customer jargon, 204
may need special knowledge, 204
tailor copy to fit prospect, 204
Copywriter's constant deadlines, 216
Copywriting alone, 310–2
Copywriting sample book, contents, 282–4
Copywriting success formula, 244
Coronet, xvi
Cosmopolitan, 66
Cost per call figures, 184
Coupons for customer response, 203
Coupon in testing copy, 252
Counter cards, 236
Counter displays, 236
Cover letter, 286, 288
Creative case histories, xiv
Creative freedom of direct mail, 186. see direct mail
Creative Strategy, preparation, 19, 39–46
effect of advertising, 40
example, U. S. Marine Corps, 42
knowledge of benefits, 40
knowledge of customers, 40
necessity to apply strategy, 46
personal profile, 41
"positioning", 40
preparation, 19
principal benefit, 41
principal objective, 42
principal target, 42
purpose of, 40
rules and procedures, 40
strategy statement, 41
tactics, 70
understanding objectives, 43
using DAGMAR, 44. see DAGMAR
what to be creative about, 46
Credit cards, 184
Criteria for seeking new business, 299
Crude creed for copywriters, 117–20
Curiosity, 6
Cut, 162
Cutty Sark, 97

D

DAGMAR, Defining advertising goals for measured advertising results, 44
Daily deadlines tax creativity, 271
Dannon Company, Inc., xiv
Dannon yogurt, 45, case study, 176
D'Arcy, Masius, Benton and Bowles, xiv
DeBeers, 97
Decals, 236
DDB Needham Worldwide, xiv, 54, 178, 241, 270
Della Femina, Jerry, 303
Demographics, 20
Department of Transportation, xiv
Determination and persistence, 6
Depth interviews, 21
Desk-top ad making, 132–5
DFS Dorland Saatchi and Saatchi, 287
Dichter, Dr. Ernest, 193, 269
Differentiate, 62
Direct approach in marketing, 183–195
Direct Mail, 185
    avoids waste circulation, 186
    catalogs, 189
    controls timing and format, 186
    coupons, 227
    efficient in reaching small groups, 194
    for political purposes, 194
    gadget mailing, 194
    has creative freedom, 186
    is "straight line" medium, 186
    marketing is like face-to-face selling, 189–90
    medium for introducing novelty and realism, 186
    offerings, 194
    pin-point targeting, 186
    responsive devices, 187
    specific forms, 194
Direct mail package
    contents, 187
    example, 188
Direct market writing
    anticipates reader questions, 190
    full sales story, 190

Direct Marketing Association, 192
Direct marketing
    feedback, 185
    media use, 185
    testing, 190
Direct selling from producer to consumer, 184
Directory of Advertising Agencies, 287
Discover Card, 35
Discrimination in learning, 26
Display of related items, 236
Display must feature product, 236
Display space is priceless, 236
Dissolve, 163
Doctor Elliott's Five-foot Shelf, 184
Dr. Pepper, 158
Dodge Colt, 24
Doe-Anderson Advertising Agency, 108, 22, 247 xiv
Dolly in, dolly out, 162
Dreier, Alex, 147
Duties of an ad agency writer, 270
Duties of company advertising department, 273

E

Easel cards, 236
ECU (Extreme Closeup), 162
Eiffel Tower, 237
ELS (Extreme Longshot), 162
Emery Worldwide, xiv, 45, 49
Empathy, 8
Emphasis on selectively, 185
Esentials of retail copy, 214–5
    news/immediacy, 215
    price, 215
    specifics, 215
    store image, 214
Esty, William Company, xiv
Ethics and Social Responsibility, 315–7

F

Fallon-McElligott, xv, 122
Familiarity in ads, 25
Farm publications, 202

Fashion ads emphasize style and flair, 240
Fashion advertising, 240
Federal Express, 49
Feedback from retail advertising, 216
Feedback in direct marketing, 185
Ferguson, James C., xiv
Fischer and Porter Company, xv
Fischer Packing Company, xiv, 244, 247
Five criteria for agency advertising efforts, 27
Five essential differences between national and retail advertising, 218
Five rules for writing internal publications, 279
Five tips for copywriters, 244
Fletcher, Alan D., 238n
Floor stands, 236
Focus group interviews, 21
Focus groups, 21
Foote, Cone Belding, xiv, 37, 52, 181, 270, 288
Forbes, 10, 202
Ford Motor Company, 58, 61
Forms of post-testing, 255–57. see Testing
Forms of pre-testing, list, 252–54
Fortune, 202
Four essentials of retail copy, 214
Freeze frame, 1, 164
French, R. T. Company, xiv
French's Mustard, case study, 172
"From Those Wonderful People Who Gave You Pearl Harbor", 303
Full and detailed information, 189
Full service agencies, 270
Fundamental truths about advertising, 214

G

Gallup and Robinson, xv
Gallup and Robinson: how interviews conducted, 258
Gallup and Robinson Readership, 258

Gallup, Dr. George, 303
Garner, James, 68
General Electric, 24
General Foods, 270
General Motors, 270
General seasonal events, 217
Generalization in learning, 26
George Washington University, xv
Gershwin, George, 147
Glossary, 319–26
Gold'n Plump Poultry, xiv, 106–7
Good Housekeeping Institute, 62, 66
Grey Advertising Agency, 302
    "Grey Matter", 302
Gribben, George, 102
Guidelines for effective copy, 204–5
    deal with specifics, 205
    example of the product at work, 205
    personalized copy, 205
    straightforward and rational, 205

H

Hafer, W. Keith, xv
Harmon, Mark, 71
Harrod's, 214
Harvard Business School, 302
Harvard University, xv
Hathaway shirts, 303
Hawthorn School of Art, xv
HCM Agency, 176
HDM Advertising Agency, xiv
HDM Dawson Johns and Black, xiv, 219–20
Headlines
    challenge or quiz, 100
    classic, 100
    curiosity, 99
    headline/picture, 85
    "how to", 101
    news, 99
    quantity, 101
    question, 100
    self-interest, 99
    subheads, 101
    unlovely example, 99
Hidden offer in split-run advertising, 254

Hints on seeking any job, 288
Hispanic markets, 267
Home Box Office, xv, 261
Home study courses, 184
Horchow catalog, 189
Hotchkiss, George Burton, 80
Housecall, Inc., 21
How to discover ideas for copy, 57
"How to get your first copywriting job", 288
"How to Put Your Book Together and Get a Job in Advertising", 287
Humility, 7
"Hunchback of Notre Dame", 158

I

"I-Am-Me" group, 21, see VALS
Illustration, 92–97
    key feature, 92
    story-telling power, 92
    uses of, 93–97
Image a great asset in retailing, 214
Imagination, 5
Industrial advertisers, 62
In-house advertising agencies, 270
Immediacy in retail copy, 214
Institute for Motivational Research, 193n
Institutional messages, 217
Instruction sheets, 236
Intelligence, 5
Integrity, 7
Interest in human nature, 7
International Cellu-cotton Products Company, 266
International Trade Center, 157
Interview, 287, 291
Ivory Soap, 24

J

Jamaica Tourist Board, xiv, 45, 73–4
Jello, 147
Jewish Hospital, xiv, 222
Job-hunting for an advertising job, 281–93
"John Caples: Adman", xvi

John Hancock, 104
Johnson and Johnson, 267
Johnson, S. C. and Son, xiv, 75
Journal of Advertising, xvi
Journal of Marketing, xvi

K

Keeping new business, 303–5
Kelly Services, Inc., xiv, 149
Kelly Services, case history, 149–50
Kemper Group, xiv
Kemper Insurance, case study, 33
Keying, 103
Kleenex, 45, 67
Kleenex Softique, case study, 37
Kimberly-Clark, xiv, 37, 266
Kimble, Keith, 86
Klepner, Otto, 97
Kobs and Draft Advertising, Inc., xiv, 261
Kraft Foods, 267

L

Layout
    cartoon, 89
    comic strip, 89
    editorial, 89
    illustration, 92
    picture-caption, 89
    picture-cluster, 92
    poster, 89
    rough, 87
    standard, 89
Learning, forms of, 26–7
Learning the lingo of your prospect, 204
Lee Jeans, 228
Letters in public relations, 278
Leyendecker paintings, 64
Light-pull tags, 236
Lincoln-Mercury Division of Ford Motor Company, xiv
Local station production help, 148
Looking for a job, 287–93
Long copy is better than short, 190
L'Oreal, xiv, 230
Los Angeles Herald Examiner, 108

M

Macy, R. H., 214, 271
Maker's Mark Distillery, xiv, 108–9
Making the most of an interview, 291–2
"Man in the Arrow Shirt", 58
Manufacturers help stores with ads, 218
Market Research, 20
Marlboro, 64
Marshall Field, 214, 217
Marsteller, Ketchum, MacLeod and Grove, 302
Marstrat Inc., xiv, 208–9
Martineau, Pierre, 22
"Mass Transit" Volkswagen ad, 246
Match cut, 163
Match dissolve, 163
Matting, 164
Maxwell House, 147
May Company, 79
Mayer, Edward N., 92
Maytag, 119
Mazda, 147
Mazda, case history, 68
McDonald's, 267
MCU (Medium Closeup), 162
Media Decisions, 202
Mediamark Research Inc., 20
Media of retailing, 217
Mental and physical stamina, 9
Mercer, Richard, 174
Mercury, case study, 174
Mercury Theatre of the Air, 140
Merchandising racks, 236
Merrill Lynch, 21
Michelin, xiv, 97, 128
Midas Muffler, 59
Miller Brewing, 267
Miller High Life, 158
Miller Light, 241
Mistakes in product naming, 266
MLS (Medium Longshot), 162
Mobile One motor oil, 244
Mobiles, 236
Motivation, 22, for smoking, 23
Motivation Research, 260
Motorcraft, 62
MS (Medium Shot), 162
Multi-page, free standing newspaper insert, 189

Musical transition, 145
Mustang, 65

N

National Georgraphic, 139
Nationals in overseas advertising, 266
Needham Harper Worldwide, illus, 55
New England Advertising Week, xv
"News business", defined 297
Newspapers carry most retail ads, 217
News release contents and rules 276–7
News releases in public relations, 275
New York Life Insurance Company, 266
New York University, xv
NFL "Fun, Food and Football" promotion, 228, 230–01
NFL Monday Night Football, 66
NFL Properties, xiv
Nielsen Market Share Data, 247
Nobilia Citizen wristwatch, 24
Norins, Hanley, 138, 157, 186, 246, 303
Northwestern University, xv
Novelty and contrast, 24
Nutshell Principle: Key to Success, 243–6
N. W. Ayer, xv, 302
N. W. Ayer ABH International, 270

O

Object of sales promotion, 226
Objectivity, 6
Observation, 5
Ogilvy and Mather, 302
Ogilvy, David, 29, 86, 193, 204, 303
"Ogilvy on Advertising", 193
O'Keefe and Merritt, 80
"Old boy" networks in job hunting, 292
Oldsmobile, 140
Osborn, Alex, 80
Oscar Meyer, 147
Osgood, Charles, 28

Outdoor posters, tips for copywriters, 245
Outside talent, 165
Overall theme in storewide promotions, 217
Over-wire banners, 236

P

Pabst Blue Ribbon, 63
Package insets, 236
Packaging Engineers, 202
Paetro, Maxine, 287
Patience, 6
Peabody, Cluett, 58
Pearl Health Services, Inc., xiv, 52
Penney's, 219–20
People Magazine, 203
Pepsi Cola, 29, 158
Pepsi Generation, 147
Perception, 23
Perry, William "The Refrigerator", 228
Persistence, an example, 290–1
Personality, 27
Personalized message, 180
Personal salesperson, 185
Person-to-person communications, 186
Persuasion
  one-sided vs. two-sided arguments, 29
  fear appeals, 29
  non-overt appeals, 29
Philip Morris, 267
Photomatics, 167
Picture/headline, 85
Pin point targeting of direct mail, 186
Placement of ads, 24
Pledge, case history, 75
Point of purchase, materials named, 236
Point system, 311–2
POP point of purchase advertising, 236
Pop-up coupons, 190
Portfolio, 284
Positioning, 35, 40
Poster advertising, various locations, 239
Posters adapt to other media, 246

Posters, marriage of picture and words, 244
Posters not subtle, 239
Preparing TV copy, 158
Preproduction meeting, 167
Pre-testing, forms, 251–2
Price essential item of information, 314
Price in retail ads, 214
Price reduction is a true bargain, 227
Prime prospects, 67
Printers Ink, xvi
Process shot, 163
Procter and Gamble, 267
Product history, 58
Product introductions in decline, 226
Product manufacture, 58
Product performance, 60
Product sales, 59
Production, forms 168–70
  film 168
  live, 163
  video tape, 169
Progressive Grocer, 202
Projective tests, 260
Promotion of mature products for quick sale, 226
Proudfoot, Alexander Organization, xiv
Psychological interviews, 260
Publicity in public relations, 277
Public relations articles, rules, 277
Public relations careers, 280
Public relations field, 274–80
Public relations writing, 274
Public relations writing, assignments listed, 275
"Pupilometer" test, 259
Purchaser plagued with doubt, 237
Purchasing Magazine, 202

Q

Quaker Oats, 270
Qualities of a copywriter, 4–9

R

Radio Advertising Bureau, xiv
Radio commercials, types
  dialog, 146

dramatized, 147
musical, 147
production spot, 146
straight, 146
Radio, writing for, 139–54
  change with television, 138
  listener preferences, 138
  medium of the imagination, 140
  picture in the minds' eye, 139
  read your copy aloud, 142
  rules for successful, 1, 141
  starting in, 142
  stress one simple idea, 139
  "The Segmented Medium", 138
  use of imagination, 138
  use of voice and music, 138
  writing for the ear, 138
Raid, case study, 181
Readers' Digest, 203
"Reality in Advertising", 303
Rear screen projection, 164
Reasons for direct marketing boom, 187
Rebates and refunds, 227
Recall method in post-testing, 257
Reeves, Rosser, 303
Reinforcement or reward, 26
Reliability of testing, 252
Repetition, 26; with variations, 29
Researching and testing ideas via sampling, 194
Responsive devices in direct mail, 187
Resume, contents, 284–6, 288
Retail advertising
  differs from national, 214
  great field for entry level, 218
  is local, 215
  is most common, 271
  is news, 214
Retail copy, four essentials, 214
Retailer is purchasing agent for community, 214
Retailing is local, 214
Riesman, David, 27
Ripple dissolve, 163
roman and italic type, 311–2
Rules for direct mail use, 192–3
Ruels for writing new business presentation, 300–1
Rules of constancy, 24

Rules of consumer, 22
Rules of learning, 27

S

Safety belt campaign, case study, 31–2
Sales and Marketing Management, 20, 202
Sales Market Testing, 255–6
Sales promotion
  boom, 226
  defined, 226
  growth, reasons, 226–7
  limitations, 229
  never substitute for quality, 226
Sales promotion techniques
  coupons, 226
  free-standing insets, 227
Sample book, 282
Sampling, 194
San Diego Zoo, 244
Schlitz, 63
Sears, 97, 119, 219
Sears Roebuck full line catalog, 189
Segue, 145
Selective perception, 29
Selectivity, 25
Self-confidence, 7
Self-discipline, 6
Self-mailing order blanks, 190
Selling strategy, 299
Semantic Differential Scale, 28
Serif and sans serif, 312
Sheaffer Pen Company, 63
Shearson American Express, 104
Shelf talkers, 236
Shih, David, hunder, literacy campaigns, 132–5
Shimmer dissolve, 163
Sikorsky, Igor, 210
Silton Company, xv
Simmons Market Research Bureau, 20
Simulated market in testing copy, 252
Simulated Market Testing, 255–6
Size of ads, 24
Slow motion, 164
Spacing/leading, 311–2
Spanish-speaking market, 266. See Hispanic
Specialty Advertising Association International, xiv, 196, 198

Specific community events, 217
Specific details in retail ads, 215
Specifics contribute to store's image for service, 216
Speeches in public relations, 278
Spencer Gifts, 189
Spiegel, xv, 219–20
Split-run in testing copy, 252
Split-run testing, advantages, 190, 255
Spuds MacKenzie, original party animal, 241
Standard Rate and Data, 66, 311
Stanford Research Institute, 20
Starch, Daniel, 256
Starch: how interviews conducted, three measurements, 256
Starch Readership Study, 256
State Farm Insurance Company, xiv, 54
Stiller and Meara, 147
Stone, Bob, 193
Store buyer makes key decisions, 216
Store policies and service, 217
Storewide promotions, overall theme, 217
Storyboard, 166–7
"Straight line medium", 186
Subjective camera, 164
Successful Direct Marketing Methods, 193
Successful retailer is an institution, 214
Sugarman, Joseph, 185
Survey of Buying Power, 20
Survivors, 21. See VALS
Sustainers, 21. See VALS
Sweepstakes
    and contests, 228
    defined, 228
    example, 228

T

TCU (Tight Closeup), 162
Teasers, 245
Television a picture medium, 158
Television concept, 159
Television copy, preparation, 158
Television production, terms, 159
Television production, types, chart, 171
Television script, form, 160–1

Television testing, 258–9
Test market, 252
Testing copy, suggestions, 251
Testing reliability, 251
Testing validity, 251
Thanksgiving Day Parade, 217
"The Store of the Christmas Spirit", 217
Theatre test, 252–3
"They grinned when the waiter spoke to me in French", 184
"They laughed when I sat down at the piano", 184
Thinking in pictures, 159
Thinking visuality, 86–9
    format, 87
    layout, 87
Thompson, J. Walter, xiv, 49, 172, 270
Tilt, 162
Timing, 165
Toll-free 800 numbers, 185
Total communication, 85
Townsend Method, 250
Tracking performance of business ads, 203
Trade ads, 202
Transit advertising, 239
Transit posters related to outdoor billboards, 239
Transparency shot, 164
Travelers Insurance, xiv, 103–5, illus. 105
Trial campaign for new products, 255
Trucking, 162
TV Art Director, 166
TV Guide, 190
Twenty ways to improve ads in specialized business magazines, 205–6

U

Uncle Mistletoe at Marshall Fields, 217
Understanding Consumer Behavior, 22
United Airlines, 147
United States Army, 47
U. S. Gypsum Company, xiv, 208–9, illus. 209
U. S. Marine Corps, xiv, 44–5, 47, illus. 48

U. S. Open, 62
United Technologies, illus. 212
University of Alabama, xv
University of Illinois, xv
University of Puerto Rico, 266
Urge Magazine, xiv, 189, illus. 209

V

Validity of testing, 251. See testing
VALS, Values and Life Styles, 21. See Standard Research Institute.
Variety of copywriting chores, 235. See copywriting
Verbal advantage, 146
Video storyboards, 241
Videotape, 156
Videotape playbacks, 170
Visa, case study, 35, illus. 35
Visa U.S.A. Inc., xiv
Visual devices, 164
Vocational Questionaire, 294–5
Voice over, 164
Volkswagen, 62, 112–3, 246
Volvo, 60

W

Walden University, xv
Wall Street Journal, 10, 122, 202, 210, illus. 124
Wards, 219
"War of the Worlds", 140
Washington, D. C. Art League, xv
Wasserman, Dick, 287
Ways to increase selling power, 191–2
Weir, Walter, 11, 142
Wesson Oil, 147
Westclox, 64
White, Gordon E., xv
Window banners, 236
Winning appeal reuseable in direct marketing, 185
Winters, Jonathan, 147
Wipe, 163
Women in the work force increasing, 185
Writers: where they work, what they do, 270–80. See

Advertising writers,
copywriters
Writing
body copy, 112
concept, 112
for advertising agencies, 270–1
for direct marketing, 273. See
direct mail
for manufacturer, 273–4
for new business, 297
for other direct marketing
media, 189
for retail advertiser, 271–2
for the ear, 138
how characters speak, 144
how to call for music, 144
how to call for sound effects,
144
identifying characters, 144
like playwriting, 142
radio copy, 140
timing the commercial, 144
Writing advertising for television,
155–70
a picture medium, 158
advertising and show business
combined, 156
basic message never changes,
158

camera terms for script, 162–5
over-riding impression, 157
register one total impression,
157
simple unity of idea, 15
Writing Business-to-business
advertising, 201–7
Writing copy for direct mail
package, 185
contains details and specifics,
187
ease of reading, 187. See direct
mail
involvement devices, 187
order form, 188
publishers letter, 188
special inducements, 187
testimonials, 187
Writing copy for local AM and
FM stations, 147–8. See
radio
Writing copy for sales
promotion, 225–9
Writing retail advertising, 213–8
Writing retail copy
as a free lancer, 272
for a small agency, 272–3
for the media, 272

Writing Yellow Page copy,
recommendations, 238–9

Y

Yellow Page ads start with a
benefit, 238
Yellow Page advertising, 238–9
Yellow Page consumers seek
information, 238
Yellow Pages, a directional
medium, 238
"Yellow Pages Advertising",
238n
Young and Rubicam, xv, 102,
174, 186, 246, 270, 303,
illus. 175
Young, James Webb, 66, 80
Yugo, 61

Z

Zayre, 228
Zenith, 61
Zoom in, zoom out, 162